THE UNSILVERED SCREEN
SURREALISM ON FILM

THE UNSILVERED SCREEN
SURREALISM ON FILM

Edited by Graeme Harper and Rob Stone

WALLFLOWER PRESS
LONDON & NEW YORK

First published in Great Britain in 2007 by
Wallflower Press
6a Middleton Place, Langham Street, London W1W 7TE
www.wallflowerpress.co.uk

A catalogue record for this book is available from the British Library.

ISBN 978-1-904764-86-1 (pbk)
ISBN 978-1-904764-87-8 (hbk)

Book design by Elsa Mathern

Chapters 1 and 2 and the editing of this book were supported by the AHRC

Arts & Humanities
Research Council

CONTENTS

ACKNOWLEDGEMENTS

The Editors would like to sincerely thank all the contributors to *The Unsilvered Screen* for their lively, and sustained, commitment to the book.

Likewise to Yoram Allon and Jacqueline Downs and the very fine team at Wallflower Press: it has been a real pleasure working with you on this one.

NOTES ON CONTRIBUTORS

BARBARA CREED is Professor of Cinema Studies at the University of Melbourne. She has published widely on film, horror and psychoanalytic theory. Her publications include *The Monstrous-Feminine: Film, Feminism, Psychoanalysis* (Routledge, 1993), *Pandora's Box: Essays in Film Theory* (Australian Centre for the Moving Image, 2004) and *Phallic Panic: Film, Horror and the Primal Uncanny* (Melbourne University Press, 2005). She is currently working on the influence of Darwinian theory on early cinema.

PETER WILLIAM EVANS is Professor in the School of Modern Languages at Queen Mary College, University of London. His publications include *The Films of Luis Buñuel: Subjectivity and Desire* (Oxford University Press, 1995), *Women on the Verge of a Nervous Breakdown* (British Film Institute, 1996) and *Bigas Luna: Jamón jamón* (Paidós, 2004). He is also the editor of *Spanish Cinema: The Auteurist Tradition* (Oxford University Press, 1999) and co-editor, with Isabel Santaolalla, of *Luis Buñuel: New Readings* (British Film Institute, 2004).

RAMONA FOTIADE is Senior Lecturer in French at the University of Glasgow. She has published several book chapters and articles on Surrealist cinema. She edited a special issue of *Screen* on Surrealist cinema (1998) as well as *André Breton: The Power of Language* (ELM Bank Publications, 1999). She is also the author of *Conceptions of the Absurd: From Surrealism to Chestov and Fondane's Existential Thought* (Legenda, 2001) and *À bout de souffle* (I. B. Tauris, 2007). She is currently working on a study of Surrealist photography and film.

DAVID GILLESPIE has taught Russian language and culture at the University of Bath since 1985. He is the author of *Iurii Trifonov: Unity Through Time* (Cambridge University Press, 1993), *The Twentieth Century Russian Novel: An Introduction* (Berg, 1996), *Early Soviet Cinema: Innovation, Ideology and Propaganda* (Wallflower Press, 2000) and *Russian Cinema* (Longman, 2003). He is currently working on the presentation of masculinity in the films of Sergei Eisenstein.

GRAEME HARPER is Professor and Director of the National Institute for Excellence in the Creative Industries at Bangor University. His other works include *Swallowing Film* (DVDX, 2000), *Comedy, Fantasy and Colonialism* (Continuum, 2002), *Signs of Life: Cinema and Medicine* (Wallflower Press, 2005), with Andrew Moor, and the *Continuum Companion to Sound in Film and the Visual Media* (Continuum, 2007). He is co-founder, with Owen Evans, of the European Cinema Research Forum (www.ecrf.org.uk) and the journal *Studies in European Cinema* (Intellect). As a fiction writer (under the name Brooke Biaz) his recent works include *Small Maps of the World* (Parlor, 2006) and *Filming Carol* (Parlor, 2007).

BRUCE JENKINS is Dean of Undergraduate Studies at the School of the Art Institute of Chicago. As a curator and critic he specialises in the interface between the moving image and the visual arts. His writings have appeared in *October, Wide Angle* and *Millennium Film Journal* and in exhibition catalogues for the Albright-Knox Art Gallery, Buffalo; Centre Georges Pompidou, Paris; the Museum of Contemporary Art, Los Angeles; Wexner Center for the Arts, Columbus; and Fundació Antoni Tapiés, Barcelona.

VAN NORRIS is Lecturer in Media Studies at the University of Portsmouth. His areas of expertise fall into Classical American animation, Hollywood Classical and Post-Classical studio production and genre, American independent cinema and pre-1990s comic books/graphic novels. He has a research background that includes examinations of American and British sitcom and screen and television comic forms.

GRAHAM ROBERTS is Senior Lecturer in Communications and Director of the Institute of Communications Studies (ICS), University of Leeds and Director of the Louis Le Prince Interdisciplinary Centre for Research in Cinema and Television. His publications include *Forward Soviet: History and Non-fiction Film in the USSR* (I. B. Tauris, 1998), *Man with the Movie Camera* (I. B. Tauris, 1999), *Introducing Film* (Arnold, 2001), with Heather Wallis, *The Historian, Television and Televison History* (University of Luton Press, 2001), *Key Film Texts* (Arnold, 2002), with P. M. Taylor and *European Cinemas in the Digital Age*, with Dorota Ostrowska (Edinburgh University Press, 2007).

MARK SCHILLING moved to Tokyo in 1975 and has lived there ever since. He has been reviewing Japanese films for *The Japan Times* since 1989 and reporting on the Japanese film industry since 1990, first for *Screen International* and presently for *Variety*. He has also written about Japanese films for many other publications, including the Japan editions of *Premiere* and *Newsweek, The Asian Wall Street Journal, Kinema Junpo, Eiga Geijutsu, Cinemaya* and *The Japan Quarterly*. His publications include *The Encyclopedia of Japanese Pop Culture* (Weatherhill, 1997), *Contemporary Japanese Film* (Weatherhill, 1999), *The Yakuza Movie Book: A Guide to Japanese Gangster Films* (Stone Bridge Press, 2003) and *No Borders, No Limits: The World of Nikkatsu Action* (Centro Espressioni Cinematografiche, 2005). He has taught at the Tokyo campus of Temple University and serves as the programmer of Japanese films for the Udine Far East Film Festival.

ANDREW SPICER is Reader in Cultural History at the Bristol School of Art, Media and Design, University of the West of England. His publications include *Typical Men: The Representation of Masculinity in Popular British Cinema* (I. B. Tauris, 2001), *Film Noir*

(Longman, 2002) and *Sydney Box* (Manchester University Press, 2006). He has also edited *European Film Noir* (Manchester University Press, 2007).

ROB STONE is Senior Lecturer and Head of the Department of Media and Communication at the University of Wales at Swansea. He is the author of *Spanish Cinema* (Longman, 2001), *The Wounded Throat: Flamenco in the Works of Federico García Lorca and Carlos Saura* (Edwin Mellen, 2004) and *Julio Medem* (Manchester University Press, 2007). He has also authored a variety of articles and chapters in edited works on Basque, Cuban and Spanish cinema.

JAN UHDE is Professor of Film Studies at the University of Waterloo, Ontario. His publications include *Vision and Persistence: Twenty Years of the Ontario Film Institute* (University of Waterloo Press, 1990) and *Latent Images: Film in Singapore* (Oxford University Press, 2000), with Yvonne Ng Uhde. He also co-edited *Place in Space: Human Culture in Landscape* (Pudoc Scientific Publishers, 1993) and is the editor of *KINEMA*, a journal for film and audiovisual media which he founded in 1993.

Graeme Harper & Rob Stone

INTRODUCTION: THE UNSILVERED SCREEN

Surrealism on film is a combination of Plato's cave and Proust's madeleine. Plato's allegory of the cave proposes that 'truth is nothing more than the shadows of artificial things': silly things that corrupt our eyes. Plato's 'shadows cast by the fire on the other side of the cave' are a precursor of the cinema that combines with the notion of 'memory-triggers' identified by Proust, who claimed that the past was hidden in some material object which we do not suspect. 'And as for that object', he wrote, 'it depends on chance whether we come upon it or not' (1957: 55).

This, in part, is Surrealism on film: the chance that shadows cast by light onto a wall might trigger memories of our primal pasts. But the Surrealists, displaying a disregard for the social stratification that certainly benefited the bourgeois Proust, went even further. They looked for 'reality', and what could broadly be called Truth, in the moments Proust had seen as relating primarily to memory. For the Surrealists these random moments *were* the hidden order, the undercurrent of life. Whereas Proust might well be placed in the same intellectual and creative realm as his contemporary, that philosopher of Intuition and the *élan vital*, Henri Bergson, the Surrealists felt that such 'epistemologists' spoke a little too much but did somewhat too little. The Surrealists' primary mode was a mode of action, but a mode of action in the realm of mysticism, action not simply concretised, but random, action thus against what they saw as bourgeois order.

This being the case, the Surrealists engaged in heightened political activity; driven partly, at least, by a belief in the importance of emotion as a response to both the political condition and to artistic output. In seeking to challenge bourgeois values they saw themselves as revolutionaries valuing destruction as a way of clearing the ideological landscape. That Surrealism and Communism were companions in the 1920s is not unexpected. That by the early 1930s prominent Surrealists such as André Breton had been expelled from the Communist Party is equally understandable. Even within their own ranks, the Surrealists were inclined to tout individualism, declare the significance of such things as desire, memory, expression and feeling, and shun party positions.

Of course, the past of Surrealist art is well-documented, elaborated upon by a number of its most important practitioners and critics. In film terms, foot for fetishised foot, more has been written about Salvador Dalí and Luis Buñuel's 17-minute-long seminal Surrealist film *Un chien andalou* (*An Andalusian Dog*, 1929) than any other film in history. Surprisingly perhaps, Buñuel was fond of recounting (though he might well have dreamt it) how he had stood behind the screen at its Paris premiere with his pockets full of stones in order to defend himself from its potentially unappreciative audience. He writes:

> I expected the worst; but, happily, the stones weren't necessary. After the film ended,
> I listened to the prolonged applause and dropped my projectiles discreetly, one by
> one, on the floor behind the screen. (1985: 106)

It was *Un chien andalou*'s success that led to Buñuel's and Dalí's entry into the Montparnasse café culture of the Surrealists led by the possessive Breton, the Dadaist whose 1924 *Le Manifeste de surréalisme* established him as gatekeeper to the clique. *Un chien andalou* oozed images of putrefaction, horror, sickly sentiment and reproach as, in no particular order, its sequences butted heads and retired hurt into their own lost worlds made from fragments of dreams and snatches of films.

In its nightmarish mix of langour and menace, Buñuel's film revealed the cinema as the true metaphor of the dream state, and made plain in this the key link between Surrealism and Freudianism. Breton himself, who had studied neuropsychology, was one of the first in France to publicise the work of Sigmund Freud, and his 1919 collaboration with Philippe Soupault on a collection of prose and poetry, *Les Champs magnétiques* (*Magnetic Fields*, 1920), was an experiment in 'automatic' writing. Its first chapter is entitled 'La glace sans tain' ('The Unsilvered Mirror').

Indeed, originally, Surrealism had not been the playground of visual artists so much as that of poets and painters. The term first appeared in Guillaume Apollinaire's *Les Mamelles de Tirésias* (1917) and then became fashionable, occupying a position not dissimilar to that attained by the word 'postmodern' in the later twentieth century. Just as hopeful of a generational difference as the term *post*-modernism, the term *above*- or *sur*-realism galvanised writers, poets, artists (as it did an array of poseurs, opportunists and charlatans) around Breton's impassioned manifesto. 'Surrealism', Breton wrote in *Le Manifeste de surréalisme*, the 'first manifesto' as it later became known, 'is within the compass of every unconscious.' So it seemed.

Atheistic, Dionysian, rebellious and revolutionary, the Surrealist movement thrived on the paradox of filling the moral, ethical and religious vacuum left in the wake of the First World War with another void of guiltless, sinless autonomy. The Surrealists favoured an orientation that was defined by dream-logic, chance, superstition, coincidence, absurdity and challenge. They aimed to recreate links with primal thoughts and emotions in order to recast human needs away from materialism, mass culture and social order towards immersion in the revolutionary hagiography of mankind's dark side. As Buñuel recalled: 'The real purpose of Surrealism was not to create a new literary, artistic or even philosophical movement, but to explode the social order, to transform life itself' (1985: 107).

Here is something of Surrealism's primary paradox. While interested in exploding the holistic social order, it was also deeply committed to personal psychology. Fascinated by the unconscious, the Surrealists explored the randomness of utterances, Freudian slips, word associations, déja-vu, coincidences and the implications of words and images rather than their literal meanings. Like-minded associates of Breton – among them Louis Aragon, Paul Eluard and Robert Desnos – made up a clique of writers, playwrights and poets who balanced between a desire for societal change and a commitment to individual empowerment.

This early group of Surrealist poets and writers might well have dissipated were it not revitalised by the visual arts and painters such as René Magritte, Max Ernst, Yves Tanguy and Joan Miró. The visibility of these artists grew so much that it later led to 'assumptions about Surrealism: that it was primarily concerned with the visual arts' (Brandon 1999: 3). Even Breton felt compelled to produce an essay entitled 'Surrealism and Painting' (1928) that sorted through contemporary artists assigning or rescinding the Surrealist qualities of each.

But, as might be obvious, it was viewing a motion picture that most approximated the dream state that the Surrealists aspired to inhabit. The Surrealist cult of cinema rejoiced in the abject emotionalism of melodrama, the brash heroism of the western and the existentialist pantomimes of the silent comics, whom the Surrealists adored for their rejection of reason and practicalities, especially Buster Keaton for his ridiculously stone-faced stoicism in the face of absurdity and Harold Lloyd for his bespectacled derring-do.

Given its dreamlike quality, film generally found many supporters among the Surrealists. In 1925, Jean Goudal writes enthusiastically: 'What cinema has produced over a quarter of a century justifies all our hopes. One does not fight the forces of the spirit' (2000: 94). The Surrealists zig-zagged from cinema to cinema down the streets of Paris and New York, celebrating Hollywood product as proletariat art that displaced the theatrical and artistic traditions of the old Europe, and adopting an excruciatingly discriminatory and controversial approach to European cinema. Abel Gance and Jean Epstein were dethroned as Keaton, Charlie Chaplin and Mack Sennett took their place. Of course, Surrealism was never a movement without its disagreements, nor one to avoid controversy. Dalí, writing in 1932, does neither when he offers a more negative view: 'Contrary to current opinion, cinema is infinitely poorer and more limited when it comes to expressing the real functioning of thought than writing, painting, sculpture and architecture' (2000: 63).

The Surrealist desire for *le dépaysement* (disorientation) did not always fit in with cinema's production ethic. Thus, perhaps, the reason that Breton's key essay on cinema 'As in a Wood' appeared as late as 1951 and why, comparatively, very few Surrealists of Dalí's, Buñuel's or Breton's generation approached filmmaking as a viable medium for their creativity. The Surrealists remained more audience than creators in that regard. In awe of the poetics of the commonplace that filled the silver screen, they were thrilled enough to have their attention drawn to details by a cut or a camera movement: a gun being slipped out of a holster, a glance between lovers, a spot of blood on a handkerchief and the dizzying collapse of all reason when they found themselves helpless between an oncoming train and the heroine tied to the tracks.

Some of the creators of the Breton generation include Georges Hugnet, Jacques Brunius, Ernst Moerman, Roger Livet, Pierre Prévert and Joseph Cornell, with slightly later entries from Ado Kyrou and Marcel Mariën. Their output was small. Notable exceptions were Man Ray and Buñuel, who had worked with Jean Epstein and was a keen student of the films of Sergei Eisenstein, Fritz Lang, G. W. Pabst and F. W. Murnau. In most cases the Surrealist films of the pre-1940s are short, and many of the films from this period have vanished.

Surrealism, as it was conceived by Breton and his contemporaries, did survive the Second World War. Just. We see in the immediate post-war period the films of Livet and Prévert, and that of Kyrou, Brunius and the earliest work of Jan Švankmajer in the 1950s and 1960s. But the movement itself had lost its strength and the term 'Surrealism' was increasingly diluted. It did not help, perhaps, when a key figure such as Dalí turned toward fascism, even at one point describing Hitler as a 'Surrealist innovator' (Nadeau 1968: 233). Nor was it useful to the Surrealists that the Second World War had a high degree of military and political sophistication compared to the First, and therefore seemed to demand not the random disregard of order, a destructiveness that the Surrealists favoured, but rather a concerted and constructive rebuttal.

The savage state that the early Surrealists sought could not be bound in the syntax of either language or film grammar; rather, in a rejection of all linearity, sense and meaning. It was in the gaps between words and images that Surrealism could flourish: in a Freudian slip, for example, or in the cinematic equivalent of an actor's spontaneous, 'in-character' movements and gestures, or a curious, even disturbing confluence of *mise-en-scène*, the overstated elements of a shot held just too long, or the detail of the camera angle, framing or movement that suggested an unsuspected thing.

Surrealism, we might say, is therefore present in such things as the Barthesian cult of Garbo's face, in James Cagney taking on what seems like the entire New York police department in a prolonged gun-battle (without ever reloading his gun) in *Angels With Dirty Faces* (1938), or in the enthusiastic extra who can be heard calling 'Goodbye Mr Massey' among the crowd calling 'Goodbye Mr Lincoln' as the train carrying Raymond Massey, as Abraham Lincoln, pulls away in *Abe Lincoln in Illinois* (1940). As contributors to this volume argue, Surrealism is discernible in the work of directors as varied as David Lynch, Humphrey Jennings, Richard Lester, Andrei Tarkovsky, Alfred Hitchcock, Joel and Ethan Coen, Julio Medem and Takashi Miike. Surrealism is there in cracks between the dislocated narratives, disassociated events and disturbing imagery of horror, science fiction, film noir, animation, documentary and any other genre, but does not often reveal itself to the bait of logic. Surrealism is also in the memories and dreams of films, in the fear and longing that they inspire and in the disorientation of the mind by the disproportionate order, importance and relevance of images and sounds.

Time has, on occasion, threatened to rob Surrealism of most of its meaning. The fact that television guides could recently celebrate a programme such as the lawyer-comedy *Ally McBeal* (1997–2002) for being 'surreal' on the basis of a crudely animated dancing baby as symbol of the protagonist's body-clock would surely be an uninviting postscript to a movement that Buñuel once claimed had the power to explode the social order. It is the intention of the contributors in this collection that such a postscript is written with greater accuracy and greater celebration.

This collection begins with an appreciation of the visual poetics of Surrealist cinema by Ramona Fotiade, who examines the free play of visual signifiers and their expression of the dream state in the films of Man Ray, Duchamp, Dulac, Buñuel and Dalí. She begins in 1920s Paris, where André Breton and the Surrealists, believing themselves to be the first generation to think spontaneously, are proposing a new world order, or at least the destruction of the old one, and explores the crisis of poetic representation brought about by automatic writing and the resurrection of Surrealism through film, which might be said to have unified the visual poetics of the Surrealist movement.

Surrealism flourishes under pressure, relishing the challenge and thriving on the destruction of its target. Rob Stone contends that the predominance of Surrealism in Spanish cinema results from an enduring protest against the dominance of Catholicism, the deep roots of the form and ideology, and a confluence with the Hispanic character. In Spain, the pre-Civil War movement of Surrealism was indelibly linked with Spanish artists (Dalí), poets (Federico García Lorca, Rafael Alberti) and film-makers (Buñuel), who embraced its call to instinctual behaviour as a medium of dissent against the stricture of the Catholic Church. In democratic Spain, Stone argues, the tradition of metaphorical cinema became more prosaic until the films of Julio Medem utilised Surrealist techniques in order to effect ruminations on fate, coincidence and a headlong immersion in the game of chance, a dearly beloved precept of the Surrealists.

Crucial to Spanish Surrealism, of course, is the enigmatic figure of Luis Buñuel, who had been exiled from Spain for most of his adult life following the Spanish Civil War and Dalí's public branding of his old comrade as a heretic. Peter William Evans thus engages with *Le Charme discret de la bourgeoisie* (*The Discreet Charm of the Bourgeoisie*, 1972), *Le Fantôme de la liberté* (*The Phantom of Liberty*, 1974) and *Cet obscur objet du désir* (*That Obscure Object of Desire*, 1977) as masterpieces which, for better or worse, would popularise and crystallise the notion of Surrealism on film. Without doubt, Buñuel's first films were hard acts to follow – even to the extent that Surrealism on film could be said to have ever after struggled to emerge from their shadow, borne out of the progressive outlook of Modernism – but Evans finds in Buñuel's final three films a fascination with the mysteries of erotic love that offers a conclusion of sorts to the Surrealist obsession with the notion, first explored in *Un chien andalou*, that love is the driving force of human existence.

To post-Second World War Eastern Europe next, where David Gillespie examines filmmakers who were traumatised by their nightmare visions of human experience, particularly those in the Soviet Union, where Surrealism was perhaps the only way to deal with real horrors, for in life there was no need to imagine the unimaginable when they had lived it. Gillespie investigates the official labelling of Surrealism as a manifestation of cultural decadence in the West but also examines its influence on Russian films of the early 1930s and on the exiled filmmaker Andrei Tarkovsky, who sought to reconcile the body and soul divide of Communist reality and its ideals in *Solaris* (1972), *Mirror* (1975), *Stalker* (1979) and *Nostalgia* (1983) but created a more universal series of sombre, reflective meditations on the pain of an unbearable existence.

Staying in Eastern Europe, Jan Uhde examines the history of the Zagreb School, which famously claimed 'to animate means to give life and soul to a design, not through the copying but through the transformation of reality'. Animation of the commonplace achieved the Surrealist aim of awarding meaning to the incongruous, and the skill of the animators created an intensity of suggestion that was subversive, magical, terrifying; never more so than in the works of Jan Švankmajer, whose *Alice* (1988) and *Faust* (1994), amongst many others, authenticate and vitalise the most disturbing imagery of fairytales.

Animation is also the subject of Van Norris's chapter on the appropriation and incorporation of popular Surrealism into classical American animation. Norris considers American 'cel' animation from its early days, primarily through its flowering in the late 1920s and 1930s, and onward to its manifestation in the 1940s and beyond. In particular, he offers a detailed analysis of the work of the Fleischer Brothers, while also touching on that of Robert Clampett and Walt Disney. Dream-logic, naturally some comedy, and the disturbing of linearity and logic loom large here. Norris's analysis is cultural as well as concerned with film art. His consideration of the role of popular animation in the deliberations on such things as anxiety, mortality and destiny highlights the primary point that popular Surrealism is found prevalently in animated form.

Following this, Graham Roberts offers an account of the use of avant-garde, Surrealist techniques for symbolic and political effect in the documentary genre, arguing that such techniques created a dangerous precedent for documentarists who might reject authenticity in favour of poetic imagery and, ultimately, propaganda.

From animation and documentary to British 'surreal fantasy' – British cinema is most often associated with the kind of social realism noted as present in the so-called 'kitchen-sink dramas' of the 1950s and 1960s; yet, as Andrew Spicer argues, British filmmakers have displayed a lively and diverse engagement with various forms of Surrealism, both in avant-garde films and within commercial genres, stretching back to Hitchcock's early thrillers in the 1920s. British Surrealism is present in *Monty Python's Flying Circus* (1969–74), which invoked the cultivation of the absurd, and in British horror films, particularly that of Hammer. It can be seen in the work of such filmmakers as Michael Powell and Emeric Pressburger, Richard Lester, Ken Russell and Derek Jarman, to name just a few. And, in the heterogeneous economy of contemporary British cinema, Surrealism informs intelligent commercial films such as *Trainspotting* (1996).

The idea that there may be something called a 'postmodern cinema' cannot be better envisaged than through a study of the cinema of David Lynch and David Cronenberg. It is here, in Barbara Creed's chapter, that the links between the playfulness and anti-historicity, the 'disrupted narratives' of Surrealism are investigated in the context of late twentieth-century mainstream cinema. And yet, Creed does not only deal with the contemporary she also considers the 'hallucinatory states' that Alfred Hitchcock sought through shocking his audience. *Psycho* (1960), she notes, could be interpreted as 'a sustained nightmare in which dream and reality are indistinguishable'. Arguing against a uniform sense of popular cinematic Surrealism, Creed nevertheless makes a case for the links made between Lynch, Cronenberg and Hitchcock in their pursuit of the 'dark side' of the Surreal.

Moving beyond 'the West' to contemporary Japanese cinema, Mark Schilling provides an account of Surrealism in the genres of horror and gangster films, examining the films of Takashi Miike, Seijun Suzuki and Teruo Ishii, among others. Schilling's historical approach gives an insight into the impact of changing national as well as industrial politics in Japan, and his close reading of a range of films asks for a reconsideration, perhaps, of the notion that Surrealist film is anti-narrative. Likewise, Schilling's analysis considers the nature of the 'national' and he suggests that the Surrealism of some 'was less borrowed from foreign sources than derived from native roots and personal obsessions'. Schilling's argument for a local manifestation of Surrealism, even if indirectly, raises the question of the origins of film aesthetics.

The penultimate chapter considers the post-digital present, and looks to the emobile future, in a study of the 'cinema of complexity'. Graeme Harper's essay focuses on twenty-first-century Surrealism and the future of film, the relationship between the non-linear 'web' of the internet and the platforms of digital disk technology emerging between the late 1980s and late 1990s, tracing their aesthetic and their philosophy back to the original Surrealist *Manifeste*. Harper suggests that, rather than view Surrealism as watered down by 75 years of movement away from the manifestos of the Surrealists, what is presented by today's post-digital age, the contemporary age of *emobilism*, is finally a physical and metaphysical manifestation of all the Surrealists sought out. While he does note that this does not represent a Surrealist utopia, he suggests that there is a need to reconsider the nature of the filmic world in order to newly consider how digitalism has been converted by the psychological, the dispositional and behavioural. As with the original Surrealists, he suggests that a new opportunity for the recognition of human agency, emotion and feeling might be upon us.

Finally, in a close postscript study, Bruce Jenkins looks at the cinema of Belgian artist Marcel Broodthaers, whose work situated itself between the still and the moving image and who was not only a maker or watcher of films but concerned with the platforms of film exhibition. Typical of his interests was his film *Un Poème ciné-matographique en l'honneur de Kurt Schwitters*, shot after-hours in the galleries of the Palais des Beaux Arts in Brussels, using 'black-and-white cinematography, kinetic camerawork' and a 'montage of close-up details'. With a honed Surrealist ideal, Brood-thaers' comedic output of some forty multifaceted films resists categorisation. They are complex, intertextual jigsaw puzzles in which the amateur, the Surrealist every-person, in the guise of Broodthaers preserves and recasts 'the art of the past (including that of his own making)'.

While critics and academics still occasionally flail in the debate of whether film reflects or affects society, the unsilvering of the screen that is propounded by true Sur-realism on film contends that society must be held open, and is so in a superior dream state, where it is possible to detect the world's true social, political, economic and cul-tural order. Detecting it, Surrealists suggest, it must then be revolted against.

As exemplified in Breton and Soupault's 'La glace sans tain' Surrealist cinema pres-ents an unsilvered screen offering no reflection to an audience except the possibility of examining, through unsettling the status quo, the Truth of their own lives; reality, that is, caught in the moments, the memories, the unexpected glimpses beyond the everyday. A sometimes dark Truth, therefore, but equally an often potent comedy of human existence.

Ramona Fotiade

FROM READY-MADE TO MOVING IMAGE: THE VISUAL POETICS OF SURREALIST CINEMA

Philippe Soupault recalled several decades after the publication of the *First Surrealist Manifesto* that 'the cinema was for us an immense discovery at the moment when we were elaborating Surrealism' (in Mabire 1965: 29). The co-author, with André Breton, of the first automatic text, *Les Champs magnétiques*, Soupault pointed at the close relationship between cinematic image and the Surrealist exploration of dreams: 'One can say that, from the birth of Surrealism, we sought to discover, thanks to the cinema, the means for expressing the immense power of the dream' (ibid.). Similarly, in the opening paragraph of a text devoted to Max Ernst's exhibition at 'Au sans pareil' in 1921, Breton hails the revolutionary advent of photography that put an end to what he globally designates as the 'old forms of expression' (1988a: 245). By this he referred, of course, not only to the demise of traditional painting, but, more significantly, to the crisis of poetic representation brought about by automatic writing, 'une véritable photographie de la pensée'.[1] Three years later, the relationship between automatism and the 'pure functioning of thought' became the basis of the first programmatic definition of Surrealism. The very notion of 'psychic automatism', which Breton employed in the Manifesto of 1924, encompasses written as much as verbal and, implicitly, visual forms of expression.

Undoubtedly, language-based experiments occupied a privileged, largely unchallenged position in Surrealist theory and practice. Yet Breton's declared interest in the free play of visual signifiers goes back to a time preceding the crystallisation of the Surrealist doctrine. The most obvious example which comes to mind is Breton's account of his 'chance encounters' with the cinema, in the company of Jacques Vaché, and their discovery of the unique *dépaysement* which the juxtaposition of random film extracts could create (Breton 1999: 902–7). The Surrealist theory of the poetic image, as the spark provoked by the sudden rapprochement between two distant realities, was already at work in the 'lyrical substance' of cinema, which prompted Breton's enthusiastic endorsement of the only 'absolutely modern mystery'.[2] In fact, it was not simply the experience of *dépaysement* that related the images of a randomly assembled film narrative to the poetic images. The two forms of expression shared the remarkable quality of inducing a state of inebriation on the viewer or the artist himself. The passive rather than active role of the subject in Surrealist experimentation with automatic techniques evolves around the idea of verbal or visual signs as intoxicating, drug-like catalysts of poetic *illumination*. Breton's remarks on the hallucinogenic effects of Surrealist images, and the addiction which they create 'in the same manner as narcotics' [*à la manière des stupéfiants*] (1988a: 337) match his description of the hypnotic trance of cinema audiences. In *Le Paysan de Paris* (1926), Louis Aragon explicitly relates the use of the *stupéfiant image* to certain disturbances of representation which determine a radical revision of reality.[3] In fact, one can say that the most important Surrealist tenets, including the theoretical elaboration of notions such as that of the poetic image, of the 'convulsive beauty', or of the *merveilleux quotidien* (to mention just a few), ultimately point to a sustained concern with phenomena of perceptual or representational distortion. Breton's retrospective analysis of the origin and aims of Surrealist experimentation in 'Le message automatique', from 1933, which marks a declared return to fundamental principles, leads up to the consideration of one single, fundamental question: the possibility of tapping into the hidden, underlying ground of all perceptual and representational processes.[4] This 'unique, original faculty' [*faculté unique, originelle*], which Breton associates with the so-called eidetic imagery in children and primitives, is significantly made to account for the hoped-for 'derangement of all senses' [*le déréglement de tous les sens*]. As a vivid mental representation of an absent object, the eidetic image defined by Quercy can modify the raw data of perception and give rise to a number of changing representations. However, Breton's over-optimistic interpretation of the concept tends to identify it with the occurrence of virtually limitless representational disturbances, hence his pseudo-scientific pleading in favour of the process of education or rather that of 'unlearning' which still needs to be carried out as far as senses are concerned – 'the education (actually the diseducation) of all the senses is yet to be accomplished' (1992a: 108). Automatism is credited by Breton with the power of re-capturing the elusive manifestations of the 'unique, original faculty', and of leading the way to the envisaged re-education of the senses.

In what follows, I would like to argue that the Surrealist conception of the object, and in particular the problematics of the found object [*l'objet trouvé*], can shed light on the use of photographic and filmic images as part of a unified visual poetics of the movement. If automatism provides 'a genuine photography of thought', it is not only because of the passive positioning of the subject in relation to the free flow of mental associations but also because of the impression that one becomes the recipient of ready-made, pre-existent images or verbal signs. Breton always insists on the fact that the subject of Surrealist experiments does not so much invent or consciously assist the emergence of such images but rather seems to come across them unintentionally. Just like a photograph, the poetic image obtained through automatic writing or drawing pertains, in a sense, to the category of the *objet trouvé*. Both techniques highlight an already existing object (or verbal sign), whose outline is revealed through a process similar to that of the development of photographic images. In *Les Pas perdus* (*The Lost Steps*, 1988b) Breton interestingly compares the effect produced by Man Ray's *rayogrammes* to the *dépaysement* induced by Duchamp's ready-mades, such as *Why not sneeze, Rose Sélvary* (1921), and ends up proclaiming the close affinity between these forms of expression and the Surrealist poetic activity:

> By means of a personal technique, Man Ray arrives at a similar result on a sheet of paper. Without any doubt this opens up the perspective of an art that has more surprises in store than painting, for example. I think of Marcel Duchamp who went to fetch his friends to show them a cage that seemed birdless and half-filled with sugar lumps. When he asked them to lift the cage, they were astonished to find it was so heavy, because what they took for sugar lumps were in fact little pieces of marble ... This anecdote paraphrases quite well the novelty of Man Ray's experiments. And it is from this point of view that it becomes difficult to distinguish them from properly speaking poetic experiments. (Breton 1988b: 300)

The *rayogrammes* and the ready-mades rely on a disquieting indetermination, which forces the viewer to reconsider his or her initial perception. But the experience of *dépaysement* is also intimately involved in psychological processes that signal the presence of an *objet trouvé*. In so far as automatism and other similar explorations of the unconscious uncovered fragments of an otherwise hidden, and inexpressible, inner discourse, the impression of estrangement created by Surrealist verbal or visual productions finds its most adequate theoretical equivalent in the Freudian notion of the uncanny. Among recent attempts at re-assessing the Surrealist doctrine, Hal Foster's study, *Compulsive Beauty* (1993), has provided the most compelling evidence in support of the idea that virtually all the tenets of the movement (for example, the configuration of *dépaysement* – estrangement; of the *merveilleux* – the wonderful aspect of everyday experience; *la beauté convulsive* – convulsive beauty; *la trouvaille* – the find) can be understood in the light of the psychological mechanism which gives rise to the Freudian *unheimlich* – 'the return of a familiar phenomenon (image or object, person or event) made strange by repression' (1993: 7). Foster's demonstration might seem reductive at times, but what I would like to take up here is his argument concerning the status of the *objet trouvé*, as the re-appearance or the re-presentation of a past event in a symbolic, altered form. According to this line of interpretation, the object that corresponds to a certain subliminal Surrealist expectation is not so much the product of a chance encounter but the result of a process of displacement and vague recognition. The *objet trouvé* provokes a disturbing feeling in the viewer precisely because it appears in the guise of an object apparently lost and regained. But the repressed memory of the experience that the object indirectly evokes defers the reference to any identifiable event or object in the past. The bewildering *trouvaille* can therefore keep its secret, while continuing to tease the subject's consciousness for possible interpretations. When Breton speaks of the revolution or the 'crisis of the object' which Surrealist experimentation brought about, he actually puts the *trouvaille* on a par with Duchamp's ready-mades and with Ernst's 'found-interpreted object' [*objet trouvé-interprété*] by virtue of their dysfunctional nature, and (one could add) of the effect of estrangement derived from the substitution of their common practical utility with a subjective interpretation:

> Such a statement justifies brilliantly the Surrealist aim of bringing about a *total revolution of the object* through various measures, including: diverting the object from its destination by attaching a new label to it and signing it, thus reclassifying it by the exercise of choice (Duchamp's 'ready mades'); ... retaining it just because of the doubt surrounding its original function; or because of the ambiguity resulting from its totally or partially irrational conditioning by the elements, entailing its dignification through chance discovery (the 'found object'), an ambiguity which is sometimes amenable to extremely bold interpretations (Max Ernst's 'interpreted found objects'); and, finally, creating it from nothing by bringing together disparate elements selected arbitrarily from the immediate data (the Surrealist object, properly so called). (1972a: 280)

In the case of ready-mades, or of the 'found-interpreted objects', the effort of replicating the uncanny aspect of the *trouvaille* almost invariably involves a radical change of perspective, or a range of techniques designed to trigger perceptual distortions. The ready-made can be achieved by the mere 're-qualification of the object' by the act of signing it as an art-object (as in Duchamp's *Bottle Rack* (1914)), whereas the found-interpreted object can, for example, create a situation of semantic and perceptual ambiguity by combining the change of perspective with a textual designation, which assigns a false utility to the object (as in Duchamp's *Fountain* (1917)). A further, and most interesting, illustration of the *dépaysement* associated with perceptual disturbances in Surrealist visual art has to do with the peculiar status of photographic and film images. Duchamp's early work, starting with his painting *Sad Young Man in a Train* (1911), was inspired by the chronophotographic experiments of Etienne-Jules Marey, which analysed the dynamic processes in humans and animals by putting together separately timed photographic images in order to represent different phases of a body in motion. Marey's successor, Eadweard Muybridge, the author of *The Human Figure in Motion* (1955), produced similar series of photographs that had a decisive impact on the early avant-garde explorations of 'moving pictures'. An explicit reference to Marey's technique comes up in a sequence of Man Ray's film *Emak-Bakia* (1926), which provides the cinematographic equivalent of Marey's sequential photograph showing the various phases of the action of a man jumping. Man Ray explicitly acknowledged that his early experiments with film were a possibility of extending his work in photography, although he preferred the static medium to the moving image:

All the films I made were improvisations. I did not write scenarios. It was automatic cinema ... My intention was to put the photographic composition that I made into motion. As far as the camera is concerned, it serves me to fix something which I do not want to paint. But it does not interest me to make 'beautiful photography' in cinema. Principally, I do not like so much things that move. (1965: 43)

Like Man Ray, Duchamp was initially interested in the possibility of creating 'a static representation of movement – a static composition of indications of various positions taken by a form in movement' (quoted in Schwarz 1969: 49). And, in fact, this spatial rendition of the different postures of a body in motion, as well as Man Ray's explorations of movement through the photographic medium, provide some of the most striking illustrations of Breton's conception of beauty as the *explosante-fixe*. Breton's definition of 'convulsive beauty' in *L'Amour fou* (*Insane Love*, 1992b) makes reference to various poetic instances of arrested motion, such as the image of an abandoned train engine, covered up by luxuriant vegetation in a virgin forest. The passage culminates with the well-known eulogy of crystals as the equivalent, in the natural world, of the 'spontaneous action' involved in the Surrealist understanding of artistic creation. G. H. Brassaï's photograph of crystals illustrates Breton's idea of the spontaneous, yet somewhat elusive, inaccessible process by which one's life and one's writing are ultimately made to coincide: 'The house where I live, my life, the things that I write: I wish that, from afar, all this appear in the same manner in which rock salt crystals appear close-up' (1992a: 681). Breton further links the poetic image, obtained through automatic writing, to the evocative power of the *trouvaille*, which displays the same spontaneity within a subconscious process leading to the material appearance of 'the marvellous precipitate of desire' [*merveilleux précipité du désir*]. This phenomenon is crucial to the Surrealist account of beauty and poetic creation. It highlights the role of the so-called involuntary poetic configurations in the natural world, or in the 'débris' of everyday existence – a notion that found illustration in the series of photographs by Brassaï published in *Minotaure*, and associated with Salvador Dalí's own interpretation of the 'found object', through his theory of the paranoïa-critique. In *L'Amour fou*, Breton uncovered the subtle, essential connection between the Surrealist conception of beauty and the various possible manifestations of a phenomenon of 'arrested motion' (including the image of crystals, coral reefs or the 'objet trouvé' itself), which gives rise to what I would call 'arrested vision'.

This brings us to the question of photographic and film images as part of the Surrealist investigation of the possibility of objectifying or externalising a mental image, whether it be a dream image or a poetic vision. Within the context of the early French avant-garde trends in cinema, the Surrealist position tended to be assimilated with the emphasis placed on the ability of the new medium to 'visualise dreams', and thus overcome the age-old contradiction between reality and imagination. During the short co-habitation period between Dada and Surrealism, filmmaking as a new means of expression attracted the artists rather than the writers of the two groups: Francis Picabia and Marcel Duchamp, Man Ray and Raoul Haussman, Viking Eggeling and Hans Richter. It is indeed doubtful whether Surrealism ever succeeded in validating its practice of automatic writing in film, although the suggestion for such spontaneous expression of one's inner visions and random associations of ideas might have initially come from the cinema, as much as from certain tenets of Freudian psychoanalysis. During the 1920s and 1930s Surrealism attempted to define its own approach to cinema in relation to competing avant-garde trends (such as Impressionism and abstract cinema), and found its distinctive theoretical basis in André Breton's article 'Surrealism and Painting', which set the emphasis on the figure of the 'savage eye', as well as on the predominantly visual nature of the medium (particularly relevant to the pre-sound era):

'The eye exists in its savage state ... It presides over the conventional exchange of signals that the navigation of the mind would seem to demand. But who is to draw up the scale of vision? There is what I have already seen many times ... there is also what I see differently from the way in which anyone else sees it, and even what I begin *to see which is not visible*. (2002: 1)

Surrealists credited the new eye of the camera with an accurate ability to capture the otherwise inexpressible, visual unfolding of dreams, thus paving the way for an unprecedented revolution in poetic language, away from the constraints of logical and verbal discourse. The analogy with painting was only partly validated by the later successful incursions into film practice (such as Luis Buñuel and Salvador Dalí's *Un chien andalou* (*An Andalusian Dog*, 1929) or *L'Âge d'or* (*The Golden Age*, 1930)), which clearly privileged movement over static images, and made use of technical innovations (dissolves, superimpositions, iris shots and so forth) not in order to highlight a self-sufficient play with forms and abstract compositions on the screen but to enhance the impression of film as visual exploration of the unconscious.

It is important to note, however, that this emphasis on the visual nature of film also characterised the earlier experiments of abstract cinema, and some of the films and theoretical writings related to Impressionist cinema. Even before the emergence of the Surrealist movement, filmmakers such as Richter and Eggeling uncovered ingenious modalities for the exploration of visual and musical rhythm through film images. Richter's series of *Rhythmus* (21, 23, 25) and Eggeling's suggestively entitled *Diagonal Symphony* stimulated similar experiments in France, where Jean Epstein and Fernand Léger became the promoters of abstract cinema, and had a decisive influence, in their turn, on the generation of Impressionist filmmakers like Louis Delluc and Germaine Dulac. The autonomy or the prevalence of visual composition and rhythm over content and logical narration inspired such Impressionist notions as 'photogénie', introduced by Delluc, and 'cinégraphie', Dulac's term, which referred to the privileged role assigned to the placement, duration and interrelation of film images.

In their search for an inherently 'cinematographic' language, Surrealists carefully distinguished themselves from abstract cinema, of which Antonin Artaud (among others) was highly critical. He argued that one cannot be moved by 'geometric lines':

> For although the mind of man may be able to conceive and accept abstraction, no
> one can respond to purely geometric lines which possess no significative value in
> themselves and which are not related to any sensation that the eye of the screen can
> recognise or classify. (1976: 150)

However, the surprising appropriation by the Surrealist movement of films directly
related to experiments in abstract cinema suggests a more ambiguous, less radical attitude to this competing avant-garde strand of early French cinema. Although Surrealism never adopted Léger's well-known *Ballet mécanique* (1924) as one of the films
which anticipated the movement, the *Short Dictionary of Surrealism*, published in
1938, included two films which illustrate Léger's use of the 'mechanical period': Duchamp's *Anémic cinéma* and Man Ray's *Emak-Bakia*, both made in 1926. More recent
film critics (White 1984; Elsaesser 1987) do not hesitate to describe Léger's *Ballet mécanique*, along with Duchamp's and Man Ray's films, as Dada or abstract experiments,
without even trying to elucidate the question of their inclusion in a list of supposedly
'Surrealist' films. The so-called 'question of attribution and contribution' (addressed by
Thomas Elsaesser) is far from clear in any of the above-mentioned cases, and needs
to be related to the specific historical context in which the various avant-garde programmes (Dada, Surrealist, or abstract cinema) struggled to impose their supremacy
in the area of non-commercial, experimental filmmaking.

The belated appropriation of Man Ray's and Duchamp's films by the Surrealists was
motivated by various reasons which had to do not so much with a shared conception
of cinematic language than with the absence of truly representative Surrealist productions. The most likely candidates for the title included Dulac's *La coquille et le clergyman* (*The Seashell and the Clergyman*, 1928) (which was not, after all, mentioned in the
Short Dictionary of Surrealism among the 'representative' Surrealist productions), Man
Ray's film based on a scenario by Robert Desnos, *L'Étoile de mer* (1928), and Buñuel
and Dalí's *Un chien andalou* and *L'Âge d'or*.

It is worth recalling Man Ray's and Duchamp's shared interest in optical illusion
and the paradoxes engendered by the kinetic extension of their experimental work
with a static medium, such as painting or photography. For both, cinema was a development of investigations that led from the pictorial representation of *Nude Descending
a Staircase* (1912) to the mechanical installations involved in the *rotoreliefs* and the
Precision Optics series (1920–26). However, according to Duchamp, the inspiration for
Nude Descending a Staircase initially came from the cinema, as well as earlier experiments in chrono-photography, independently carried out by Marey and Muybridge:

> This definitive version of *Nude Descending a Staircase* ... brought together in my
> mind various interests, among which the cinema, still in its early days, and the
> separation of the static positions in Marey's chronophotographs in France, and in

Eakins' and Muybridge's in America … I completely gave up the naturalist appearance of the nude, and kept only the twenty or so different static positions in the successive act of descending. (1975: 222)

Having explored the decomposition of movement through painting and installation works, Duchamp would ultimately adopt film itself as a medium, only to expose, once more, in playful manner, its facticity and reliance on optical effects. Between 1920 and 1926 Man Ray collaborated with Duchamp on various projects, including *Rotary Glass Plates* (1924), sub-titled *Precision Optics*, and the production of Duchamp's film, *Anémic cinéma*. This short experiment in cinematography consists of a succession of images of rotating disks with spiral lines which alternate in a slow rhythm with disks containing spirally-printed verbal puns. As Elsaesser remarks, the technique developed by Duchamp involved the synchronisation of two machines: the recording camera and the revolving motor that spins the disk (1986: 24). One could further argue that the film camera functions in this case more like a photographic, static recording mechanism, and the movement remains confined to the repetitive pattern of the revolving disks. In a similar manner, Man Ray made *Retour à la raison* (1923) partly without a camera, by applying his technique of the Rayograph to the film celluloid: 'On some strips I sprinkled salt and pepper, like a cook preparing a roast, on other strips I threw pins and thumbtacks at random: then I turned on the white light for a second or two, as I had done for my still Rayographs' (1963: 260).

The objects and motorised installations which preceded the making of *Retour à la raison* and *Anémic cinéma* highlight Man Ray's and Duchamp's concern with the effects of motion on perception, and especially with processes of optical illusion. For *Disks Bearing Spirals* (1923), Duchamp used ink-drawn lines on five paper plates to create the impression of continuous concentric circles when the mechanism rotated. In fact, one of the most striking and distinctive aspects of Dada films (in particular films such as *Emak-Bakia* or *Anémic cinéma*) is their self-referential comment on the process of filming. The recurrent motif of the eye in Man Ray's *Emak-Bakia* (starting with the shot showing the author's eye reflected upside-down in the camera lens, and ending with the famous final shot of Kiki, who has a second pair of eyes painted on her eyelids) points to the mechanical, artificial, yet also disorientating aspects of photographic and film images. The illusion involved in the cinematic transposition of continuous movement is denounced, and the author tends to emphasise the contrived nature of the process of recording and projecting moving pictures on a screen. Man Ray, for example, uses not only the image of the eye in the camera lens (in order to highlight the tension between 'normal vision' and 'cinematic vision'), but mostly the contrast between static images and so-called 'moving images' – sometimes his Rayographs interestingly comment on this deliberate disclosure of the illusion of movement in the medium of film.

The use of perceptual distortions in Rayographs such as *Distorted House* (1923) reminds one of similar scenes from *Emak-Bakia* (in particular those using an unusual

360-degree pan shot of waves on the beach), but also some scenes from the middle part of *L'Étoile de mer*. Man Ray occasionally refers to photographic techniques he experimented with (such as solarisation), and it is not surprising to notice the strong similarity between some of his early work with static images (especially Rayographs) and shots from *Emak-Bakia* (for example, the close-up of the dahlia flower, the image of the crystal and the shadows of hands).

The understanding of representability and vision in film seems to provide the only conclusive criteria for qualifying abstract films as either Dada or Surrealist. One could say that the so-called Dada films not only break the cinematic illusion by constantly pointing at the mechanical, technical side of film production (the discontinuity and static or repetitive character of images behind the apparent continuity), but also represent empirical reality as half-abstract, as a simulacrum or an illusion in itself. The undermining of the illusion of movement in film is coupled with an undermining of what seems to be the illusion at work in normal, real-life processes of perception and representation. *Emak-Bakia*, like the other Dada-related films, ultimately tends to show, as Mimi White remarks, that 'perception and recognition are more "abstract" than we think' (1984: 46). In fact, what needs to be said about the production of abstract films, related or not to Dada, is that they share a rudimentary understanding of movement in terms of purely intellectual analysis and mechanical reproduction which applies not only to the camera (as source of the illusion of movement in film image), but also to the perceiving subject, considered as a highly complex apparatus itself and as a source of illusion. This mechanistic conception of mental processes is radically opposed to the role assigned by Surrealism to imagination in the constant interaction between dream and reality, which makes the subject a real being in the world insofar as its vision constitutes a real order of things rather than a mere simulacrum. In contrasting Man Ray's *Emak-Bakia* and Buñuel and Dalí's *Un chien andalou*, for example, one has to admit that the latter relies on a 'recognisable' reality within which it explodes conventions and artificial boundaries with the imaginary. Neither the so-called 'first avant-garde' nor the 'abstract cinema' ever satisfied or came to identify completely with the Surrealist programme. In the case of the 'first' or the 'Impressionist' avant-garde – including filmmakers such as Abel Gance, Marcel L'Herbier, Delluc and Dulac – the interest in the technical innovations and in the autonomy of the visual 'language' of cinema went along with an affiliation to Impressionist painting, Impressionist music, or to the psychological novel. In contrast to the conception of 'psychological film' and 'subjective cinema' developed, for example, by Germaine Dulac, the use of shots linked through dissolves in Buñuel and Dalí's *Un chien andalou* implicitly undermine the psychological characterisation of the realist film, and the related literary conventions of the psychological novel. One such instance is the inexplicable, illogical transformation of underarm hair into a sea urchin, or the unresolved mystery of the box with diagonal stripes containing an envelope and a tie with the same pattern. Dissolves here play on the viewer's frustrated expectation, on the absence of any elucidation or conventional psychological reference to the previous and/or following shots. The Surrealist interpretation of film as 'conscious hallucination' that bridges reality and imagination, and explores the absurd and the irrational of everyday existence, effectively challenged both the formalist approach of pure or abstract cinema (as represented by Léger, Richter, Eggeling) and the aesthetics of Impressionist cinema. The major objections made to these trends by Surrealist commentators (such as Artaud and Desnos, in particular) were, first, that they paid excessive attention to formal aspects at the expense of content and, secondly, that their 'modernist' technique remained attached to conservative moral and political tenets. By criticising literary and theatrical adaptations for the screen, Surrealism promoted the idea of a cinema inspired by daily life situations, which would radically contradict common perceptions, moral conventions and religious beliefs. The new language of film had to illuminate equally disquieting, unfamiliar topics in order to achieve a truly 'revolutionary' impact, thus heightening the impression of 'reality' and, at the same time, disclosing images that the eye has not yet seen.

Breton's interpretation of Man Ray's experiments (in *Le Surréalisme et la peinture*) (*Surrealism and Painting*, 1928)) establishes a significative correlation between the *dépaysement* aimed at by Surrealist objects and the spectral, 'negative' quality of photographic and cinematographic images, which reveal the paradoxically immaterial presence of perceived reality:

Almost at the same time as Max Ernst, but in a different and, at first sight, almost opposite spirit, Man Ray also derived his initial impetus from photographic precepts. But far from entrusting himself to photography's avowed aims and making use, after the event, of the common ground of representation that it proposed, Man Ray has applied himself rigorously to the task of stripping it of its positive nature, of forcing it to abandon its arrogant air and pretentious claims ... The same considerations apply, indeed, to the taking of cinematographic images, which tend to compromise these figures not only in an inanimate state but also in motion. The photographic print, considered in isolation, is certainly permeated with an emotive value that makes it a supremely precious article of exchange ... nevertheless, despite the fact that it is endowed with a special power of suggestion, it is not in the final analysis the *faithful* image that we aim to retain of something that will soon be gone for ever. (2002: 46)

The photographic image acquires the unique value of a 'precious article of exchange' [*précieux objet d'échange*] only in as much as it transcends the mere reproduction of reality, in order to become the faithful yet indeterminate, and therefore disquieting, reminiscence of an irretrievable object of desire. This particular understanding of the optical illusion, which the Surrealist photographic and cinematographic vision alludes to, perfectly matches Breton's definition of the 'found object' and of the 'objects with symbolic functioning' [*objets à fonctionnement symbolique*] in relation to the production of objects of oneiric origin, as 'genuine materialisations of desire' [*(des) véritables désirs solidifiés*] (2002: 32). In an article published in *Minotaure*, Man Ray analyses the obscure, subconscious charge of photographic images with reference to processes of 'oxidation of emotional residues', captured on paper thanks to chemical reactions and the action of light. His account of the relationship between personal recollection and what one could call the photographic remnants of past events adds further support to the idea that photographs (and, by extension, film images) display the same uncanny configuration of repressed desires as the *objet trouvé*:

> Seized in moments of visual detachment during periods of emotional contact, these images are oxidised residues, fixed by light and chemical elements, of living organisms. All plastic expression is nothing but the residue of an experience. The recognition of an image that has tragically outlived the experience, and continues more or less clearly to remind one of the event like the intact ashes of an object consumed by the flames, the recognition of this barely visible and fragile object and its identification in the spectator's mind with a similar personal experience excludes all possibility of psychoanalytical classification or of assimilation to an arbitrary ornamental system ... Any effort shaped by desire must also draw on an automatic or unconscious energy that supports its fulfilment. (1933: 1) [5]

Man Ray's final reservations concerning the psychoanalytical interpretation of the momentary emotional overlap between a present impression and a past, vaguely remembered event, point to the undeniable shortcomings of any theory which, like Hal Foster's systematic use of the uncanny as an all-encompassing hermeneutic device, ends up explaining away the Surrealist *merveilleux* (and its correlate, *dépaysement*), by reducing it to Freudian repression and compulsive repetition of the same. Such an approach has limited applicability, if only because it lends itself to obvious criticism on at least two major accounts: firstly, Breton had no knowledge of the Freudian doctrine of the *unheimlich* (since the original essay was completed in 1919, but was not translated into French until 1933, a time when the most important points of the Surrealist conception had already been elaborated); secondly, the ideological and practical manifestations of the movement aimed to transcend the mere aestheticisation of pathological compulsion. The simulation of madness, and the adoption of psychoanalytical techniques for the exploration of the subconscious in Surrealist experiments deliberately ignored the therapeutic finality of Freud's theory. Whether Breton was or was not fully aware of the implications and the current developments of psychoanalysis during the 1920s and 1930s, the fact of the matter is that the doctrinal texts or the activities designed under the influence of Freudian ideology were always meant (and always actually functioned) as second-degree pledges of allegiance – in the sense that the imported material was neither to be read literally nor to be absorbed as one indivisible block of knowledge. One can also mention Breton's equally personal reading of Hegel as an example of the selective manner in which Surrealism appropriated various theoretical discourses of the time. However, Breton's ambivalent relationship to Freudian psychoanalysis can help clarify the function assigned to the cinemato-graphic image within a wider Surrealist poetics of visual communication, and in op-position to earlier Dada investigations into optical illusion. The recurrent use of purely abstract shapes arranged in rhythmical patterns (such as in Léger's *Ballet mécanique* or in Man Ray's *Retour à la raison* and *Emak-Bakia*) was neither creative enough nor 'marvellous' according to the Surrealist sensibility. For Breton and the Surrealist film-makers or writers for the screen, the mechanics of compulsion and repetition (which a psychoanalytical critic would associate with Léger's 'mechanical period', or the similar occurrence of such shots in Man Ray's *Emak-Bakia*) had nothing fascinating or excit-ing in themselves. One can no doubt notice that the small number of films that Sur-realist artists produced or recognised themselves in were not merely trying to provide an aesthetic justification for the display of pathological, manic behaviour. The place of the uncanny *objet trouvé* in the economics of the Surrealist film narrative (for ex-ample, the starfish in Man Ray's eponymous *ciné-poème*) corresponds to a discourse of transgression, and an attempt at expressing something which, whether consciously or unconsciously, remains unattainable. Breton's own search for the elusive, lost origin of both perceptual and representational phenomena points to the same transgressive aspiration towards a visual poetics more akin to the sublime (in its simultaneously en-chanting and terrifying aspects) than to the classically beautiful. Madness itself is not aestheticised as a purely mechanical, repetitive, and ultimately sterile, monologue.

The Surrealist understanding of photographic and filmic images as part of a radi-cal (philosophical and aesthetic) re-assessment of the relationship between dreams and reality, imagination and visual perception, madness and reason, brings us back to Breton's article on Max Ernst which speaks of recollection not as mere reproduction, but actual creation or invention of the past. The phenomenon of *dépaysement* is thus achieved within the framework of processes of memory which underlie both percep-tual and representational phenomena:

> It would be equally sterile for us to reconsider the ready-made images of objects (as in catalogue figures) and the meaning of words, as though it were our mission to rejuvenate them. We must accept these conventions, and then we can distribute and group them according to whatever plan we please ... It is the marvellous faculty of attaining two widely separate realities without departing from the realm of our experience; of bringing them together and drawing up a spark from their contact ... and of disorienting us in our memory by depriving us of a frame of reference – it is this faculty which for the present [holds the attention]. (1978a: 7–8)

One cannot help thinking of the analogy between Breton's remarks and Brassaï's in-terpretation of Proustian recollection as 'the recurrent preoccupation with the latent, or what could have been and what has not been, what is buried; and yet close at hand, beneath reality'. In *Marcel Proust sous l'emprise de la photographie* (*Proust and Photog-raphy*, 1997), Brassaï provides the best indirect description of the Surrealist artist when he refers to the author of *Remembrance of Time Past* (*À la recherche du temps perdu*, 1912) as the photographer of mental images, with his own being as the sensitised plate.[6] From this perspective, creating rather than simply recollecting the past might be a way of escaping the mechanics of compulsion and repetition. Beyond the arrested motion of photographic images, the *dépaysement* of memory itself restores the movement and the filmic temporality of the *camera obscura* of subconscious desires.[7]

Notes

1 'The invention of photography dealt a deadly blow to the old forms of expression, in painting as well as in poetry, where automatic writing, which appeared at the end of the nineteenth century, is a genuine photography of thought' (Breton 1988a: 245). All translations are the author's unless otherwise indicated.

2 'There is a way of going to the movies as others go to church and I think that, from a certain angle, quite independently of what is playing, it is there that the only absolutely modern mystery is celebrated' (Breton 1999: 904; fragment translated in Matthews 1971: 2).

3 'The vice called Surrealism consists of the excessive and passionate use of the image narcotic or, more specifically, it refers to the uncontrolled prompting of the image for its own sake, and for what it entails as to the representation of unpredictable disturbances and metamorphoses: because each image, each and every time, forces one to revise the entire universe' (Aragon 1926: 83).

4 'All the experimentation here would be of a nature to demonstrate that perception and representation (which to the ordinary adult seem radically opposed) are merely products of the dissociation of *one original faculty*, of which the eidetic image gives us an idea and of which one still finds a trace among primitives and children. All who have striven to define the true human condition have aspired, more or less confusedly, to regain that state of grace. I say automatism alone provides access to it' (Breton 1978b: 109).

5 'In 1924, for instance, when I suggested that objects seen in dreams should be manufactured and put into circulation, I envisaged the assumption of concrete form by such objects ... far more as a means than as an end. I certainly hoped that the multiplication of such objects would entail the depreciation of those objects of often dubiously accepted *usefulness* which clutter up the so-called real world; such a depreciation seemed to me a prerequisite for the unleashing of the *powers of invention* which, within the limits of our present understanding of the dream process, must surely be vitalised by contact with dream-engendered objects representing pure desire in concrete form. But the aim I was pursuing went far beyond the mere creation of such objects: it entailed nothing less than the objectification of the very act of dreaming, its transformation into reality' (Breton 1965: 277).

6 'In the light of photography I discovered a new Proust, someone like a photographer of the mind, who considered his own body as a highly sensitised plate; he was able to

capture and store thousands of impressions during his youth and, when he set out to remember the past, he devoted all his time to developing and fixing these impressions, thus making the latent image of his whole life visible in the gigantic photograph that is now the *Remembrance of Time Past*' (1997: 20).

7   This chapter was completed with support from the AHRC.

Rob Stone

EYE TO EYE: THE PERSISTENCE OF SURREALISM IN SPANISH CINEMA

Catholicism celebrates self-control and saves all its anguish for sin, but Surrealism is the opposite. The importance of Surrealism for Spanish filmmakers, as well as for writers and artists, can therefore be understood by its inversion of the precepts, techniques and arts associated with 500 years of obeisance to clerical hegemony. The eruption of Surrealism in Spain in the 1920s was a rallying cry to sensualists and revolutionaries that allowed them to conceive of creativity beyond the censure of the Church. Where clerics ordered propriety, decorum, respect and faith, the Surrealists exhorted spontaneity, instinct, scandal and atheism. The artists Pablo Picasso and Salvador Dalí, the poet and playwright Federico García Lorca, the poet Rafael Alberti and the filmmaker Luis Buñuel were all, at one time or another, advocates of the anti-faith. Yet, while for most it was a creatively fruitful phase, for Buñuel it became its own religion, though even he strayed when the more extreme philosophy of the Marquis de Sade turned him on to more radical tastes. The appeal of Surrealism lay in its advocation of liberty from clerical and political doctrine. During the four decades of the Francoist dictatorship (1939–75), when freedom was only possible in a dream-state, the challenge of recreating such liberty in the waking world was abetted by Surrealist means of expression. And when the dictatorship ended, and the liberation of instinct in the cultural and consumerist free-for-all made Surrealist subterfuge redundant, there arose a new challenge of making Surrealism newly relevant to those who were already liberated.

Paul Ilie (1968) argues that Spanish Surrealism was largely a voguish use of language and style copied from the French. C. B. Morris contends that although the ideology and practice came from France, 'Surrealism was a resilient springboard for a number of Spanish writers in the 1920s and 1930s' (1972: 160). These writers made it their own as they explored a very different and quite specific Spanish reality by challenging the subconscious, and vice versa; for by exploring their subconscious they also challenged their reality. However, the roots of Spanish Surrealism go far deeper than the arrival of the writings of André Breton from France in the 1920s. The paradox of spiritual strength and physical weakness is a theme that informs the nineteenth-century art of Francisco de Goya y Lucientes, whose portraits of degenerate nobility and the wretched poor have in common the baggage of earthly desires and the burden of heavenly retribution. Dig deeper and there are links with the Spanish mystics of the seventeenth century, Saint Teresa of Avila and Saint John of the Cross, whose erotically-charged poetry employed the metaphysical strategy of stepping from the real to the unreal in order to express the conflict between spiritual longing and physical desire.

Transcendence was always frustratingly out of reach for the saints, which only compounded their tortuous understanding that metaphysical strategies really were successful in the transubstantiation of bread and wine into the body and blood of Jesus Christ during Holy Communion. Indeed, this sacrament has always informed the atheism of those Spanish Surrealists who recognised something divinely profane in its supposedly holy carnality, cannibalism and vampirism. García Lorca and Dalí, for example, reworked its motifs and symbolism into their respective poetry and paintings, while the most extreme parody of its pretension is the *tableaux vivant* of Leonardo Da Vinci's *The Last Supper* that Buñuel creates out of beggars and whores in *Viridiana* (1961), a film banned by the Vatican and burnt by the Francoist state.[1]

An absent father

To many of the Spanish writers, artists and filmmakers known collectively as the Generation of 1927, Surrealism was an attempt to express the workings of the subconscious mind as a corrective to propriety and censure. Film was an important factor in the battle between instinct and reason because it allowed for the cultivation of the incongruous. The movement and transformation of images reflected the dream-state by imitating rapid eye movement in its flickering frames per second. Poets such as García Lorca and Alberti were delirious with going to the pictures and revelled in the outsize celebration of metaphors for reality that played upon the screen.[2] However, though both García Lorca and Alberti incorporated cinematic conventions and language into their poetry, they aimed not to make films but to appropriate a cinematic aesthetic as a framework for their own poetic sensibilities. In contrast, Buñuel believed that film had the potential to be the truest medium of Surrealism and to prove it made *Un chien andalou (An Andalusian Dog*, 1929) with Dalí.

The film's 17 minutes of nonsense, carnage, wit and melancholy dispensed with narrative logic and aesthetic comfort in an attempt to provoke, enrage and inspire. This most influential Surrealist film disregards aesthetics and therefore destabilises critical response because it responds to its own criteria. Buñuel's infamous slicing of the eye liberated the subconscious and insisted upon the cinema screen as a repository for the stuff of dreams. His Spanish contemporaries promptly transposed the malignant connective tissue between his imagery into that of their poetry and plays, but rarely ventured into film.[3] As Robert Short puts it, *Un chien andalou* 'turned out to be a very hard act to follow' (2003: 7). But the liberalism proffered by Surrealism and the Second Republic (1931–36) was but a brief taste of liberty snatched away by the Spanish Civil War, when Nationalist forces killed García Lorca, subdued a self-serving Salvador Dalí and forced Buñuel into exile in New York and later Mexico City. Subsequently, the influence of Buñuel on Spanish cinema has most often been overstated, for his early shorts were unseen outside the elitist film society *Cineclub Español* (1928–31) and his many years of work in the lower reaches of studio-bound Mexican melodrama went unheeded. It was not until *Los olvidados* (*The Young and the Damned*, 1950) reached the Cannes Film Festival that his reputation as a Spaniard operating beyond the reach of the Francoist dictatorship resurrected him as a rallying point for dissident Spanish filmmakers such as Carlos Saura.

Metaphorical cinema

Saura's earliest features had subscribed to the Italian Neorealist aesthetic but the films he developed in collaboration with the producer Elías Querejeta and the writer Rafael Azcona utilised symbolic characters within a metaphorical narrative that required audiences to interpret the images so as to read between the lines. If the narrative, characters, dialogue and images were deciphered correctly the audience could construct a critique of the Francoist dictatorship that had been rendered cryptically so as to avoid censorship. Symbolism, similes and metaphors were the hieroglyphic language of this *cine metafórico* ('metaphorical cinema') that utilised Surrealist tactics, techniques and tricks such as symbolism and shock, imbuing objects with meaning beyond their practical function or empirical purpose, and dream-imagery. *La caza* (*The Hunt*, 1965), which Guy Wood (2005) has proven duplicates imagery from the paintings of Dalí, *Peppermint frappé* (1967), *Stress es tres, tres* (1968), *La madriguera* (*The Warren*, 1969), *El jardín de las delicias* (*The Garden of Delights*, 1970), *Ana y los lobos* (*Ana and the Wolves*, 1972) and *La prima Angélica* (*Cousin Angelica*, 1973) all shared an intense focus on the private psychological chaos and trauma of their protagonists; yet, by recognising the essentially symbolic nature of these characters, it was possible for an audience to extrapolate a metaphorical critique of the society which they shared with these distorted reflections of themselves. Thus, the individual Hell of Saura's protagonists was revealed as the collective Hell of like-minded Spanish people.

Saura, Querejeta and Azcona used film as a weapon against a society that propagated faith in Francoism as a logical, longed-for continuation of a centuries-old crusade. Franco's Spain was a regime manufactured in the likeness of the kingdom of the Catholic kings of the fifteenth century and its own omnipresent iconography was dedicated to signifying the resurrection of this glorious Catholic past. The yoke and arrows that signified the Catholic Kings, for example, were reinstated as the insignia of the Falangists, the sole political party under Franco, who took for himself the medieval title of *caudillo*. Displacement of such imagery was impossible in a totalitarian regime. However, the immobilisation of the imagination created an interrogative void that, in turn, powered the paradox that this void could only be filled by imagination. In other words, ordering someone not to think of something ensures only their focus and obsession, the same traits that characterise the films of Carlos Saura. In *El jardín de las delicias*, for example, a senile, wheelchair-bound patriarch observes the role-playing of his desperate family who wish him to recall the combination of his safe, but the isolated lunacy of this 'dictatorial' madman comes to dominate by the film's last scene in which his family are wheelchair-bound in imitation of him. In *Ana y los lobos* the three sons of a noble family are represented as a crazed hermit, a uniform fetishist and a pervert and obliquely represent the sacred trinity of the dictatorship: the Church, the Military and the Family. And in *La prima Angélica*, a soldier breaks his arm and has his cast set in a manner suggestive of a military salute, thereby turning the sacred symbol of the regime into a sacrilegious figure of fun.

Another surrealist element of these films was their investigation of memory and fantasy. Instead of accepting the assertion that Francoism was the culmination of 500 years of a supposedly glorious Spanish past, Saura invoked a Proustian recognition that spontaneous memories could encapsulate an entire life. In *The Warren* a housewife is prompted by her inheritance of furniture from her family home to role-play memories of her childhood, and in *El jardín de las delicias* a precise reconstruction of childhood is specifically designed to jog the memory of a senile adult. In *La prima Angélica* an adult of the 1970s is thrown back into a Civil War childhood by such stimulii as feeling sick during a car ride. Thereafter, though surrounded by children, he is played by the same adult actor (José Luis López Vázquez), whose shuffling, mournful characterisation is a symbol of an entire generation infantilised by Francoism. Rather than national pride, Saura held that alienation and fragmentation characterised his generation of Spaniards in the context of the never-ending dictatorship. Deprived of any future, memories were a way to recapture a childhood born to war and an innocence lost to fascism. As the Surrealist writer John Hawkes remarks, 'fiction should achieve revenge for all the indignities of our childhood; it should be an act of rebellion against all the constraints of the conventional pedestrian morality around us' (2007). The consequent rationale for Saura's imagery and narrative convolution was that the audience's recognition of their reflected infantilised selves would reacquaint them with their true selves and therefore liberate the essence of their being. For Saura, as for Proust, these moments showed that art, in response to censure, might offer the spiritual equivalent of an alternative but truer reality. As for Proust, this was a technique by which 'the fragmented self is healed by the activity of the rediscovery of lost time via the emergence of spontaneous memories' (Chessick 1987: 33). The tactic coincides with Freud's notion that memories in the unconscious are unaffected by time and therefore continue to exert the same pressures in any stage of adult life: the function of Saura's films was ultimately to awaken those memories in order to stimulate reflection, debate and protest, even revolution.

Morris rightly laments the consequence 'if Buñuel's contribution to the spread of Surrealism in Spain were to be judged solely on his advocacy and use of visual shock' (1972: 30), but his legacy and influence is also evident in Saura's provocative, dream-like narratives incorporating flashbacks, flash-forwards, fantasies, nightmares and daydreams, and the recurrent motif of mirrors that prompted reflection on the nature of the self, as well as an intertextual recourse to Spanish art and literature that was designed to prompt subconscious responses from his audience. The vertiginous descent into the self that Surrealist practices demanded suggested the possibility of discovering a secret, hidden, forbidden territory that was far beyond the reaches of Francoism. However, any explicit attempt to follow Breton and Buñuel in revitalising psychic forces against the dictatorship was clearly dangerous at a time when both scripts and finished films were submitted to the censor and its board of ecclesiastical hawks. In response, Querejeta developed a technique of submitting a dummy script that could be 'corrected' (the official term for 'censored') and returned with a filming permit. He then produced the film that he and his collaborators always intended to make and made sure it reached a foreign film festival before returning it to the censor for belated classifying, thereby, as Querejeta puts it, 'putting the censor in the position: "The film's finished, what can we do?"' (in Stone 2001: 7).

This tactic was employed when Juan Antonio Bardem and Saura combined to persuade Buñuel to return to Spain to make *Viridiana*. The state approved a script that seemed to eulogise a Catholic sense of duty and sacrifice in its tale of a novice nun (Silvia Pinal) who leaves her convent but finds fulfilment in helping the poor. It even welcomed back Buñuel because it was believed that his growing international reputation could be relocated in Francoist Spain or, at worst, could be manipulated as a symbol of how tolerant and supportive the dictatorship was at a time when it desperately needed to impress foreign investors of an improving record of human rights. However, *Viridiana* was promptly denounced by the Vatican after its screening in Cannes. Instead of an uplifting tale of a do-gooder, Buñuel had made a blackly comic treatise on the evil that men do, in which our heroine is a blank idiot whose unfailingly generous practices result in her uncle's suicide, his house being overrun by malicious beggars, her rape by a murderous leper and the general crumbling of all she and Church-backed Francoism hold dear until she sees the errors of her ways, lets her hair down and joins her lascivious cousin in a guiltless *ménage à trois*. Blasphemy was most blatantly served in the aforementioned parody of Da Vinci's *The Last Supper*, but profanity was also present in incidental imagery and asides. Just as the Surrealists believed in challenging mediocrity but were transfixed by the ennui of the everyday, so they understood that mundane objects inspired affective responses to daily routine and therefore, if utilised correctly, could disturb and prompt sinful thoughts. In *Viridiana*, for example, a holy crown of thorns is thrown upon a bonfire: shocking – except it is just a circle of twigs; while a supposedly pious rendition of the Angelus is ruined by a cacophony of roadworks. In one blackly comic sequence worthy of Buster Keaton, Viridiana's cousin takes pity on a dog tied to a cart and buys it from the owner, but as the cart trundles off another comes by with an almost identical dog. Good deeds are irrelevant, people are rotten, and the only devotion worth a damn is that of sexual desire and longing.

Buñuel hurried back into exile and the entire Spanish film industry was strangled with regulations. The few examples of metaphorical cinema that followed *Viridiana* went largely unseen in Spain by a public who preferred the more prosaic escapism provided by the generic delights of comedies, melodramas and musicals. Instead, the *cine metafórico* of Saura and his like was mostly tolerated by the dictatorship as a cynical symbol of its tolerance towards dissidence. It may be argued that such films were not made for Spaniards but for foreign intellectuals and critics, who could flatter themselves on their code-breaking capabilities as much as by expression of their political bleeding hearts. Saura's *Peppermint frappé*, for example, was barely released in Spain, but did play a key role in the uproarious Cannes Film Festival of 1968, when members of the *Nouvelle Vague* reacted to rioting in Paris by attempting to stop the coincidental screening of Saura's film. Enthused, Saura joined the protestors in hanging on to the curtain, but in the ensuing scuffle his star and common-law wife, Geraldine Chaplin, was punched in the face by Jean-Luc Godard. *Cine metafórico* may have found its revolution abroad, but its Surrealist elements actually limited the scientific truth of the picture for the domestic audience, for whom symbolism, metaphysics and abstraction were just fiddling while Spain burned. *Cine metafórico* created an alternative reality that excited the unconscious mind, but the fantasy on-screen was easily dismissed as irrelevant because the language of metaphor, as opposed to that of the state, was too elusive. What was missing was a recognisable, collectively agreed-upon point to the whole venture: a punchline.

Black humour

As the regional languages of Basque, Catalan and Galician were declared illegal and prohibited from being uttered in school, song or on-screen, so the dictatorship enforced control of expression that curtailed the ability of creative persons to utilise ordinary language in their art. The Basque songwriter Mikel Laboa, for example, sang of his oppressed cultural identity by means of anguished, non-verbal cries.[4] Elsewhere, the word *rojo* (red) was outlawed for fear of its communist overtone; though such absurdity received its rightful response in Luis García Berlanga's *Bienvenido Mister Marshall* (*Welcome Mister Marshall*, 1953), wherein the three lights that villagers imagine shining through their fountain are described as 'yellow, blue and ... coloured'.[5] Humour, the blacker the better, is a characteristic Spanish response to hardship. It is for this reason that Italian Neorealism, though a massive influence on dissident cinema, was also derided for its sentimental response to poverty by Spanish filmmakers who substituted black humour, which dispensed with respect for reason and infuriated those who ascribed to it.

Surrealism does not presuppose a link between intelligence and reason in the target of its humour and, indeed, uses humour to prove their disassociation. In his *Anthologie de l'humour noir* (*Anthology of Black Humour*, 1972b), Breton writes of transcendence attained by the operation of intelligence beyond the limits of reason as something akin to poetic intuition, but also celebrates humour as a product of juxtapositional chance. As J. H. Matthews explains, 'through use of intelligence, man can expect the practice of black humour to achieve, more effectively and with less delay, the act of surmounting the real' (1976: 93). This act, akin to transcendence, was exactly what opponents of Francoism desired. In Luis García Berlanga and Juan Antonio Bardem's *Esa pareja feliz* (*That Happy Couple*, 1951), a young, poor, but happily married couple win a competition to be treated like royalty for a day and are chauffeured at breakneck speed around shops, restaurants and places frequented by the wealthy middle classes. The humour from juxtaposition allowed by Breton was everywhere in this comedy of manners, not least in the scene where the bewildered couple find themselves in a hall of distorting mirrors at the funfair and are horrified by their apparent transcendence: 'It's a mirror? Just as well. I thought that's what we were like.'[6]

Berlanga and Bardem were schooled in Spanish theatrical traditions and film theory respectively. Together they made *Bienvenido Mister Marshall*, in which a grotty Castilian village must employ Andalusian disguise in order to impress visiting American dignitaries. The juxtaposition of poverty and riches, the reality of a backwards Spain and the fantasy of a progressive, Francoist nation, the knockabout laughs of the venture and its deeply melancholic resolution informed a comedy that was blackest in the sequence given over to the dreams of its protagonists. A shot of characters leaving the village cinema is accompanied by a voice-over (Fernando Rey) that explains how film-watching has banished the habitual preoccupations of this audience; but the subsequent illustrations of their dreams reveal how the experience has also removed their conditioning and prejudices, replacing them with expectancy and potential, demonstrative rather than affirmative images, suggestion rather than persuasion. The deaf and bumbling mayor dreams himself into a western, where the saloon 'shoot-em-up' is conducted via a garbled approximation of English and concluded with play-gun pops. The local priest dreams of his participation in a holy procession but is arrested by the FBI who interrogate him in front of the McCarthyist anti-communist committee. And the prim schoolmistress plays a cheerleader in her dream, in which she is ravished by her entire team of players: or at least she would have been if that scene had not been cut. The irony was that dreams are indicative of freedom and desire, but here all they revealed was how the collective subconscious of the inhabitants of this village had already been colonised by Hollywood. An imagination that was stifled by the threadbare fantasies of nationalist Spanish propaganda found no redemptive reality in the American equivalent.

In *Calle Mayor* (*Main Street*, 1956), *Plácido* (1961) and *El verdugo* (*The Executioner*, 1963) black comedy provided an intelligent, subversive means of realising dystopias that was ideal for depicting Francoist Spain. Black humour treats intellectual power with respect, while ridiculing authority based on arrogance. Black humour, as Breton described, was '*par excellence* the mortal enemy of sentimentality' (1962: 21), especially the nationalist, Francoist kind. Bardem's *Calle Mayor* begins with the cruel joke of a coffin being delivered to a man who is very much alive, and then delves into sadism with the story of a spinster who is courted by a handsome youth so that he can dump her for the amusement of his friends at the annual town dance. Berlanga's *Plácido* tells of a charitable campaign to make rich families adopt a vagrant for Christmas.[7] The scattershot farce involved excruciating juxtapositions of poverty and riches that included poor guests ungratefully dying at the table. Blackest of all, Berlanga's masterful *El verdugo* presented an apprentice executioner in the pay of the Francoist state, whose ridiculous efforts to avoid having to perpetrate his trade include stopping arguments in the street. In the film's vicious conclusion, the executioner is plied with drink and manhandled to his duty behind the anonymous but dignified prisoner. As a black comedy, this was startlingly devoid of light and therefore, as Berlanga intended, representative of the society it depicted.

The Surrealist effect of these films was not about aesthetics; for Surrealism on film does not thrive by becoming art but by cultivating the incongruous and performing the impossible. These depictions of an alternative reality to that propagated by the jingoistic *Noticiarios y Documentales* newsreel was a way of discrediting Francoist society; for in place of crusading war films, biopics of saints and priests, musicals with warbling child-stars and flamenco-flavoured melodramas, these few examples of dissident cinema invited their audience to attach significance to their humour and interpret jokes as metaphors and allegories of their existence.

Surrealism was arguably an ingredient and aftertaste of the most overwrought melodramas, such as Luis Saslavasky's *La corona negra* (*The Black Crown*, 1951) and the exploitation films of Jesús Franco Manera, better known as Jess Franco (though the Internet Movie Database lists 67 known pseudonyms for this most prolific of directors), who worked mostly in liberal France or Italy on films such as *La isla de la muerte* (*Eugenie: The Story of Her Journey Into Perversion*, 1970) and *Vampyros lesbos* (*Lesbian Vampires*, 1971); but the final film to be considered truly Surrealist during the dictatorship was Buñuel's *Tristana* (1970). Ostensibly a faithful adaptation of what Buñuel described as the worst novel by Benito Pérez Galdós, this excuse to return a supposedly penitent Buñuel to Spain proved tantamount to a terrorist attack. Perhaps, more than any other film by Buñuel, *Tristana* dispenses with aesthetic considerations in order to examine the moral, psychological and physical trauma of the young, eponymous virgin (Catherine Deneuve). Traded as commodity between the two Spains of an impoverished, aged gentleman (Fernando Rey) and a wealthy young rogue (Franco Nero), Tristana finally succumbs to cancer and has to cope with a false leg, which fascinates Buñuel who thereafter affords it the film's few close-ups. Objects such as this may be designed for a purpose, but when they are separated from that workaday destiny by Surrealist endeavour they become the focus for perverse and cruel thoughts. The Surrealists believed that staring at an object for long enough prompted it to acquire significance far in excess of its function, and the close-up was the cinematic equivalent of the stare. Buñuel therefore hid his bomb in plain sight, daring the censor to react to the image, but without stating explicitly what, if anything, was symbolised by the orthopaedic leg. The Surrealist dare was to see how the censor reacted. Unable (or unwilling) to say exactly what it found so disturbing about the film, the censor banned it for a reference made to duelling.

In Tristana's false leg the Surrealist object was not subconscious but explicit. However, its meaning was nonetheless latent because it was withheld and therefore dangerous, disruptive and malignant because it prompted thoughts of decay, perversity and sado-masochism that emerged from a subconscious response to its importance, not least by Alfred Hitchcock who – as Buñuel recounts – was jealously enraptured by its provocation (1985: 195). Whereas the latent content of the image inspired the pleasure principle, the manifest content of its social and political context was debased. What was left after the leg was removed and *Tristana* was banned was the residue of a single, spent subjectivity, that of Francoism. All this from an artificial leg? The deployment of this Surrealist tactic can too often result in a parlour game for pseuds, but the distinction between latent and manifest content that is illustrated by this catalyst is vital to an understanding of Surrealism and its appearance in dissident Spanish cinema during the dictatorship, because only latent content is associated with imaginative freedom and infinite potential. Like a dream of political and creative freedom that emerges from consideration of Spain's potential beyond Francoism, the image of the leg is so charged with possibility that it overwhelms its contemplators with notions of chance, many of which relate to erotic desire. Matthews states that 'it is thanks to chance, apparently, that poetic liberation is effected in its purest form' (1976: 3). Desire therefore created a Surrealist objective out of post-Franco Spain and fetishised any object that might promise the beginning of liberty, even an artificial leg.

Juxtaposition: Post-Franco Spain

The weirdness of Surrealist imagery was tailor-made for the outlandish but increasingly fashionable pose of young consumers in the aftermath of Spain's transition to democracy, though the philosophies and practices of the art were also maintained by those whose rejection of reason was born of a compulsion to challenge this mask of gaiety. In the midst of the rampant capitalism that followed victory for the Spanish Socialist Worker's Party (PSOE) in 1982, those with Surrealist tendencies or affiliations were arguably more indebted to the Marxist reorientation of Surrealist ideology than their forebears. André Breton's view of Marxism as 'la plus grande chance de libération des classes et des peuples opprimés' ('the greatest opportunity for freedom of the oppressed classes and peoples') (1949: 134), therefore seemed naïve to those who understood that tyranny was not only the expression of capitalism but of any hegemony, ranging from the fascism of the dictatorship that had birthed them to the socialism of the democracy in which they lived. However, just as the transition to democracy signified political self-determination, so did it allow for freedom of expression and a consequent liberation of instinct. Thus, the subversive ideology of Surrealism, if not its aesthetic trappings, was largely redundant in such movements as Madrid's deliberately outrageous *movida* and the Barcelona School, from where had emerged low-budget genre films by Catalan directors such as Vicente Aranda. Horror had always had its claws into Surrealism, with the more preposterous representations of monsters and ghouls providing a superficial frisson of contact with the unknown that usually peters out after a few nightmares; but in films such as *La novia ensangrentada* (*The Bloody Bride*, 1972) Aranda employed absurdity as a way around censure. A film such as *Clara es el precio* (1974) was extravagant and shocking, but beneath its veneer of meaning-lessness there was nothing meaningful anyway; for the film's unintelligibility was its purpose. Aranda claimed he had 'sacrificed conventional coherence for the cinemato-graphic and phenomenological possibilities of each action' (in Hopewell 1986: 69). It was as if Surrealism was being retrained for peacetime, de-clawed and made ready to be reinserted into society like the ETA terrorists who were granted their amnesty. The challenge to make Surrealism newly relevant depended upon the ability of artists and filmmakers to recognise that oppressive forces emanated equally from a society that placed its values in freedom.

Imagination was once more the key, its powers rescued from films of the transi-tion such as Víctor Erice's *El espíritu de la colmena* (*The Spirit of the Beehive*, 1973) and Saura's *Cría cuervos* (*Raise Ravens*, 1975) that had painfully detailed the loss of wonder in a child's gaze as metaphor for the quashing of creative power in Spain. In their sad portraits of the infant Ana (played in both films by Ana Torrent), the imagination and its capacity to reach new territories of fear and thrills were shown as stifled in a land dedicated to distracting its citizens from ideas of escape and otherness. Then, Surreal-ism had been sharpened and strengthened by contact with an omnipotent foe; now, following the revoking of censorship by royal decree in November 1977, Surrealist imagery was a flimsy slap against the easy target of Catholicism in post-dictatorship Spain.

One indomitable exception was Iván Zulueta's *Arrebato* (*Rapture*, 1979), a feverish and abrasive display of horror conventions filtered through the paranoid psychothera-peutical self-diagnoses of a drug-addled film director, who confronts his damaged psyche by reacquaintance with his childhood and vampirically captures his alter ego by filming himself while asleep. Perverse to the point at which the subject's love of the cinema fills the void left by the filmmaker's lack of concern for his own life, *Arrebato* culminates in the character's escape to an unexplored area of existence that is rendered by the use of Super-8, speeded-up film and a fractured, frenetic montage that links the experience of drugs with that of watching film. Like the work of a Spanish Ken-neth Anger, *Arrebato* delivers hallucinatory imagery that demands its inclusion in any study of Surrealism in Spanish cinema, though the nature of a work that is midway bet-ween experimentation and exorcism is perhaps more appropriately understood as the autobiographical flare-and-fade of its director, who studied at Madrid's Offi-cial Film School during the dictatorship and participated in New York's Arts Students League at the time of Andy Warhol, John Cassavetes and indeed Kenneth Anger. His subsequent estrangement from the cinema was only partially stayed by his brilliant design-work on the film posters of others, including that for the delayed Spanish release of *Viridiana* in 1977 and those for Pedro Almodóvar's comparatively restrained *Laberinto de pasiones* (*Labyrinth of Passions*, 1982) and *Entre tinieblas* (*Dark Habits*, 1983).

Nevertheless, the spectacularly kitsch juxtapositions of Catholic, pop and trash culture that punctuate the features of Pedro Almodóvar, in whose early, funny films the Church was a figure of fun rather than fear,[8] prompt accusations of Surrealist tactics in films such as *Entre tinieblas*, in which a convent decorated in a kitsch mix of sacred and profanely pop iconography is the refuge of an ex-novice drug addict on the run from the police, who finds redemption and lust in the company of the lesbian Mother Superior, the drug-addled Sister Manure, the sex-mad Sister Rat and Sister Sin, who enjoys an intimate relationship with her pet tiger. In *La ley del deseo* (*Law of Desire*, 1987) the once-sacred family unit of Francoism is re-created from a homosexual, his transexual brother and this brother's daughter Inmaculada (so-named for her immaculate conception) by his ex-wife played by real-life transexual Bibi Anderson. The deeply compassionate film ends with a *pietà* of the homosexual and his psychotic bisexual lover in front of a burning altar decorated with saints, tacky souvenirs and Hollywood figurines. The key to the humour was juxtaposition, though this became gradually darker in Almodóvar's films of the 1990s, when disillusionment with democracy and the fall-out from the drug- and sex-fuelled excesses of the *movida* soiled the once-carefree mood.

By *¡Átame!* (*Tie Me Up! Tie Me Down!*, 1989) Almodóvar was seeking to reconcile his wayward characters with the more traditional elements of Spain. The film opens on multiple images of the Virgin Mary and the Sacred Heart of Jesus Christ before cutting to the story of psychopathic Ricky (Antonio Banderas) and his soulmate and captive Marina (Victoria Abril), an ex-junkie porn star. True love wins out and the final sequence sees this couple reunited with the traditional, rural family unit, though all the mundane ceremonies and moral conventions that entailed seemed to betray the director's earlier flirtation with Surrealism in favour of a grown-up consideration of the damage it caused. Elsewhere, Surrealism in post-Franco Spanish cinema was similarly separated from its sting. The Catalan director Juan José Bigas Luna, for example, employed playful irony to contrast Catholic and Surrealist iconography in *Jamón, jamón* (1992) and treated them equally, with a keen eye for the erotic potential of both, clearly relishing rather than reviling a joyous, all-encompassing celebration of Spanishness. 1992 was also the year of Spain's enthralment to David Lynch's television series *Twin Peaks*, which was screened by the Tele 5 television channel in what seemed like five-minute segments between half-hour advertising breaks that turned Surrealism into just another object of consumerist desire.

Surrealism rising: Julio Medem

The place of Surrealism in modern creative endeavour is often reduced to a commodity or style. Surrealism requires the participation of the spectator and, therefore, cinematic Surrealism especially requires the production of spectacle, which would be without value if it only referred spectators to the known. Matthews describes the reciprocal relationship of the spectator as 'a re-creation on the plane of responsiveness which treats the material presented as perhaps no more than the starting point, merely the exciting cause of poetic experience' (1976: 190). However, by the early 1990s, the Romantic ideal of democracy had lost its way amidst too many scandals of political corruption, making cynicism, passivity and depression the most characteristic response.[9] It was also at this time that the Basque filmmaker Julio Medem revisited Surrealism upon Spanish and Basque cinema as a way of reviving dreams and examining what had gone wrong. His 1991 debut *Vacas* (*Cows*) dealt with the rivalry between three generations of Basque farmers as seen from the viewpoint of their cows and it resembled a paranoid dream of the Basque Country in which Romantic and Surrealist ambitions for the nation collided. In *Vacas*, as in Buñuel and Dalí's *Un chien andalou*, close-ups of the cow's eye provide a portal between the conscious and the subconscious that is exploited by Medem juxtaposing the subjectivities of man and cow in order to challenge the authority of the historical perspective.

In the four chapters and cyclical narrative of *Vacas* Medem presented a Surrealist interpretation of a romantic object of desire: the Basque nationalist dream of a rural Basque utopia. As desire creates a Surrealist object, so Basque nationalism had turned the Romantic ideal of Basque nationhood into an expression of the suppressed Basque subconscious, precisely because the pleasure it afforded was heightened by being forbidden under Francoism. A desire to render on film this vision of a rural Basque utopia also made the perspective of Medem's enquiry historical, the function of which was 'to illustrate how ... the expression of romantic literary attitudes lends itself to interpretation in the light of Surrealist goals' (Matthews 1976: 15). Most obviously in *Vacas*, Medem looks back to Romanticism, but uses Surrealism, which Breton considered the heir to Romanticism, to re-establish contact with the past.

As a child, Medem had become aware that filmmaking created a space and time that was open to infinite, manipulative possibilities. This imagined world on Super-8 had revealed itself as an arena for tangible representations of his subconscious and thus a medium for the realisation of illusionary places, times and relationships. Essential to an understanding of Medem's Surrealist credentials is his scholarly adherence to Nietzsche and Freud. Nietzsche's *The Birth of Tragedy* (1872) convinced him that non-rational forces reside at the foundation of all creativity and reality and inspired him to see human interaction in terms of non-rational forces such as coincidence, fate, duality, irrational outbursts and subconscious impulses that he subsequently deciphers by reference to Freud. It is also notable that the greatest literary influences on Medem are magic realism, a close associate of Surrealism, which revels in the paradox of the union of opposites like life and death as well as the tensions that exist in South American literature, where they illustrate the conflict between the extremes of a pre-colonial past and a post-industrial present, and in contemporary Spain, where the transition from dictatorship to democracy effected a similar collision of opposites.

In *Vacas*, *La ardilla roja* (*Red Squirrel*, 1993), *Tierra* (1995), *Los amantes del Círculo Polar* (*Lovers of the Arctic Circle*, 1998), *Lucía y el sexo* (*Sex and Lucía*, 2001) and even his documentary about the Basque conflict, *Pelota vasca: la piel contra la piedra* (*Basque Ball: The Skin Against the Stone*, 2003), Medem combined ideas of duality, existentialism, psychopathology, metaphysics, mysticism and Surrealism in films that are a product of their interaction. Medem is a fabulist whose ideas for an improved sense of reality lead to his use of film as a metaphysical plane and as such he maintains the association of Surrealism with Spanish cinema. Indeed, it is possible to trace Medem's evolution through the three phases of Surrealism's evolution – the Freudian, the metaphysical and the Marxist – whereby his films can be seen to demonstrate the evolution of incidental dream-imagery (*Vacas*, *La ardilla roja*, *Tierra*) through structural metaphors (*Los amantes del Círculo Polar*, *Lucía y el sexo*) towards a cumulative politicisation (*Pelota vasca* and its long-gestating sister-project *Aitor*).

Medem writes by assuming the subjectivity of his characters and employs the Surrealist trick of automatic writing, 'very fast, automatically, without worrying about the style, just enjoying the sensation of exploring the intimate lives of others' (Medem 2001: 9). As he writes, he transposes real actions and personal experiences into the metaphysical plane of his films, thereby employing a method of protracted self-analysis that allows this metaphysicist to move between real and fictional worlds. As he admits, 'I know I achieve this with my films. To do this I have to apply logic and technique, but my first ideas are always these moves from reality to fiction.'[10] His films are therefore full of fantastical relationships that exist because of the emotion invested in them. There is Jota's creation of Lisa, the perfect girlfriend, out of the amnesiac Sofía in *La ardilla roja*; Otto's Ana and Ana's Otto in the juxtaposed subjective retelling of events in *Los amantes del Círculo Polar* and, most optimistically of all, Lucía's recreation of her post-traumatic self in *Lucía y el sexo*. Perhaps what most allies Medem with Surrealism is his love of chance, a theme that he has explored in films that meditate on fortuitous meetings, symmetries and collisional coincidences. The Surrealists added caveats to their manifestos that allowed for both black humour and coincidence as a result of juxtaposition and were thrilled when opposites not only reacted, but attracted, for these exceptions proved the rules of a universe defined by irrationality and resulted in what Jean Cocteau called 'the appearance of a tragic gag' (1992: 133). Imagine, for example, if after a million juxtapositions in his paintings of a pipe (*Ceci n'est pas une pipe* (*This is not a pipe*, 1929) and an apple (*Ceci n'est pas une pomme* (*This is not an apple*, 1964)), a tired and emotional Magritte had accidentally or automatically betrayed his own treason of images by painting a cat and writing 'this is a cat' below. Medem has similar fun with equations: in *Tierra* a man named Ángel meets his guardian angel (now what are the chances of that?) and the Nietzschean conflict that ensues is also echoed in the luck of Otto and Ana in *Los amantes del Círculo Polar*, soulmates who have the fortune to meet each other and the bad luck of being step-siblings when they do.

In his second manifesto of Surrealism, Breton admitted that 'we [the Surrealists] are quite willing, historically, to be considered today as the tail, but then such a prehensile tail, of Romanticism' (1962: 184). This admission was pragmatic, even opportunistic. Surrealists look backwards for selfish reasons, hoping to justify their questions by finding universal, cyclical incidents of their asking. Where Surrealist filmmakers aspire to a shift from concrete reality to the intangibility of a world beyond reason they find liberation in the infinite and therefore often end up going around in circles, happily trapped in a cyclical patterning that is characteristic of Medem's features. In his films and his long-cherished script for *Aitor*, which links several incidents of torture to a protagonist accompanied by a choir comprised of ghosts of victims of the Basque conflict, Medem continues to mix ever-shifting patterns of ordinary events and descriptive details together with supernatural and dreamlike elements.[11] Thus, his work may be situated in a particularly Spanish tradition of Surrealist filmmaking that has never lost its way amidst meaningless fantasy, but has stayed focused on the aim of revolution by maintaining an ironic, suspicious and determinedly political stance amidst all its magic, metaphors, black humour and coincidences. It is for this reason that Surrealism's challenge to both political oppression and freedom alike has never been compromised, but remains persistent in Spanish cinema.[12]

Notes

1   All but one copy was destroyed; the only remaining copy was smuggled out of Spain by the director's son, Juan Luis Buñuel, who hid the reels under bullfighting paraphernalia in the back of his Pyrenees-bound van. Author's interview with Juan Luis Buñuel, Paris, November 2001.

2   For García Lorca, the cinemas that he frequented during his stay at Columbia University on his journey to New York (1929–30) offered spectacle that outstripped even that of the metropolis in the midst of the Wall Street Crash. Of the cinema he wrote, 'I am a fervent supporter because one can create wonders' (1994 (VI): 1092).

3   Dalí collaborated with Buñuel on the Sadean follow-up *L'Âge d'or* (*The Golden Age*, 1930) and continued to explore the extent of Catholic damage of subconscious thought in his paintings, while García Lorca distilled cinematic notions into his theatrical works and poetry and wrote one script entitled *Viaje a la luna* ('Trip to the Moon').

4   Laboa can be seen performing in this way in Julio Medem's *Pelota vasca: la piel contra la piedra* (*Basque Ball: The Skin Against the Stone*, 2003) as accompaniment to images of the bombing of the Basque town of Guernica during the Spanish Civil War.

5   This evasive last adjective was also invoked in the circumventory telling of such tales as Little Coloured Riding Hood, which was cryptically recounted by the humorist Forges, who mixed up all the syllables but kept the sing-song rhythm of the telling. Impossible to translate, Forges' original went like this: 'ba i tacirupeca jaro por el quebos, *ta-ra-ri*, *ta-ra-ra*, docuan cedi "¡Joder! ¡El bolo!"'

6   Author's transcription and translation.

7   The film's working title was 'Seat a Poor Person at Your Table'.

8   The reference to the famous criticism made of Woody Allen by aliens in his *Stardust*

Memories (1980) is intentional, for Almodóvar was often compared to Allen in the early part of his career. For a comparison of his representations of the Catholic Church in his later films, see the paedophile, predatory, murderous monks of *La mala educación* (*Bad Education*, 2004).

9   On 12 January 1991 Alfonso Guerra had been forced to resign as vice-president following a scandal involving his brother. In March 1992 the governor of the Bank of Spain, Mariano Rubio, resigned over insider training. In November 1992 the High Court ordered a search of the central offices of the ruling PSOE as part of an investigation into illegal financing of the party through the FILESA company.

10 Author's interview, Madrid, 23 April 2004.

11 This reference to *Aitor* is to the second draft of the script, given to the author by Medem on 23 April 2004.

12 This chapter was completed with support from the AHRC.

Peter William Evans

AN *AMOUR* STILL *FOU*: LATE BUÑUEL

All that we see or seem
Is but a dream within a dream.
                    – Edgar Allan Poe

The final scene of *Cet obscur objet du désir*, Luis Buñuel's last film, shows Mathieu (Fernando Rey) and Conchita (Angela Molina/Carole Bouquet) peering through a shop window in a Parisian arcade, studying a woman repair, after the manner of a famous painting by Vermeer, a bloodstained torn garment. As they watch, we see them mouth inaudible words while we hear the music of Wagner's *Die Walküre*, moments before they walk away, perhaps to be killed by the terrorists' bomb that serves as the film's dramatic epilogue, a Parisian *Götterdämmerung*.

Buñuel refers to his love of opera in *Mon dernier soupir* (*My Last Breath*, 1982), especially Verdi, Puccini and, above all, Wagner, whose music is a constant motif in his films, most famously the *Liebestod* melody from *Tristan und Isolde*, added years later by him to the soundtrack of *Un chien andalou* (*An Andalusian Dog*, 1929). But, as Agustín Sánchez Vidal (1993) has noticed, Wagner also makes appearances in *El ángel exterminador* (*The Exterminating Angel*, 1962) through the character of Leticia, known as 'la Valkyria'; through the feminised version of Tristan in *Tristana*; in the discussion of *Tristan und Isolde* by the defecating diners in *Le Fantôme de la liberté* (*The Phantom of Liberty*, 1974); and in the recasting of Siegmund and Sieglinde as Mathieu and Conchita in *Cet obscur objet du désir*. The common thread is fascination with the mysteries of erotic love. *Un chien andalou* begins the cycle of Buñuel lovers drawn to each other by irresistible forces leading to fraught relationships between incompatible individuals unable to overcome the imperatives of a compulsive desire. In alternating the passionate intensity of Wagner's *Liebestod* with the jauntier rhythms of two Argentine tangos, Buñuel acknowledged the ambivalently sacred and profane drives of tormented lovers submerging themselves both willingly and reluctantly in a love-hatred that brings mutual destruction as well as redemption.

In *El ángel exterminador* Silvia Pinal's Mexican *Walküre* is a troubled presence. *Tristana*, too, adheres to the pattern of compulsive relationships, most darkly exemplified through Tristana's failure to break free from her attachment to Don Lope, her much older husband and former guardian whom she murders. *Cet obscur objet du désir* ends, in a sense, where Buñuel began: to a Surrealist obsession with the notion, first explored in *Un chien andalou*, that love is the driving force of human existence.

Unlike the paintings of Salvador Dalí, his collaborator on *Un chien andalou*, which draw more directly on Freud's symbols in *The Interpretation of Dreams* (1900), Buñuel is fascinated less by precise meanings than by mystery and the opaque landscape of the unconscious:

> The element of mystery, essential to all works of art, is generally lacking in films. Authors, directors and producers take great pains not to trouble our peace of mind by closing the marvellous window of the screen to the liberating world of poetry. (2000b: 138)

Human desire, largely male but also female, is the overarching subject in late as well as in early Buñuel. But where does 'late' begin? In his first collaboration with Serge Silberman and Jean-Claude Carrière (*Le Journal d'une femme de chambre* (*Diary of a Chambermaid*, 1964))? With *Belle de jour* (1966)? Or in the 1970s with *Tristana*, a film that breaks the partnership with Silberman and Carrière to team Buñuel up for the only time with Julio Alejandro and Eduardo Ducay? Buñuel himself thought of *La Voie lactée* (*The Milky Way*, 1969), *Le Charme discret de la bourgeoisie* (*The Discreet Charm of the Bourgeoisie*, 1972) and *Le Fantôme de la liberté* as a trilogy, significantly leaving out *Cet obscur objet du désir*, which seems, owing to its more conventional narrative structure, less 'late' aesthetically than the trilogy. Perhaps arbitrarily, I shall take 'late' Buñuel to mean literally the last three films, *Le Charme discret de la bourgeoisie*, *Le Fantôme de la liberté* and *Cet obscur objet du désir*, arguing that in these one finds all the characteristics of a phase that evolves in the late 1960s, the origins of which lie to some extent in his earliest collaboration with Silberman and Carrière, even though no radical break ever takes place with earlier stages of his work. As Linda Williams (1981) has pointed out, the view – of critics like Pauline Kael and Penelope Gilliatt – that Buñuel matured into mellowness is as untenable as that of the uncomplicated 1920s iconoclast. The very least that can be said of late Buñuel is that the smoother and sunnier the manifest content of these films the more troubling their latent meanings. For all their different thematic and formal perspectives all three films return to the topic of *amour fou*.

For Buñuel, as for all the Surrealists, love is an irresistible force, but one that invariably makes fools of lovers. Francisco in *Él* (1952), Archibaldo in *Ensayo de un crimen* (*The Criminal Life of Archibaldo de la Cruz*, 1955) and Don Jaime in *Viridiana* (1961) head for disaster by pursuing torrid idols of love. In each case Buñuel is careful to expose not only the irrational behaviour of grown-up men but also the childish origins of their adult predicaments. In *Él* Francisco (Arturo de Córdova) is a husband whose paranoid jealousy is partly readable as the result of a mind misshapen by over-identification with the father. The violence towards his lovers in *Ensayo de un crimen* is prompted by Archibaldo's (Ernesto Alonso) buried hostility towards his mother. In both cases the tormented desires of the adult play out dramas of punishment and revenge against sinning parents. Buñuel's female protagonists though often, in contrast to the men, emerging triumphant from skirmishes with their objects of desire, are driven unconsciously by childhood demons. *Susana* (*The Devil and the Flesh*, 1950), *Le Journal d'une femme de chambre*, *Belle de jour* and *Tristana* are all films where patriarchal figures experience the supplications as well as the wrath of designing women. In these cases, characteristically for a director who never lost interest in the socio-political agenda of Surrealism, desire is to some extent defined by yearning for release from the traditions of religion-dominated cultures and ideologically-determined notions of role and gender. In some films – for example, *Susana*, *Belle de jour* and *Tristana* – a woman uses her sexuality to wrest control from a man, becoming in the process at times a nightmarish apparition of female empowerment. In *Susana* this self-conscious deployment of female sexuality, as the anti-heroine (Rosita Quintana) sets about enslaving in turn all the men in the *rancho* household, before being returned to the infernal reformatory from which she has fled, is ultimately construed by her detractors as diabolical. In *Le Journal d'une femme de chambre* Celestine (Jeanne Moreau) not only takes the lead in steps to capture Joseph (Georges Géret), the suspected child-killer, but also marries one of the pillars of the establishment in order, one suspects, to take advantage of his power and wealth. In *Tristana* the heroine's treatment of her guardian/husband Don Lope is a perverted form of *amour fou* by which she is both enslaved and revolted. Significantly, Tristana's failed attempts to liberate herself from the law of the father by eloping with the young painter, and her return to Don Lope – whose cries for help on his deathbed she cruelly ignores – highlight the vice-like grip on the woman of parental authority. Another of Buñuel's characters for whom liberty is only a phantom, Tristana had long ago become too much the feminised version of her guardian's patriarchal conformism to be truly free.

The power of the unconscious is often stressed in Buñuel's films through dream or daydream. Sometimes, as in *Le Charme discret de la bourgeoisie*, the boundaries between dream, daydream and reality are clearly drawn; at others, as in *Belle de jour*, the distinctions are blurred. Though made at a time when Surrealism was no longer the provocative force it had been at the outset of Buñuel's career, *Belle de jour* remains true to the movement's irreverence and capacity for unsettling the viewer. As Buñuel himself comments, the film is in part an exploration of the darker corners of sexual perversion: 'Le film me permettait aussi de décrier assez fidèlement quelques cas de perversions sexuelles' ('The film also gave me the opportunity to describe quite accurately various types of sexual perversion') (1982: 298). The scene of the flashback to Séverine's (Catherine Deneuve) abuse as a little girl by the workman is readable in a variety of ways, but at the very least it invites speculation on the notion that Séverine's desires are affected by memory. The scenes at the brothel are a form of self-harm, exemplifying theories and clinical evidence that this is often a woman's way of coping with sexual abuse. Séverine's supposed blow for freedom – looking for it in a brothel, however 'soignée' and chic, surrounded by agreeable working-girl colleagues – is ultimately as futile as the sniper's *acte gratuit* as he picks off the innocent bystanders on the streets of Paris.

The brothel is still a space which – for all her enflamed sexuality (lesbian as well as heterosexual) – is, as Michael Wood (1992) also argues, a patriarchal setting, whose Madame has introjected the outside world's ruling values. The discipline administered by Madame Anaïs (Geneviève Page), to which Séverine submits, is the authority of the patriarch. Moreover, the *amour* almost *fou* that Séverine feels for the dandyfied gold-toothed hoodlum cannot shake off an allegiance to her conventional, bourgeois husband Pierre (Jean Sorel), whose side she will never leave.

The exposure of Séverine's contradictory desires is achieved through a blend of dream, daydream and reality, an aesthetic shaped by psychoanalytical accounts of identity that continued to fascinate Buñuel in his last three films. Even if, as Buñuel argued, Surrealism as a political force ended in failure, its impact on his own cinematic art remained as potent at the end as at the beginning of his career:

> I'm often asked whatever happened to Surrealism in the end. It's a tough question, but sometimes I say that the movement was successful in its details and a failure in its essentials. Breton, Eluard and Aragon are among the best French writers in this century; their books have prominent positions on all library shelves. The work of Ernst, Magritte and Dalí is famous, high-priced and hangs prominently in museums. There's no doubt that Surrealism was a cultural and artistic success; but these were precisely the areas of least importance to most Surrealists. Their aim was not to establish a glorious place for themselves in the annals of art and literature, but to change the world, to transform life itself. This was our essential purpose, but one good look around is evidence of our failure. (1985: 123)

Le Charme discret de la bourgeoisie

In *Le Charme discret de la bourgeoisie* the twin themes of *amour fou* and politics are conveyed through Buñuel's most elaborate dream imagery since *Belle de jour*. Curiously, though, his lovers have become so sophisticated their erotic drives have been sabotaged by fussy etiquette. Largely through their unconscious – the dreams, daydreams and slippages, sometimes displaced onto minor characters – and through the political gestures of young radicals, Buñuel's characters here show signs of revolt against the enervating impulses of a decadent society. Among the group of friends constantly inviting one another to meals and other social gatherings, only the Sénéchals (Stephane Audran and Jean-Pierre Cassel) seem capable of rising above the *comme il faut* manners of their class, still apparently drawn passionately to each other, willing to delay attention to their guests in their smart salon by first satisfying their libido in the garden. The Thévenots (Paul Frankeur and Delphine Seyrig), by contrast, are an ill-matched pair, Simone involved in an affair with Miranda's ambassador to France, François unable to confront his cuckolder except in dreams. These sophisticates pursue an affair, hardly *fou*, failing to risk all for love, Raphael too wedded to a life of diplomatic privilege, Delphine preferring the pleasures of a clandestine liaison, having become, like Séverine in *Belle de jour*, too lost to the comforts of her own class, unable or unwilling to risk scandal by ditching her husband for an uncertain future with her lover. The nearest the pair get to public exposure of their furtive romance occurs at her lover's apartment where, even then, Simone prefers to use the opportunity of her husband's unexpected appearance to emerge from his bedroom rather than remain concealed until his departure in order to resume her Sadean encounter with Raphael. Simone's reaction is readable in at least two ways: either as a calculated attempt to humiliate her husband, or as a declaration of priorities, the valuing of her death-dealing status as a bourgeoise over a life-affirming passion with her Latin lover. The latter seems more probable. Whatever the motivation, the scene succeeds in confirming the suspicions of François, in whose dream of revenge against his betrayer Buñuel achieves his most brilliant projection of the workings of the unconscious. The equivalent of the *mise-en-abyme* narratives of Jan Potocki's *The Manuscript Found in Saragossa*, a favourite text of his, or Poe's 'A Dream within a Dream' (1849), this most elaborate of the six dreams, reveries or quasi-dreams of the film, seems inspired by *The Interpretation of Dreams*. The division of the dream in two movements, the first of which is attributed to Sénéchal, as well as the displacement onto other characters in the dream of hostility towards Raphael, adheres to Freud's remarks on condensation and transference in discussion of latent and manifest content. In the first part of the dream the group of friends discover they are not dining at the Colonel's home, but on stage, actors in a production of Zorrilla's *Don Juan Tenorio*. The significance of the choice of play refers to Buñuel's often-quoted approval of what he considered its *amour fou* and Surreal qualities (Moix 1983: 14), as well as to the equation in Thévenot's dreaming mind – filtered through Sénéchal's – of Raphael with Don Juan, the notorious rake. Yet again, though a Don Juan, Raphael makes no real sacrifices for love, continuing to pursue Mme Thévenot clandestinely, refusing to compromise more profane desires. For this, as well as for his betrayal of friendship, he is humiliated in the second part of Thévenot's dream – and now dreamt directly by the dreamer – when finally at the Colonel's home the insults against Raphael's country, Miranda, reach a crescendo that prompt his shooting of the Colonel. The dreamt gunshot leads to Thévenot's awakening from the dream, and he explains that 'je rêvais, non que Sénéchal rêvais...' ('I dreamt, no I dreamt Sénéchal dreamt that...') to a wife whose flagging sexual response is confirmed not only through her dalliance with Raphael but also by preference for sleeping apart from her husband in a single bed.

Le Fantôme de la liberté

Buñuel's taste for formal inventiveness substitutes experiments in dream imagery with complications of narratives stitched together through chance, or the 'hasard', so revered by the Surrealists. For Buñuel, 'chance governs all things; necessity, which is far from having the same purity, comes only later' (1985: 171). Perhaps for that reason *Le Fantôme de la liberté* is his favourite film: 'If I have a soft spot for any of my movies, it would be for *The Phantom of Liberty*, because it tries to work out this theme' (ibid.). In pursuit of liberty and mystery, the film adheres to no conventional pattern. In taking aim at the bourgeoisie, religion, political and social injustice, Buñuel weaves narratives that move from a Bécquer-inspired story set in Spain during the Napoleonic invasion to episodes set in contemporary France.

At first glance appearing to abide by the laws of chance, the film is of course the dramatisation, precisely through its careful structure, of the impossibility of chance and liberty. The title, after all, refers to liberty as a phantom, an apparition caught in an in-between world, between life and death, earth and heaven, freedom and enslavement. As in the multiple narratives of *La Voie lactée*, and the dream sequences of *Le Charme discret de la bourgeoisie*, *Le Fantôme de la liberté* sees Buñuel identifying himself more fully than, say, in the Mexican films with the European art-movie auteurs whose artistic liberties may set them apart from classical Hollywood directors, but for whom sovereignty also remains limited in various ways, circumscribed by commercial, aesthetic, psychological and other circumstances.

The episode at the inn, with its key incident of the incestuous *amour fou* of the nephew and aunt, illustrates this principle. Here, a number of characters are brought together *par hasard* in an inn that recalls the work of Cervantes. Among the motley group of characters friars are scandalised when the exhibitionist Monsieur Bermans (Michel Lonsdale) and his dominatrix lover Mlle Rosenblum (Anne Marie Deschott) perform before them an act of sadomasochism. Through the regressive antics of this unlikely couple, as through the illicit romance between aunt (Hélène Perdrière) and nephew (Pierre-François Pistorio), Buñuel warns that sexual desire is determined by tendencies that imprison the seekers of liberty, chained as they are to Oedipal memory. The warning is delivered in an earlier scene, where the Napoleonic captain's passion for Doña Elvira is expressed not only as necrophilia – the desire of a living man for a dead woman – but as Oedipal yearning, an assault on the patriarchal authority of the Church, since the libidinal gesture is performed while the lifeless beloved is on her knees, praying beside the statue of her husband. Suddenly the stony hand of the deceased strikes the head of the transgressor.

This Oedipal moment is a prelude to the liaison between aunt and nephew. François introduces his aunt to Monsieur Bermans as 'ma mère', an older woman who belongs to a long line of glacial Buñuel blondes: Viridiana, Séverine, Simone Thévenot, Leticia, the *Walküre* and others. Her pallor makes her an almost perfect object of necrophilia. In *Belle de jour*, for instance, the mutual passion of Pierre and Séverine is to some extent inspired by morbidity. Pierre is attracted to a woman whose appearance is cadaverous, a woman devoid of colour, often dressed at home in white or pallid colours, and his own profession as a doctor identifies him routinely with illness and death. His own physical features and gestures align him with passive, almost lifeless forms of behaviour, and reciprocate the anaemic nature of Séverine's desire. Buñuel's attraction to pallid hues, claustrophobic milieux and characters whose behaviour recalls the lifelessness of corpses or statues, is indebted to his 'Master', the Marquis de Sade, in whose writings love is invariably associated with death.

Lisa Downing (2003) has rightly drawn attention to the one-sidedness of the argument by Elisabeth Bronfen (1992), who restricts her discussion of necrophilia to male treatment of women, but her point about necrophilia as a form of punishment by men of what are regarded as faithless, cruel or wanton women, seems appropriate in the context of Buñuel's incestuous lovers, the aunt and nephew (and the brother and sister, appearing later) in *Le Fantôme de la liberté*.

The sexual attraction of François for his aunt undoubtedly derives some of its most intense pleasure from the contravention of social taboo. François is, additionally, regressing to childhood, illustrating Freud's notion in *On Sexuality* (1981) that perversion represents the first phase of the erotic drive in the infant. François' desire for his aunt could also be partially explained as pleasure derived directly from the precariousness of his object of desire, and of his relationship to it. The surrender of identity in the act of love prefigures terminal disintegration in death, and represents for many of Buñuel's lovers – such as Don Jaime in *Viridiana* or Alejandro in *Abismos de pasión* (*Wuthering Heights*, 1954) – a victory over mortality and the empirical world.

The presentiment of mortality is perhaps what ultimately drives Séverine, the *Walküre* and, here, the ageing aunt to these necrophilic men. In the case of the latter the Oedipal implications provide an additional frisson of pleasure, one, moreover, associated with a need to punish the aunt/mother for arousing such feelings. François' hectoring treatment of his aunt/mother is followed by a momentary attempt to murder her by placing a pillow on her face as she lies in trepidation on the country inn bed, an act from which he eventually recoils, an *amour fou* that stops short of *liebestod*.

Cet obscur objet du désir

Reverting to a less experimental 'Surrealist' form – avoiding, say, the overlaps of dream and reality of *Le Charme discret de la bourgeoisie*, or the complications of narrative in *Le Fantôme de la liberté* – *Cet obscur objet du désir*, a film not devoid, however, of narrative inventiveness, focuses more consistently on the topic with which Buñuel began his cinematic odyssey in *Un chien andalou* and *L'Âge d'or* (*The Golden Age*, 1930)): *amour fou*. It draws on *La Femme et le pantin*, Pierre Louys' 1898 novel, already screened as *The Devil is a Woman* (Josef von Sternberg, 1935), and chronicles the lives of two individuals, a middle-aged man and a young woman, inescapably linked to each other by the perverse destiny of a fateful passion. Though the core of

the film is *amour fou*, Buñuel does not fail, as usual, to provide extenuating circumstances to explain the vicissitudes of desire. While, as Víctor Fuentes notes *à propos*
Le Fantôme de la liberté (2000: 191), the Napoleonic war defines not only through
reason and enlightenment, but also havoc and destruction, the meaning of modernity, so in *Cet obscur objet du désir* contemporary realities are seen through the veil
of that *inquiétude*, a kind of politicised form of Baudelairean anguish, so common in
the work of the Surrealists. If the origins of Surrealism lie in the post-Dadaist reaction
to the First World War, the sources of *inquiétude* overshadowing *Cet obscur objet du*
désir are the rise of terrorism, both global (for example, the Middle East) and local
(for example, ETA). The narrative of *Cet obscur objet du désir* is punctuated by the
explosion of bombs, readable not only perhaps in narrowly political terms but as a
more general comment, in line with the politics of the eye-slicing opening of *Un chien*
andalou, on the failure of Western civilisation to overcome prejudice and injustice.
The explosion with which the film closes is linked to a fanatical religious group – and
is in that sense true to Buñuel's irreverent humour – but, following on from strains
from *Die Walküre*, its aim is wider: autobiographical, perhaps, as well as aesthetic and
socio-political.

In keeping with the spirit of Surrealism, *Cet obscur objet du désir* is another of
Buñuel's (penultimate) inward journeys of self-scrutiny. The film's confessional form is
underlined by the casting in the last of his four key roles in a Buñuel film of Fernando
Rey. The actor is on record as saying that Buñuel thought of him in some respects as
a dark alter-ego, the more negative, more decadent middle-aged alternative to Paco
Rabal, his 'sobrino', the younger, wish-fulfilment version of a self. Less psychotic than
Arturo de Cordova's Francisco in *El*, a heightened variant of the jealous self so vividly
portrayed in Jeanne Rucar de Buñuel's autobiography, *Una mujer sin piano* (1991), Fernando Rey's characters reflect the drives of a Sadean sensibility, moving through the
suicidal melancholia of Don Jaime in *Viridiana*, the corrupt liberalism of Don Lope
in *Tristana*, the suave tyranny of Don Raphael in *Le Charme discret de la bourgeoisie*,
to the love-crazed bourgeois wanderer of *Cet obscur objet du désir*. Rey is Buñuel's
modern Orpheus descending into the underworld of his own unconscious. In all the
films Rey, like Buñuel – forever after 1939 an exile – is either an outsider or a wanderer.
An outsider in *Viridiana* and *Tristana*, he is, in the former, out of time in the new
Spain represented by his illegitimate son; in the latter a liberal at odds with, but finally
defeated by, his conservative heritage. In *Le Charme discret de la bourgeoisie* he is a
Latin American in Europe, and in *Cet obscur objet du désir* he is neither wholly 'Mateo'
nor 'Mathieu', but a liminal mixture of the two, club-class man, at ease anywhere and
nowhere in luxurious international settings. An exploration of the underworld of his
own identity, the journey also becomes an attempt at redeeming Conchita from both
a humble background and petty bourgeois morality. In rescuing Conchita, Mateo/Ma-
thieu also projects onto his split object of desire the dividedness of his own subjectivity,
and exposes the Oedipal nature of his passion, since he woos Conchita not directly
but through her mother. His love for Conchita cannot be fulfilled, remaining forever

unsatisfied, a vivid illustration of post-Freudian accounts of the lover's inability ever to attain his object of desire.

As Mateo/Mathieu pursues his aim, he fails to take account of the objective reality of Conchita, of changing times, of shifts of power in post 1960s feminist-driven relations between the sexes. The difference in age between them makes each guilty of misperception of the other's reality. Like his failure to distinguish between the Conchita of Carole Bouquet and Angela Molina – a confusion enhanced by Buñuel's happy decision to replace Maria Schneider with two actresses – Conchita's alternating form of addressing him as either 'Mateo' or 'Mathieu' reveals the mismatched focus of their obscure desires. What resists obscurity is that for all their differences, mutual needs condemn them to each other's eternal company.

Their love, not explained, is highlighted through allusion to Wagner's great opera *Die Walküre*. After endless humiliations and reconciliations, Mateo/Mathieu and Conchita are reunited on the train from Seville to Paris. He feels compelled to explain to his fellow first-class compartment travellers the row with Conchita that has climaxed in a water fight. At their journey's end, these seemingly incompatible lovers are seen strolling down a Parisian arcade, still inseparable, still affectionate, still squabbling. Like Baudelaire's *flâneur*, they stroll down the arcade, as Walter Benjamin puts it, *à propos* the Baudelairean prototype, observing the phantasmagoria of the city and its commercial centres of luxury (1999). They enter a 'Réprographique' shop and, at Mathieu/Mateo's insistence, drift towards a shop where through the window a woman is seen in the pose of a Vermeer painting repairing a garment, while the arcade loudspeaker announces, after news of the Archbishop of Siena's death, that a musical interlude would follow. The music is one of the most lyrical moments in *Die Walküre*, as Siegmund and Sieglinde – the separated twins – ignorant of their family bond, sing of their mutual passion:

Siegmund: ...was mich berückt / errat ich nun leicht / denn wonnig weidet mein Blick. (... What enchants me / I can easily tell / for rapturously my eyes gloat on you).

Sieglinde: Wie dir die Stirn / so offen steht / der Adern Geäst / in den Schläfen sich schlingt! / Mir zagt es vor den Wonne / die mich entzückt! / Ein wunder will mich gemahnen: den heut zuerst ich erschaut. (Look how your forehead broadens out and the network of veins winds into your temples / I tremble with delight that enchants me / It reminds me of a miracle: though I first saw you today, I've set eyes on you before).

Siegmund: Ein Minnetraum / gemahnt auch mich: / in heiß Sehnen / sah ich dich schon! (A dream of love comes to my mind as well: burning with longing I have seen you before).

In this fragment from his panegyric of love, Siegmund concentrates on Sieglinde's physical beauty, on his visual pleasure. While also extolling Siegmund's beauty, Sieglinde moves on to sing of the irresistible force that draws them together, and of dreams. The irresistibility of their love conforms to the Buñuelian pattern – in keeping with a general tendency in Surrealism – that love is a destiny from which no lover is ever willing or able to escape; perhaps even, remembering Buñuel's Catholic origins, a duty.

However many humiliations Conchita heaps on him – culminating in his exclusion from the house he has bought her, and in whose patio he is sentenced to watch, from outside the locked iron-grilled gate, her passionate surrender to her young lover, El Morenito – Mathieu/Mateo remains a martyr of love, ever willing to forgive his *belle dame sans merci*, hoping forlornly for fulfilment of a desperate longing. The scene in the arcade, like the episode involving Conchita and El Morenito in the Sevillan patio, may well be, as Paul Sandro argues (1987: 154–5), a meditation on the compulsion to tell a story, but it is surely also about the pathos of *amour fou*.

In Buñuel's more extended treatment of *amour fou* – as in *Un chien andalou*, *L'Âge d'or*, *Él*, *Tristana* or *Cet obscur objet du désir* – there is a prevalent aura of anguish, the reflection in microcosm of the wider *inquiétude* that governs the world, a sense of unease in part inspired by de Sade's view of a universe at war with itself. The lover yearns, is indeed compelled to yearn, for a never-to-be-fulfilled ideal of love. More usually, violence, humiliation and degradation, not happiness, are the fruits of erotic love. Through this union the lover renounces the world and seeks redemption through love. Like Sieglinde, Mateo/Mathieu is a dreamer, his attachment to Conchita – recalling the incestuous love of Sieglinde and Siegmund – not just a Sadean transgression of the laws of nature and culture, but also a defiance of the world. His love for Conchita, his contempt for marriage as an institution that would pollute their love, falls short of the ideal. His failure to recognise the uniqueness of either version of Conchita (Wood 1981) – a sin against the individuating process of true love, as opposed to indiscriminate lust – his allegiance to bourgeois norms and etiquette in his wooing of the young woman (approaching her mother to authorise the relationship), and even his insistence on physically consummating his passion, compromise the purity of his *amour fou*, a condition that occasionally seems to have more of the medieval *loco amor* about it – a frenzied lust – than the force of *amour fou* and its disdain for worldly values.

In some ways, comically, Conchita's refusal to surrender her virginity to Mateo/ Mathieu preserves the courtly ideal, taking perverse pleasure from his frustration, and his everlasting obsession. These shortcomings, and the opportunities they afford for humiliation, lighten through Buñuel's characteristically corrosive humour the gravity of theme. Comedy allows for a mixed response, enabling Buñuel to push the viewer away from the pathos of content, giving the film here, as throughout his work, the distant perspective and necessary detachment that lead to greater understanding.

David Gillespie

NIGHTMARE AS PHANTASMAGORIA: SURREALIST SUBTEXTS IN RUSSIAN FILM

Surrealism and Soviet film

It is hardly surprising that Surrealism has not been a major force in Russian and Soviet cinematic culture, largely because that culture was dominated by the demands of an aggressive political ideology that imposed on it the 'basic method' of socialist realism for five decades or so. Soviet art was meant to be positive and forward-looking, and illogicality, the subconscious, Freudianism and fantasy all met with official disapproval (although the latter could be acceptable if it was 'optimistic', or pointed to a harmonious future). Certainly, from 1934 to the death of Stalin in 1953 it was impossible to make films that did not conform to the Party line on Russian history and Soviet social development, although Sergei Eisenstein, in the second part of *Ivan Groznyi* (*Ivan the Terrible*, completed 1946, shown only in 1958) came as close as anybody to subverting the historico-mythological foundations on which the Stalinist state had sought to legitimise itself. Indeed, Eisenstein seems to be the one Soviet director deeply impressed by Surrealism, especially during his 14-month stay in Mexico from December 1930 to February 1932, as Anne Nesbet, quoting André Breton, has remarked:

> Under the influence of Mexican art and 'the actual, astonishing, linear structure of the stunning purity of the Mexican landscape', Eisenstein began to produce drawings remarkable for their line, the speed in which they were produced and their sheer quantity: 'they were drawn almost automatically. But how obscene they were!' Where the Surrealists had called for automatic writing, Eisenstein responded with automatic drawing. In some respects, however, he was closer to the Surrealist cast of mind during his stay in Mexico than at any other time, for here he basked for a time in what André Breton had called in 1924 'the light of the image', and for once came close to simply revelling in 'reason's role being limited to taking note of and appreciating, the luminous phenomenon'. (2003: 129–30)

There is not much evidence of Surrealist influence in Eisenstein's subsequent work on his return to the Soviet Union, and he failed to complete his film in Mexico.[1]

Socialist realism demanded of the artist a 'truthful, historically concrete' depiction of reality 'in its revolutionary development', that is, a realistic (as interpreted by Party ideologues) portrayal of social processes and historical conditions, but with a clear indication that conflicts can be resolved in the here-and-now or not too distant future, opening up the 'radiant future' for the benefit of all mankind. It was, in other words, not reality as it was in actual fact, but reality as it ought to be, and one day will be. Stalin's cultural spokesman, Andrei Zhdanov, made this explicit in his speech at the First Soviet Writers' Conference in 1934: 'Soviet literature should be able to portray our heroes; it should be able to glimpse our tomorrow. This will be no utopian dream, for our tomorrow is already being prepared for today by dint of conscious planned work' (1977: 21–2).[2]

This ideological credo remained in force until the collapse of the Soviet Union in 1991, although it is clear that after the death of Stalin artists took it upon themselves to erode its aggressive edge and generally make it increasingly irrelevant to cultural production. Nevertheless, even in the post-Stalin years the Party and the literary establishment militated against all forms of stylistic experimentation, alternative views of reality and history, and the adoption of foreign or 'alien' ways of cultural expression. To be sure, Surrealism, with its emphasis on the subconscious and irrational, was seen as a manifestation of cultural decadence in the West, a symptom of the 'crisis in Western culture' and by direct ideological implication a harbinger of the coming collapse of a discredited socio-political system.[3]

Yet there are some unmistakeable traces of Surrealist influence in some films of the early 1930s, no doubt informed by the work of Luis Buñuel and Salvador Dalí before Soviet cultural isolationism really set in under Stalin. Alexander Faintsimmer's *Poruchik Kizhe* (*Lieutenant Kizhe*, 1934), based on a 1928 novella by Iurii Tynianov, is set in the troubled reign of Pavel I, son of Catherine the Great. The Tsar is portrayed as an incompetent and eccentric buffoon, in himself an absurd symbol of the inanities of Russian Autocracy. But it is the lieutenant who represents true absurdity, as he does not actually exist and was dreamt up spontaneously by a military scribe to hide his own error in cataloguing the ranks. Rather than admit the mistake, the whole military apparatus connives in concealing the fact that Kizhe is an invention. Kizhe is blamed for raising a false alarm and sentenced to a hundred lashes, but since there is no physical body to take the punishment, it is perpetrated on a cannon (the sight of able-bodied men energetically thrashing the phallus-like barrel is open to obvious Freudian interpretation).

Kizhe's star comes in the ascendancy when he is promoted to the rank of colonel, and then general. He becomes engaged to be married, but when he does not turn up, the ceremony nevertheless carries on without his actual presence: 'the lieutenant is secret, he doesn't have a figure', his perplexed bride is told, and she then proceeds to kiss the air in the absence of her spouse. When it is announced that he is dead, he is to be buried with full military honours, but, created by the military to hide its own absurd incompetence, 'Kizhe' is reduced in rank by the Tsar and given a private's funeral.

Poruchik Kizhe is not only a satirical swipe at the irrational excesses of the Tsarist court, but it also has a sinister prophetic ring to it: in a few years time individuals who fell foul of the authorities would be declared non-persons, and historical figures who joined the lists of the repressed or undesired would be air-brushed out of photographs, chronicles and official accounts. The film plays around with notions of reality and absurdity, its seemingly 'correct' ideological reading of Russian history undermined by its playful illogicality, and the exuberance of its own quirkiness.

If *Poruchik Kizhe* is 'difficult to categorise … a genuine oddity' (Kenez 1992: 227), an even stranger film is Abram Room's *Strogii iunosha* (*A Strict Youth*), completed in 1936 but banned until after Stalin's death because of its 'Formalist' features. The charge of Formalism in Stalinist culture was a serious one, and could lead not only to artists losing the right to have their work published, but even to arrest and imprisonment as 'class enemies'. It is easy to see why this film upset Party critics, with its meandering plot and lack of ideological conviction, as well as the ambivalently presented 'positive' and 'negative' heroes. Instead, the film draws attention to itself as a self-consciously visual experience, with irrational juxtapositions, seemingly meaningless dialogue, and some startlingly innovative imagery and camera angles. Moreover, the boundary between dream and reality is deliberately blurred, if not occasionally entirely eroded.

Strogii iunosha was a play written by Iurii Olesha, who also wrote the screenplay. Olesha is the author of a celebrated novella, *Envy* (*Zavist*), published in 1927, which takes as its theme the inability or unwillingness of men of aesthetic sensitivity to fit into the new society born in 1917, and abounds in contrasting images of sight and blindness, perception and ignorance. The play *Strogii iunosha*, published in 1934, develops the theme of 'old' men in the 'new society', and concentrates on the relationship between an affluent surgeon, Iulian Stepanov, his younger wife Masha and her potential lover Grisha Fokin. At the end of the play the relationship of Grisha and Masha is dominant, with Stepanov abandoned as he prepares to travel to London for an international medical conference. The film, however, ends with a final resolution promoting harmony and social progress as Stepanov and Masha remain together. Olesha's play contains the verbal repetitions of Room's film, as well as the emphasis on purity, athletic youth and the values needed in the 'classless' new society. Olesha's play is complex and playful, but Room's film is incomparably more ingenious. It is full of visual tricks and in-jokes, such as allusions to the films of Eisenstein. The occasional use of inter-titles to explain the narrative reminds us of silent movies of the Soviet 'golden age'.

Whereas some of the film's dialogue is deliberately absurdist, eye-catching details include the erotically-charged juxtaposition of half-naked athletic bodies and Roman sculptures, as well as the muscled men taking part in chariot races. There are arresting contrasts of colour and imagery, such as white floors and walls offset by characters dressed in black or the outline of a black grand piano. Social inclusion and exclusion are suggested by shots through windows and mirrors, or characters filmed either standing in front of or behind bars and railings. The ghost-like, dreamy and erotic nature of this reality is emphasised as a man walks through a garden of gigantic flowers, suggesting decadence, and when Grisha and Masha kiss for the first time in a concert hall the floor suddenly changes into a pool of rippling water. Although Stepanov and Masha are eventually reconciled, the real interest of this film is its idiosyncratic visual style, which sets it apart from anything else in Soviet cinema of the 1930s, and which even today offers a remarkably rich and varied viewing experience.[4]

However, below the surface (re)conciliation of husband and wife there is a deeper subterfuge. Both the play and the film include scenes of characters walking up or down staircases, suggesting the possibilities of social progress in the new society, but, more sinisterly, movement in the opposite direction. The final image of Stepanov leading his wife back into the distinctly vaginal image of the entrance to their home has a clear Freudian significance, however, as Masha abandons a future with the youthful and athletic Grisha for the security of home with the older, more corpulent but materially more affluent Stepanov. Masha therefore chooses the past over the future. More sinister semiotic allusions include the discus-throwing sportsman Kolia with the letter 'D' printed on his shirt: this letter suggests the leading sports complex 'Dynamo', which during much of Soviet rule was under the tutelage of the secret police. Masha's future is consequently being decided not only by the Komsomol activist Grisha, but the NKVD, too. The frequent repetition by a girl of the refrain 'Neuzheli ty ne ponimaesh'?' ('Do you really not understand?') is directed at those who are not fully in tune with the new society, and has a clear resonance in the culture of the time. In Grigorii Aleksandrov's ideologically impeccable *Tsirk* (*The Circus*, 1936) the American performer Marion Dixon finally comes to true awareness of Soviet reality as she marches with the massed ranks on Red Square, and her 'now I do understand' marks the narrative and ideological closure of the film. In the new society, acceptance and acceptability are based on being able to 'understand' that the future is built on the present, and that progress is inexorable and directed from above.

Both the play and the film of *Strogii iunosha* gently subvert the ideological priorities of Stalinist politics. The same precocious young girl insists that the new society must be based on people's desires, none of which should be refused: 'It is necessary to fulfill all desires for man to be happy. Do you really not understand? And if desires are not fulfilled, then man becomes unhappy. You can't suppress desires. Supressed desires provoke bitterness. That is the theory. If you want to sit on a step then sit on it' (Olesha 1934: 76). It is not suggested that Grisha is envious of Stepanov's wealth, and he denies that socialism means that everyone should be 'levelled', but he, the man of the future, does not deny that socialism means 'inequality', simply agreeing that in a classless society 'one man cannot have power over another' (Olesha 1934: 77, 80).

The Stalinist equation of physical perfectibility and spiritual contentment was expressed by the 'founder of socialist realism and originator of Soviet literature' Maxim Gorky in the slogan 'a sound mind in a sound body'. In other words, physical perfection in humans is a coda for the workings of the machine, and the equation of man and machine, as in Dziga Vertov's *Chelovek s kinoapparatom* (*Man with the Movie Camera*, 1929), itself a symbol for social progress in the dynamically evolving and growing city. As if on cue, towards the end of the film a Gorky lookalike beams approvingly at the athletic young people. However, the device is artifical and transparently contrived, and positivist ideology is subverted at the very end of the film. Masha chooses Stepanov, whose name 'Iulian' suggests the Julian calendar adopted by Julius Caesar but abandoned by Russia in 1918, and rejects Grisha. The name 'Grisha' is the diminutive of Grigorii, recalling the Gregorian calendar proclaimed by Pope Gregory XIII and adopted in 1582 by most European countries, and in 1918 by the new workers' state. Masha, therefore, is going back in time, history and politics.

It is therefore easy to see why these two films of the 1930s were not only 'difficult', but potentially subversive in ideological terms.[5] In an age where realism was the accepted (and enforced) medium, they foregrounded absurdity, illogicality and even the subconscious, thereby provoking questions about the empirical reality around them. These films were very much the exception to the norm of standard socialist realist fare, and further suggestions that the brave new world born in 1917 was a phantasmagoric illusion had to wait until the twilight years of Soviet power in the late 1980s, when the powers-that-be allowed all sorts of nightmare visions on to the screen. However, we should not forget the occasional foray into fantasy and allegory in the relatively liberal 1960s, such as Elem Klimov's *Dobro pozhalovat, ili postoronnim vkhod vospreshchen* (*Welcome, or Unauthorised Access Prohibited*, 1964), with its flights of adolescent imagination literalised, and Gennadii Poloka's *Respublika ShKID* (*The Republic of ShKID*, 1966), a *Lord of the Flies*-like political allegory where children take over a school and where the dynamics of power structures are explored with unsettling effect. In Soroka's film we come close to anarchy and social collapse, but closure brings about (somewhat artificially) social cohesion and stability, largely through the rehabilitation of the rebellious Jewish boy Iankel, whose initial inner turmoil gives way to a need for love and acceptance.[6]

The nightmare relived: the 'glasnost' years

The unsavoury underbelly of Soviet society was exposed to all in the socially chaotic yet culturally exhilarating years following Mikhail Gorbachev's accession to power in 1985. His policy of perestroika, begun shortly after he became the General Secretary of the Communist Party, was designed to make Soviet society democratically more accountable and economically more efficient. Experts to this day are unable to agree whether the policies Gorbachev set in motion were actually designed to bring about the end of the totalitarian state, or whether the collapse of the Soviet Union in 1991 was an unfortunate if unforeseen result of his intention to instigate reform from above on a stagnating economy and inflexible political structure. Still, collapse it did, and filmmakers were among the first to make explicit that what for decades had been taken as a resilient and stable society moving steadily toward economic prosperity and social harmony was, in fact, built on lies, coercion and illusion.

Karen Shakhnazarov's *Gorod Zero* (*City Zero*, 1988) offers a crystallisation of social thought in this period. With a stellar cast featuring some of the biggest names of Soviet stage and screen in the 1980s (Leonid Filatov, Armen Dzhigarkhanian, Evgenii Evstigneev and Oleg Basilashvili), it begins with the engineer Varakin (Filatov) getting off a train in a provincial backwater and, in true 'Twilight Zone' fashion, walking into what seems a parallel universe. As he gets off the train, he is alone in the dark on the station, and similarly alone in the street, before being picked up by a taxi and taken to his hotel. All around him is gloomy, empty space. The next day he makes his way to the factory he is meant to visit in order to negotiate the sale of air-conditioners, but he is not expected. The manager's secretary strolls around her office naked, her nakedness not noticed by anyone but Varakin. The director of the factory (Dzhigarkhanian) is not even aware that his own chief engineer died eight months previously. Varakin's situation becomes increasingly bizarre. He has lunch in a restaurant which is about to close for its own lunch break, and is offered a cake in the shape of his own head. He is forced to watch as it is sliced up to a musical backdrop from the group on stage, playing for him, the only customer. When he refuses to eat it, the chef shoots himself, and as the only suspect Varakin is summoned to the police.

In the lines of the Eagles' 1977 hit 'Hotel California', he can check out any time he likes, but he can never leave. There are no tickets or trains back to Moscow, a child tells him he will die there in the year 2015, and the police will not allow him to leave the town. He takes a taxi to look for another railway station out of town and comes across the local museum, whose curator (Evstigneev) shows him round the various stages of human history, from Troy and ancient Rome to the Gulag, the forced labour camps, the War with Germany (1941–45), and the Moscow international festival of youth in 1957. This latter event was the first signal that post-Stalinist society was opening up to the West, although the curator reminds him that Soviet citizens could still be arrested for conducting relationships with foreigners at that time. The unsettlingly lifelike image of Attila the Hun was created through a DNA sample, and other realistic statues include the Ukrainian nationalist Nestor Makhno and a young Joseph Stalin. Varakin is told that many famous people were born in this town, embracing the highlights of Soviet technical achievement and the whole span of Soviet history, from the Revolution to the present.

Varakin is treated to a historical and philosophical reflection on Russia, Europe and democracy by the town Prosecutor (played by the actor-director Vladimir Men'shov), who insists that Russia must remain strong and united in the face of new threats, the most significant being rock 'n' roll. Introduced into the town in 1957, the year of the youth festival, it clearly marks the influx of Western ways and the end of cultural isolationism. To the writer Chugunov (Basilashvili) rock 'n' roll is the real criterion of progress, a vibrant contrast to the rotting oak that is the symbol of the town's historical lineage, now more than a thousand years old. Indeed, as he announces to a jubilant crowd, rock 'n' roll can help overcome the vestiges of Stalinism, stagnation and subjectivism! At the end of the film Varakin tries to flee, but he ends up alone and adrift in a boat on a fog-bound river, going nowhere.

Shakhnazarov's film is a witty and absurdist mixture of illusion and reality, but with symbolic references to Russia's past, present and future. When Varakin is interrogated by the police, he is told that the cook Nikolaev did not kill himself, but was in fact murdered, and, just as in a totalitarian police state, everything Varakin says in his defence is twisted and distorted. 1957 is seen as a key year, when the Iron Curtain was breached for the first time. Varakin is a simple man caught up in increasingly bizarre events, and is mistaken for the cook's son. He is even forced to dance rock 'n' roll in homage to his 'father'. The issue of fatherhood is also mentioned by the museum curator in the form of the historical pretender False Dmitrii. This was the name given to three men who, during the Time of Troubles (1598–1613) variously claimed to be the son of Tsar Ivan IV (the 'Terrible'). Fatherhood is related to sovereignty and statehood throughout Russian culture, most notably in Pushkin's historical novel *Kapitanskaia dochka* (*The Captain's Daughter*, 1836). The Russian Tsar was traditionally called the 'little father' of his people, and so paternity and statehood have consistently been linked in Russian political thought. One of the film's more obvious metaphors is the ancient oak tree in the forest, under which the great hero Dmitrii Donskoi, conqueror of the Mongols at Kulikovo Field in 1380, once sat. When people start pulling off its branches, it is a clear sign that the old ways are no longer respected, or even relevant.

Shakhnazarov's film revolves around notions of truth and its mirror image, objective reality and its illusion. Only Varakin sees that the secretary is naked, only he notices that the cake is in the shape of his own head, and only he thinks that the cook committed suicide. Perhaps Varakin is, indeed, the son of Nikolaev the cook, and it is his stable domestic life in Moscow that does not exist. After visiting the past in the town's museum, he is told by a young boy of his future, and even what will be written on his gravestone. The films asks: in this period of cultural and political tumult, just what is the relationship of past and present, where is truth and where is falsehood? As Varakin is stranded at the end of the film, surrounded by mist and water, so, too, the film remains open-ended, as if unwilling or unable to offer a definitive comment on this decisive moment in Russia's history.

A much more unsettling picture of community values is provided by Iurii Mamin's *Bakenbardy* (*Sideburns*), released in 1990. At the beginning of the film an unnamed community is in a state of anarchy, as youths run riot and scandalise the older generation. Order and propriety are re-established only with the arrival by boat of a group of young men with long sideburns and dressed in nineteenth-century garb: Pushkin look-alikes. One form of oppression, though, replaces another, as these youths emphasise the dominance of literary values over all others, muscle-bound thugs recite Pushkin's epic poem *Mednyi vsadnik* (*The Bronze Horseman*, 1841), and in one hilarious scene a sculptor is forced to recast with great dexterity his bust of Lenin into that of Pushkin.

Mamin's film is a clever deconstruction of Russia's much-vaunted dependence on its literary culture, which leads, in the absence of any politically legitimising institutions, to a cultural totalitarianism. Followers of Alexander Pushkin and Mikhail Lermontov battle it out for the soul of Russia, and social order is finally re-established at the end as the Pushkin followers have their sideburns shaved off. As in Shakhnazarov's film, reality and nightmare are blurred, all too easily interchangeable.

Both Shakhnazarov and Mamin subvert accepted truths and realia, revealing inanity and absurdity that lead to the victory of chaos and anarchy much feared by those who yearn for a strong state. Both directors give a knowing wink to a native audience that would intuitively understand the many hints and allusions to their nation's history, culture and politics. Similarly irrational excursions into the border between reality and illusion can be seen in other films of the period, especially Oleg Teptsov's *Gospodin oformitel'* (*Master of Decoration*, 1988), an adaptation of Alexander Grin's 1925 short story *Seryi avtomobil'* (*The Grey Motor Car*), and Mark Zakharov's *Ubit' drakona* (*To Kill the Dragon*, 1989), an adaptation of Evgenii Shvarts's political allegory *Drakon* (*The Dragon*, 1943). Both adaptations emphasise the surreal and absurd dimensions of the original texts.

Teptsov's film is set in the early years of the twentieth century, leading to the First World War, a cataclysmic time that was to have disastrous consequences for Russian history. The director's blurring of the concrete and imaginary, what is and what seems to be, represents the erosion of art and reality. It is the beginning of the end of a way of life, then as in the late 1980s. This allegorical allusion brings Teptsov's film close to Alexander Sokurov's *Skorbnoe beschuvstvie* (*Mournful Indifference*, 1986), based on George Bernard Shaw's play *Heartbreak House* (1920), a similarly disparate series of images suggesting chaos, dislocation and the end of a world.

Shvarts's play is an allegory about the good knight Lancelot challenging and, despite huge odds, eventually killing the dragon that has terrorised a town for 400 years. However, instead of thanks from the townspeople, he is soon forgotten as the corrupt mayor and his son take the credit and impose their own dictatorship on the town. In the final act Lancelot returns and has the mayor and his son arrested, but he is aware that the metaphorical Dragon, the monster of fear and acquiescence, will take some time to vanquish: 'And all of us, after long work and torment will be happy, very happy at last!', are the play's closing words (Shvarts 1999: 339). The play is an allegory of Nazism and its ultimate defeat, although during the Thaw years (1953–64) it came to be interpreted also as a sign that the dragon of Stalinism had been destroyed. Zakharov's film takes the allegory one step further, to suggest the destruction of the whole Soviet system. The dragon's kingdom may be made to look like a fascist state, with soldiers and guards dressed in black leather and Nazi helmets, but even here Zakharov allows himself satirical liberties. Surreal cinematic touches abound, as people appear unexpectedly and in strange places, there are startling juxtapositions of people and statues or suits of armour, and shots of long, dark passages and dungeons. The dragon asks Lancelot why he wants to fight for the freedom of townspeople who do not know what freedom is, and, indeed, fear it. Men such as Friedrichsen are prepared to accept any-thing for a quiet life and the semblance of stability, even if it means their own castra-tion (an all-too-painful symbol of political disempowerment).

The tyrannical dragon assumes many guises, and his plane that attacks Lancelot both looks and sounds like an enemy fighter jet from George Lucas's *Star Wars* (1977). When the townspeople think that the dragon has been slain, they immediately inter-pret their new-found 'freedom' as a licence for wanton violence, pillage and all-out anarchy. In fact, Lancelot does not kill the dragon, it continues to thrive in the form of a schoolteacher surrounded by adoring children (not unlike the pictures of a paternal, caring Lenin looking down on children that used to adorn Soviet streets). The end of the film sees Lancelot and the dragon head off into the snow for yet another duel. Russia's history of terror and oppression does not end: 'Now will begin the most inter-esting time', says Lancelot.

Both films by Teptsov and Zakharov feature fantastical plot twists and surreal im-ages, where the boundary between reality and nightmare, sanity and madness, is barely palpable. In Zakharov's film, the mayor proclaims himself President, announcing that he is a hero because he had suffered from insanity during the dragon's rule, thereby linking himself to the Soviet dissidents incarcerated in psychiatric hospitals during the Brezhnev years (1964–82). The traumas of terror and insanity, above all, are caused by the acquiescence and tacit encouragement of the masses, who remain, in Lancelot's words, 'slaves', 'non-people', 'sheep' and 'a herd of cattle'. Moral condemnation comes from, of all people, the mayor/President (played by the great comic actor Evgenii Le-onov), who says to his son: 'And now you will be asked who, during the difficult years, were the time-servers, and who suffered spiritually, at whatever cost to their health.' What price de-Sovietisation, indeed?

Andrei Tarkovsky: dream, memory and identity

The films of Andrei Tarkovsky stand apart from the general corpus of Soviet cinema through the originality and bravery of the director's individual vision, and his fierce affirmation of the personal. As we have seen, Surrealist subtexts embed themselves in political narratives throughout much of Soviet cinema history, but Tarkovsky's dreams and flights of fantasy simply reinforce the integrity of his highly personal criteria. It is not unusual to see a Tarkovsky film, beginning with his first feature, *Ivanovo detstvo* (*Ivan's Childhood*, 1962) where fire and water are in the *mise-en-scène*, to incongru-ously unreal effect; indeed, such shots easily carry his signature. Similarly, in this first film dream and reality become almost indistinguishable, with a flooded forest through which Ivan has to wade to get to his own lines, ghostly German figures passing by in the night and a war plane that has nose-dived at a right-angle into the earth among the arrestingly vivid, but semi-real, images. Is the scene when his mother is shot Ivan's own dream, or a memory, or, indeed, neither, simply a directorial narrative device to establish context and background?

Dreams/memories feature in other films. In *Solyaris* (*Solaris*, 1972) Kris Kelvin (Donatas Banionis) is visited by the 'ghost' of his former wife, Hari (Natalya Bondarchuk), as his subconscious interacts with the ocean on the planet Solaris, and he struggles to deal with a reality that is, in fact, an unreality. Again, are the scenes of his family life on earth actually a memory, or a dream, an unrealisable fantasy? In *Zerkalo* (*Mirror*, 1974), his most personal film, dreams and memories are almost indistinguishable from the real world throughout the film; fire and air, and even living animals, possess qualities that should be beyond them, and incongruities litter the narrative.[7] Human life is irrational and subject to perverse swings of the imagination, not readily controlled and adapted by external forces. Indeed, the body itself is transformed into an object that can defy gravity: in *Zerkalo*, as in *Solyaris* and *Zhertvoprinoshenie* (*The Sacrifice*, 1986), human bodies in loving embrace and gliding through air become a metaphor of sexual love.

The relationship of dream and reality is at the heart of *Stalker* (1978), and the whole film itself can be viewed simply as a dream (or nightmare, given the plot's apocalyptic implications). *Stalker*'s now-celebrated dream sequence takes in all manner of artifacts from twentieth-century life, including religion and war, and *Stalker* warns us that without understanding of one's fellows and personal self-abnegation modern man is doomed. In *Nostal'giia* (*Nostalgia*, 1983) the relationship of reality and dream/fantasy becomes so contradictory as the writer Gorchakov tries to embrace the very different cultures of Italy and Russia that the final frame literalises his dilemma. Gorchakov sits behind a pond looking at the camera, against a Russian rural backdrop, but framed by the arches of a Catholic cathedral, as a Russian folk song is heard on the soundtrack.

Dream and fantasy are an important part of Tarkovsky's cinematic thought, for it is in an individual's dreams of his past that the real truth of personality is revealed; similarly, with fantasy the truth of the present and the future is affirmed. Dream, fantasy, imagination, religious faith and the intricacies of the subconscious and the soul are what make us human, and what we must cling on to as we go into the technological future. As Vida T. Johnson and Graham Petrie have noted:

> Dreams are central to Tarkovsky's imaginative achievement because they bypass all that he felt was most inhibiting and destructive in the contemporary world – the scientific rationalism, the materialism, and the mindless faith in technology that he and his favoured characters reject – and speak directly to what is both most private and universal within us. (1994: 241–2)

Given the mechanisms and ideology that controlled the development of Soviet cinema, it is not surprising that there is not a solid body of work that can be labelled 'Surrealist', in the French or Spanish contexts, and such a corpus would have been unthinkable. Yet what is astonishing is the wit and imagination displayed by various, and very different, directors that points to the absurdity, even nightmarish illogicality, that lies beneath the surface of this society. Some directors, even in the 1930s, played with notions of truth and falsehood, reality and illusion, dream and fantasy. In the 1960s and 1970s Andrei Tarkovsky emphasised the private realm of existence, rejecting the ideological and political, and merged dream and reality to create an intensely personal aesthetic experience and an assertion of all that he saw was human. In the 'reconstruction' years of Gorbachev's reform process, the nature of historical truth came under increasing scrutiny, and political reality itself soon disappeared. Directors such as Mamin, Shakhnazarov and Zakharov could see that one world was threatening to give way and collapse, but could not have foreseen what it would be replaced by. That, too, is pure Surrealism, but not, as yet, treated as such in the cinema.

Notes

1   Eisenstein would later be harshly negative towards Surrealism. In his memoirs, for instance, written in 1946, he favourably compares his own 1929 film *Staroe i novoe* (*The Old and the New*) ('that speaks of the socialist system of statehood in the ascendancy') with Buñuel and Dali's *Un chien andalou* (*An Andalusian Dog*, 1929), where the latter is 'a film that totally and consistently reveals the prospects for the collapse of bourgeois consciousness in "surrealism"' (1997 (II): 327). Elsewhere he equates Surrealism and Futurism as 'equally distanced in both ideology and form from what we have done and from what we do' (1997 (I): 199), and allows himself some caustic personal gibes at André Breton (1997 (I): 198, 200).

2   Alexander Solzhenitsyn lampoons the forward-looking ethos of socialist realism in his novel *Cancer Ward*, where the would-be literary zealot Aviette tries to persuade the impressionable young Dema on its virtues: 'Now, my boy,' she said, turning back to Dyoma to finish with him. 'You must understand this. Describing something that exists is much easier than describing something that doesn't exist, even though you know it's going to exist. What we see today with the unaided human eye is not necessarily the truth. The truth is what we *must* be, what is going to happen tomorrow. Our wonderul "tomorrow" is what writers ought to be describing today.' 'But what will they describe tomorrow, then?' The slow-witted Dyoma frowned. 'Tomorrow? ... Well, tomorrow they'll describe the day after tomorrow' (1978: 311–12).

3   The *Bol'shaia sovetskaia entsiklopediia* gives the following definition of Surrealism: 'Continuation of the traditions of the romantic-anarchic rebellion against the emasculated spiritual values of bourgeois civilisation, imbued with a banal rational sensibility, was complemented in Surrealism by the pretension to change fundamentally the accustomed structure of intellectual activity and even public life, while liberating those latent impulses that lie deep in man's subconscious from the power of the intellect. The consequent reinterpretations of Intuitivism and especially Freudism served as the philosophical basis for efforts to drive reason from artistic thought, to assert the chaotic arbitrariness of subconscious "insights" in creative work, and this made Surrealism one of the extreme embodiments of the crisis of the irrational in Western culture' (vol. XXV, p. 152, col. 444).

4   Kazimiera Ingdahl notes the relationship of reality and dream in the 'play': 'The architectonic beauty and harmony of the house symbolise the absence of conflicts and reflect the peaceful immobility of nature. Olesha's obvious intention is to use this montage of natural and architectural imagery to communicate as a reality the illusion of an ideal society ruled by scientific genius' (1994: 111). For a sustained close reading of the relationship of the play and the film, see Jerry T. Heil (1989) *No List of Political Assets: The Collaboration of Iurii Olesha and Abram Room on 'Strogii iunosha [A Strict Youth]'*, Munich: Otto Sagner.

5   Boris Shumiatskii, head of the Soviet film industry from 1930 until his arrest in 1938 (he was executed as an 'enemy of the people'), included *Strogii iunosha* in the list of films he labelled as 'mistakes', in his campaign against Eisenstein's film *Bezhin lug* (*Bezhin Meadow*, 1936): 'Therefore with all such manifestations of rotten liberalism in this respect we must conduct a decisive struggle' (in Parfenov 1999: 45).

6   Gennadii Poloka relates that the film did reflect the end of a way of life: 'At the end of the thaw a part of our society collapsed. This was conveyed in *The Republic of ShKID*: Iankel' is the story of compromise in the hope for forgiveness' (1996: 214).

7   Natasha Synessios distinguishes between dreams and memories, also touching on the sur-reality of Tarkovsky's dreams: 'The space of the dreams does not have the warm, comforting glow of the space of the memories; it reveals an unconscious which is at odds with the fond memories of childhood Tarkovsky sought to recapture' (2001: 75).

Jan Uhde

JAN ŠVANKMAJER: GENIUS LOCI AS A SOURCE OF SURREALIST INSPIRATION

The Czech filmmaker and visual artist Jan Švankmajer (b. 1934) is one of the most significant living directors of non-mainstream and experimental film animation. During the four decades of his filmmaking and artistic career, he has produced over thirty shorts and features. Švankmajer's work displays exceptional philosophical depth and brilliant formal invention which has earned him worldwide respect in the animated film domain.

A major influence on Švankmajer's film style is Surrealism, specifically its Czech variety, which he has also helped to shape through his creative contribution. Another important source of his inspiration is Mannerism, which has prompted Michael O'Pray (2007) to describe him as a 'Mannerist Surrealist'. Acknowledging this context, Švankmajer's imagination has also substantially drawn from the physical and spiritual environment closest and most familiar to him – the city of Prague, and the region of Bohemia with its history, mystery, magic, suffering and centuries-old culture. It is the influence of this 'spirit of a place' on the Surrealist Švankmajer which will be discussed in this chapter.

A recognised artist

After years of relative isolation during the totalitarian Communist rule in Czechoslovakia, Švankmajer has, since 1989 when this collapsed and the country became a democratic state, received well-deserved praise both at home and internationally. In his own country, where his work has been called 'revolutionary' (Poš 1990: 138), Švankmajer is now considered to be the undisputed heir of his famous compatriot, the animator and book illustrator Jiří Trnka. Julian Petley ranks him, along with the Polish-born directors Jan Lenica and Walerian Borowczyk, as 'one of the key animators to have emerged in Eastern Europe since the war' (1986: 188). Švankmajer has also been compared to Yuri Norstein, the Russian master animator whose contemplative *Skazka skazok* (*Tale of Tales*, 1979) was named the best animated film of all time at the Los Angeles Olympic Arts Festival.

During his career, Švankmajer has received over fifty prizes and awards at international festivals and countless other honours. Among the most prestigious was the Grand Prix at the Animation Film Festival in Annecy for his *Možnosti dialogu* (*Dimensions of Dialogue*, 1982) – a film which may be considered his best work. Annecy has always been appreciative of Švankmajer: in 1985, Jack Lang, then the French Minister of Culture, suggested *Možnosti dialogu* be used as the most eloquent example of Annecy's festival contribution to animated film. In 1997, the Czech animator was honoured with the Persistence of Vision Award at the San Francisco Festival for his lifetime work. A lion's share in supporting Švankmajer's artistic vision in the English-speaking world, especially during his most difficult years of government-imposed isolation, must go to British producer Keith Griffiths of Koninck, and the Illuminations Films production company.[1]

Today, Švankmajer and his style have become a model for other filmmakers. Timothy and Stephen Quay, two American experimental animators working in Britain, owe much to him.[2] The Quay brothers publicly acknowledged their mentor and source of inspiration by naming their 1984 short *The Cabinet of Jan Švankmajer*. The work of Tim Burton, particularly *The Nightmare Before Christmas* (1993), which he scripted for Henry Selick, adopts the spirit of the Czech animator's films; so does Selick's *James and the Giant Peach* (1996), a mix of live-action film and stop-motion animation. Back home in the Czech Republic, the brilliant Jiří Barta (*Krysař/Pied Piper*, 1985; *Club of the Discarded*, 1989) developed his style under Švankmajer's influence which he himself confirms: 'Švankmajer was a great inspiration, because his aesthetic and imagination were very attractive to me' (in Ballard 2003).

Throughout his career, Švankmajer has concentrated on stop-motion, three-dimensional animation. Most animators of his generation have preferred the anthropomorphic cartoon popularised by Disney: their drawn characters look, act and speak like humans, and are confronted with similar problems and situations. Švankmajer sees things quite differently: 'I don't like the cartoon and I prefer to place my imaginary world into reality' (in Ciment & Codelli 1989: 45). Švankmajer's signature technique has been 3-D animation combined with live action. His style is unique but his professional background links him with the centuries-old traditions of Czech folk puppetry.[3] Moreover, he had first-hand experience with the experimental 3-D animation of his famous compatriots of the preceding generation, Karel Zeman (*Vynález zkázy/A Deadly Invention*, 1958; *Baron Prášil/The Fabulous Baron Münchhausen*, 1961)[4] and Jiří Trnka (*Sen noci svatojánské/A Midsummer Night's Dream*, 1959; *Ruka/The Hand*, 1965). Comparing and confronting them has helped in forming Švankmajer's own style. The latter also reveals influence by other Eastern European filmmakers, such as Lenica and Borowczyk, but particularly Ladislas Starewicz, the Polish-Lithuanian pre-First World War pioneer of 3-D animation, with his shorts featuring insect skeletons, better known in Eastern Europe than in the West.[5]

Like Norstein, Švankmajer, oblivious to trends and fashions, rejects modern animation techniques and technologies. He remains outside the computer animation world, preferring plain, common materials: paper, stone, wood, clay, metal, fabric. He is attracted by articles of everyday use, found objects, dolls, figurines and puppets as well as products of the early industrial age: simple mechanisms and devices and early automata manufactured from elemental materials, which to him suggest originality, ingenuity and accomplished craftsmanship – today's *objets d'art*. In more ways than one, the Czech animator is on the opposite end of the spectrum of most of the hi-tech animation dream factories of North America. Yet swimming against the current is never easy: since gaining recognition in the West in the 1980s, Švankmajer has begun to prefer the feature film, a format more suitable to the prevailing distribution and exhibition patterns.[6] In addition, the proportion between animation and live-action in his features has been slowly changing in favour of the latter.[7]

In the Surrealist orbit

Surrealism has been an important factor of Švankmajer's work and, one also could say, of his life. He calls himself a 'militant Surrealist' (in Hames 2007: 63). Mainstream art historiography considers Surrealism an art movement of the first half of the twentieth century, now relegated to history; yet in the Czech Republic, the movement survived the Second World War and even the years of Communist repression.[8] It was sustained particularly by the country's dedicated Surrealist community, the Prague Surrealist Group (now the Group of Czech and Slovak Surrealists). Švankmajer and his recently deceased wife Eva[9] have been members of this group since 1970.[10] Only a couple of people from the second generation of the Surrealist group remain today, yet quite a few young people have joined, indicating that Surrealism still has something to offer to today's artists.

Surrealist themes, imagery and techniques are inseparable from Švankmajer's film style as well as most of his extra-filmic activities: in the 1970s, for example, he created a series of imaginative collages and the so-called tactile experimentations which examined the relationship between senses, especially sight and touch. The artist's commitment to Surrealism was undiminished even in the darkest years of the post-invasion period when the movement was criticised by Communist ideologues and practising Surrealists were often persecuted.[11] In fact, in 1979, he and his wife Eva edited a voluminous *samizdat* anthology of this group's creative activities entitled *Otevřená hra* ('Open Game').[12] In 1989, they began publishing *Analogon*, the cultural, artistic and literary magazine of the Surrealist group.[13]

The significance of Švankmajer's Surrealist link becomes more evident when examining the graphic and plastic characteristics of the artist's style and imagery, prominently displayed in his films. It also penetrates into his thematic and narrative range, and directorial style. The Czech animator has also drawn inspiration from proto-Surrealists and artists who influenced the Surrealists or were admired by them. Besides the already mentioned Mannerists, others include Giuseppe Arcimboldo, Pierre Ch-oderlos de Laclos, Edgar Allan Poe, Lewis Carroll, Horace Walpole, Luís Buñuel, Fed-erico Fellini and Franz Kafka:[14]

Unlike conventional animated films in which images often serve as mere illustra-tion to the narrative-driven, dialogue-based plot, Švankmajer's Surrealist perspective allows him to foreground colour, movement, frame composition and other visual ele-ments which in his films acquire paramount importance; in most of his animation the image overshadows the narrative. The artist's blending of the ordinary, the unreal and the surprising is a known Surrealist technique and Švankmajer makes generous use of it. In *Byt* (*The Apartment*, 1968), for example, the legs of a chair grow or shrink when somebody sits on it; a fork about to spear a sausage suddenly undulates.[15] When the main character hits a solid masonry wall with his fist, his entire arm disappears inside the wall and cannot be extracted. This moment echoes a scene in Jean Cocteau's Sur-real feature *Orphée* (1949), in which Orpheus walks into a mirror with outstretched hand: instead of breaking it, he moves right through it and into another dimension.[16] Furthermore, Švankmajer's film debut *Poslední trik pana Schwarcewalldea a pana Ed-gara* (*Last Trick*, 1964) includes images of a beetle crawling from the head (actually a wooden mask worn by the performer) of one of the characters, a not-to-be-missed reference to the Surrealist icon from *Un chien andalou* (*An Andalusian Dog*, 1929) by Buñuel and Dalí.[17]

The surreal of the quotidian

Surrealist techniques involving unexpected imagery and twists of plot have been successfully applied to film, especially by Buñuel, since the 1920s.[18] Švankmajer, like Buñuel, was confronted by a totalitarian regime whose political and social manifes-tations were often 'surreal'.[19] Unlike Buñuel, he decided against exile; thus he had ample opportunity to experience the absurdities and horrors of totalitarian reality. He was banished from filmmaking for six years (1973–79).[20] Even when allowed to shoot, his movies were censored, sometimes prohibited and their exhibition restricted. Švankmajer's technique of combining 3-D animation with real action was an apt tool for reflecting the surreal of the quotidian which saturated his life and the lives of most people around him.

The blending of real action with animation is accomplished mostly through edit-ing. Švankmajer also uses rapid-montage and momentary big close-ups[21] intercut with the principal action, a technique also employed by Borowczyk.[22] This produces a pow-erful effect, such as in Švankmajer's early (predominantly live-action) short *Zahrada* (*The Garden*, 1968): the viewer is virtually assailed by the big close-ups of one of the character's Adam's apple; this causes an otherwise innocuous conversation between two characters to appear disquieting. This juxtaposition of live-action images and ani-mated ones has a disorienting, frustrating and sometimes threatening effect on the audience. In *Možnosti dialogu* for example, a clay head suddenly sticks out its tongue

– a real tongue; in *Mužné hry* (*Virile Games*, 1988) and *Jídlo* (*Food*, 1992), violent de-molitions of the characters' faces and bodies alarm the viewer before he realises that an actor was swiftly replaced by a clay model or a paper cutout.

This editing technique, which suggests inspiration by Buñuel and Dalí's famous opening shot of their Surrealist experiment *Un chien andalou*,[23] allows the director to play cat-and-mouse with his audience, sometimes to satirical effect: in *Smrt stalinismu v Čechách* (*Death of Stalinism in Bohemia*, 1990) a gypsum Stalin bust is placed on an operating table and a scalpel cuts into it, revealing real bowels within. A hand pokes inside and pulls something out of the bloody mass. A real umbilical cord is cut. The object pulled out of this head/womb is a small gypsum bust of the Czech Communist president Klement Gottwald (1896–1953), known as a Stalin puppet. The bust is care-fully washed, placed upright on a table and given a slap to which it promptly replies with the real cries of a baby.

Genius loci

One of the strongest and most interesting influences on Švankmajer's work has been Bohemia's rich cultural landscape and especially its capital Prague, whose magic has captivated many artists, including the early twentieth-century French poet, novelist, playwright, critic and proto-Surrealist Guillaume Apollinaire. Before the First World War Prague was a multicultural city in which the Czech-speaking majority co-existed in a peaceful but competitive relationship with the German and Jewish minorities. Prague's Jews found themselves in a kind of double isolation. Not accepted as equal by the Germans with whom they shared a common language, they were shunned by Czech nationalists who considered them 'Germans'. This simmering cultural cauldron helped to produce an atmosphere favourable to artistic creativity as shown in the works of Franz Kafka, Max Brod, Franz Werfel, Rainer Maria Rilke and others.[24]

It would be difficult to imagine Švankmajer without Prague, a city in which he was born and where he has spent most of his life. His work reflects in one way or another the singular, often inscrutable atmosphere of this city which prides itself on its long, rich and sometimes dark history. The filmmaker's interest, however, does not belong to the modern, contemporary Prague; its crowded streets and avenues, cars, subways, fast-growing shopping centres and thousands of international tourists – his is rather the city's old quarters and legends: the Old Town, the Lesser Quarter and the shadows of the thousand-year-old Jewish ghetto with their mysterious past, reflected in many of his films.[25] If the camera ventures into the streets of contemporary Prague with their cars, trams and crowds, this 'normality' suddenly seems odd, like a mere transition between two 'real' parts of the movie. Švankmajer is also attracted by the historical atmosphere of Bohemia's monuments and structures, both famous and forgotten – be it the Ossuary of the Cistercian Sedlec Monastery, or an anonymous castle ruin.

Švankmajer's own life seems to be bound to Prague's historical core. He lives in two adjoining houses in Hradčanská Street in the tiny Nový svět (New World) neighbourhood, just outside the Prague Castle walls. The 'New World' name, given to the cluster of brightly-coloured cottages, is a kind of misnomer, as this is one of Prague's most ancient areas, similar in many ways to the Zlatá ulička (Gold Lane) within the Prague Castle walls, one of the city's most famous tourist attractions. The houses, which belonged to alchemists centuries ago, are now converted into a single dwelling which is also the home of the Surrealist gallery Gambra,[26] established by the Švankmajers. The houses' thick walls conceal a maze of rooms whose doors are so low that visitors must constantly mind their heads. The kitchen appears much closer to an alchemist's laboratory than for modern cooking. Moreover, the entire house is like a gallery, stuffed with precious artefacts and objets trouvés. One can easily imagine that at night the place assumes an autonomous existence and becomes a functioning part of Švankmajer's magic film world.

The historical background of Švankmajer's unconventional home ties the filmmaker personally and emotionally with one of the most mysterious and artistically stimulating periods of Prague's history: the second half of the sixteenth century, during the reign of the eccentric Hapsburg Emperor Rudolf II (who ruled between 1575 and 1611). Unlike the Emperor Charles IV of the Luxembourg Dynasty (1346–78), a more practical visionary who made Prague a showpiece of his Holy Roman Empire, the moody Rudolf was not a great ruler. He was, however, a lover and sponsor of the arts and sciences which included the fashionable practices of alchemy and astrology. Emperor Rudolf invited famous astronomers such as Tycho Brahe (1546–1601) from Denmark, his assistant Johannes Kepler (1571–1630), the German astronomer and natural philosopher, and artists from all over Europe to his Prague court. Among them was the Italian Mannerist genius Giuseppe Arcimboldo (1527–93), whose revolutionary painting style became a major inspiration for Švankmajer's films. Rudolf's fabulous 'cabinet of curiosities' (or 'art collection' in modern idiom) was perhaps the best in Europe.[27]

It was in the Rudolphine era that Renaissance ideas clashed with those of the receding Middle Ages and with maturing Baroque sensitivity. This was also the epoch of great post-Columbian discoveries and Europe's colonial expansion. Science was growing out of magic but their mutual boundaries were not yet clearly defined. The Rudolphine Prague became a pulsating European hub of artistic creativity. In its fertile multicultural atmosphere, imagination flourished. Popular fantasy, horror and magic tales born in this period included Faustian stories as well as the legend about the Golem, a clay colossus brought to life by the Rabbi Loew who summoned his magic powers to protect the city's Jewish community but was unable to control the Golem's destructive impulse, not unlike the Frankensteins and robots of recent science fiction literature and cinema.

Already in the early years of film history, the alluring mysteries of the Rudolphine era and Prague's mysterious presence provided inspiration to filmmakers. The impression they made on the German pre-Expressionist cinema, for instance, is clearly visible in the early psychological horror *Der Student von Prag* (*The Student from Prague*,

1913)[28] by Hanns Heinz Ewers and Stellan Rye (two more films on the same subject followed in 1926 and 1935), and Henrik Galeen's and Paul Wegener's *Der Golem* (*The Golem*, 1915, the first of many film versions of the legend).

Švankmajer's film style, too, has frequently drawn inspiration from Prague, particularly from the Prague of Rudolf II and the style of Rudolf's Italian court painter Arcimboldo who painted composite images and portraits out of objects such as vegetables, flowers and trees. Arcimboldo's collage-like style and his *trompe d'œil* technique have fuelled the imagination of Švankmajer since the beginning of his career. More than once, the Czech animator confirms the sources of his inspiration by making explicit references to them in his films: for example, he dedicated his *Historia Naturae, Suita* (1967), a film whose collage of images seems to have come straight out of a sixteenth-century cabinet of curiosities, to Rudolf II, Arcimboldo's patron. The Italian Mannerist's profound influence on Švankmajer is displayed most eloquently in his 20-second video *Flora* (1989, made for MTV). In *Možnosti dialogu*, the film's first sequence ('Material Dialogue') portrays a confrontation between three Arcimboldian heads composed, respectively, from fruit and vegetables, kitchen utensils and drawing tools. *Možnosti dialogu* and *Flora* are two of Švankmajer's most evident tributes to Arcimboldo, whose paintings *The Librarian* (c. 1566), the portrait of a man constructed from books, and *Flora* (c. 1591), the portrait of a woman composed from flowers, were obvious inspiration for the two films. Furthermore, the juxtaposition of Švankmajer's Arcimboldian collage with a subject rooted in Prague, a city at once historical and modern – exemplified in the feature *Lekce Faust* (*Faust*, 1994) – points to sources of inspiration tied not only to a person or a period, but to the atmosphere of a place. In short, to the genius loci.

A more recent Prague also appears in the shorts *Do pivnice* (*Down to the Cellar*, 1988), *Mužné hry* and the feature *Otesánek* (*Little Otik*, 2000). In these films, large, scruffy nineteenth-century houses are the settings of Švankmajer's dark stories and mysterious happenings. He explores the bizarre, the sensual, the dreamlike and the dark, hiding under the surface of mundane reality. This perspective, dear to most Surrealists, finds a perfect expression in *Do pivnice*, considered by the director as his 'proto-Alice'.[29] In this simple story a small girl descends to the cellar of an old apartment house to bring back a basket of potatoes. This becomes an impossible expedition as the girl is gripped by fear of darkness, isolation and the black cat which sneaks into the cellar with her. In the cellar, her imagination conjures strange characters and situations: an old man in a bed of coals; an old woman baking coal briquettes, then using it as fuel for her baking oven; the potatoes mysteriously rolling from her basket back to their crate. A most important stylistic component of this film (shot mostly as live-action) and the physical source of the movie's disturbing atmosphere, is the setting – the gloomy, dilapidated and very real Prague apartment house whose dark cellar becomes the little heroine's 'rabbit hole'.

Prague has given Švankmajer another creative stimulus: Franz Kafka (1883–1923), a German-speaking Jew who has become an icon of alienation, absurdity and twentieth-century horrors. Kafka's influence on Czech culture has been profound. In May 1963, one year before Švankmajer's film debut, the former Communist Czechoslovakia rediscovered Kafka at the ground-breaking Franz Kafka Liblice Conference, initiated by Eduard Goldstücker (1913–2000), a Czech scholar, statesman and well-known Kafkalogue.[30] In the country's intellectual circles, Kafka was suddenly a hot topic but also somewhat risqué: the Communist authorities did not like the obvious implications of his bleak, absurd and hopeless world – a silent indictment of the brave new world created by them. At about the same time, Pavel Juráček (1935–89), one of the directors of the budding Czechoslovak New Wave, produced a brilliant absurdist short *Postava k podpírání* (*Josef Kilian*, 1963), about a man who rents a cat from a rent-a-pet store. When he brings the cat back the next day, the shop is gone and nobody can even remember having seen it.

It is therefore no wonder that the world of Kafkaesque absurdity became the focus of Švankmajer's *Zahrada*. Unlike his preceding films, *Zahrada* is a live-action film, using mostly outdoor settings. Its impact is drawn from its strange subject, amplified by occasional disturbing intercuts of big close-ups of the human body. The story is about a subtle confrontation of views between two middle-aged male characters – an apparent conformist who has built for himself a comfortable life in an agreeable country home, and his taciturn opponent, probably an old friend, who has not done so well. Švankmajer reveals the manipulative nature of the former through a most original metaphor: the 'fence' encircling the successful man's property is actually a living chain of silent, obedient people. The passive guest friend is gently forced to join the fence. The filmmaker presents this scene in a matter-of-fact way: there is even a padlock at the fence's human 'gate'. The absurdity of the situation is invested with an explosive political charge which could hardly be overlooked by anyone.

Švankmajer has also made use of atmospheric locations outside Prague. When looking for suitable ruins to shoot *Zánik domu Usherů* (*The Fall of the House of Usher*) in 1981, he and his wife purchased a deserted small chateau in Horní Staňkov, a locality in southwestern Bohemia, which became their country house and 'Surrealist Central'. In this secluded haven he produced some of his best-known works, including *Možnosti dialogu* and his first feature *Něco z Alenky* (*Alice*, 1989), inspired by Lewis Carroll's *Alice in Wonderland* (1865). This partially dilapidated and mysterious house served Švankmajer as a place of refuge in times of political pressure; a brief glance at it leaves no doubt about its power as a source of Surreal inspiration. A decade later, in 1991, Švankmajer and his producer, Jaromír Kallista, purchased a defunct cinema in the village of Knovíz, about thirty kilometres from Prague. There they established a studio and film production company, Athanor,[31] to produce original Czech films. *Lekce Faust*, *Spiklenci slasti* (*Conspirators of Pleasure*, 1996) and *Otesánek* were produced by Athanor.

For his 'horror documentary' *Kostnice* (*The Ossuary*, 1970), Švankmajer turned to one of Bohemia's most unique and bleakest monuments, the Ossuary of the Cistercian Sedlec Monastery in Eastern Bohemia, which contains the bones of up to 70,000 people buried there since the Middle Ages. In 1870, after a decade of work, the bones were assembled by the Czech artist František Rint into a variety of shapes and objects including skull pyramids and crosses; one chandelier contains every bone of the human body. They have been installed into the crypt of the Cistercian chapel as a *memento mori* for the visitors to see. Švankmajer filmed this extraordinary exhibit in black-and-white and in documentary style, using his 'Arcimboldian' rapid-montage. As a result of censors' pressure, two soundtracks were produced for this film, both of which are quite fitting.[32] Among Švankmajer's films, *Kostnice* is the one in which the director exploits the haunting 'spirit of the place' to the fullest.

Conclusion

For Jan Švankmajer, one of the most original and accomplished Czech filmmakers, Surrealism has been a major inspiration during his four-decade-long filmmaking career. Equally important to his art is the genius loci of his native city Prague, and that of Bohemia, with their long history, glory, beauty and scars of suffering. This cultural landscape has been home to the Mannerists, Giuseppe Arcimboldo, the alchemists, the Inquisition, Czech folk tales and puppetry, Kafka's bleak visions and forty years of totalitarian regime, all of which have blended with the artist's Surrealist perspective. The result is a unique animated style with the power to transform the commonplace into haunting images of extraordinary force and beauty.

Notes

1   Keith Griffiths co-produced a number of Švankmajer's films; during the totalitarian regime in Czechoslovakia this often had to be done secretly. Koninck Studios (founded in 1979) has worked closely with many independent and avant-garde filmmakers, including Jan Švankmajer, the Brothers Quay, Chris Petit and Patrick Keiller.

2   American-born twins Stephen and Timothy Quay (b. 1947) have acknowledged an important influence upon their work by Švankmajer. Their films include *The Street of Crocodiles* (1986) and *Institute Benjamenta* (1995).

3   Švankmajer studied puppetry at the AMU (School of Dramatic Arts) in Prague between 1954 and 1958. He also worked with avant-garde stage productions such as the *Semafor* theatre, the *Činoherní klub* and the internationally known *Laterna Magika* which successfully combined stage and film techniques.

4   Zeman's *Vynález zkázy* for example, based on the eponymous novel by the French nineteenth-century science fiction writer Jules Verne, combines live actors with animated background recalling the period illustrations of Verne's books.

5   (Ladislas) Wladyslaw Starewicz (1892–1965) is considered to be the inventor of the 3-D stop-motion animated film. Starewicz used real (dead) beetles and puppets in his films, which include *Strashnaya mest* (*A Terrible Revenge*, 1913). His *La Voix du rossignol* (*Voice of the Nightingale*, 1923) combines animation with live-action.

6   Švankmajer's first feature was *Neco z Alenky* (*Alice*, 1988). Since 1994, he has produced only features: *Lekce Faust* (*Faust*, 1994), *Spiklenci slasti* (*Conspirators of Pleasure*, 1996), *Otesánek* (*Little Otik*, 2000) and *Šílení* (*Lunacy*, 2005).

7   This tendency was emphasised by Švankmajer's *Otesánek*, a contemporary horror-comedy based on a popular Czech fairytale recorded by the revered Czech poet and collector of folk songs and tales, Karel Jaromír Erben (1811–70). *Otesánek* is not his first film dominated by real-life action; he has used such an approach also in *Zahrada* (*The Garden*, 1968), *Byt* (*The Apartment*, 1968) and the short *Do pivnice* (*Down to the Cellar*, 1983).

8   Surrealism was officially denounced as undesirable during the Czechoslovak Communist era; artists were required to conform to the official style – Socialist Realism.

9   Eva Švankmajerová (1940–2005) was a well-known Surrealist painter, ceramic artist and poet. She collaborated with her husband on a number of projects, including the films *Neco z Alenky*, *Lekce Faust*, *Spiklenci slasti* and *Otesánek*.

10 The Prague Surrealist Group was founded in 1934. Among its founding members were the Czech painter, photographer and poet Jindřich Štyrský and Toyen, a leading Czech Surrealist who played a significant role in the International Surrealist movement; the Prague group was in close cooperation with André Breton's group in France.

11 A manifesto was published in January 1977, signed by 230 prominent Czech intellectuals. Called Charter 77, this 'loose, informal and open association of people' was committed to human rights and requested the Czech Communist government to observe them. The regime replied with a repression campaign directed mainly against the country's intellectuals and artists. Václav Havel, who later became the country's President, was one of the Charter 77 signatories.

12 The leading personality in this group was, until his death, Vratislav Effenberger (1923–86); other members included Karol Baron, František Dryje, Jiří Koubek, Albert Marenčin, Emila Medková, Alena Nádvorniková, Martin Stejskal and Ludvík Šváb. The anthology, professional in appearance, was published clandestinely as a paperback, with 210 pages and 89 black-and-white illustrations. The print run was 100 copies.

13 Actually, *Analogon* had been established in 1969 by Vratislav Effenberger. The first issue was published in May 1969 but it was quickly banned by the post-invasion Communist government. After twenty years of silence, the journal was resuscitated in 1989.

14 In 1928, Buñuel wrote a script for Jean Epstein's *The Fall of the House of Usher* (1928); the same subject matter was also filmed by Švankmajer. Švankmajer was inspired by Poe in *Zánik domu Usherů* (*The Fall of the House of Usher*, 1981) and *Kyvadlo, jáma a naděje* (*The Pit and The Pendulum*, 1983); by Carroll in *Žvahlav aneb Šatičky slaměného Huberta* (*Jabberwocky*,) *Alice* and *Do pivnice* (*Down to the Cellar*); between 1973 and 1979, he also adapted Walpole's celebrated Gothic romance *The Castle of Otranto* (1764) as *Otrantský zámek* (1977).

15 Such 'living objects' appear in a number of Švankmajer's films.

16 Jean Cocteau (1889–1963), French poet, filmmaker, novelist, dramatist and designer, was a leading member of the Surrealist movement in France. The word 'surrealism'

coined by Guillaume Apollinaire was meant to describe Cocteau's modern ballet *Parade* (1917), a collaboration with Erik Satie, Pablo Picasso and Léonide Massine.

17 In a scene from *Un chien andalou*, a swarm of live ants issues from the palm of one of the characters.

18 Buñuel used this technique in his other films, too, including *El ángel exterminador* (*The Exterminating Angel*, 1962), *Le Journal d'une femme de chambre* (*Diary of a Chambermaid*, 1964), *Belle de jour* (1966), *Tristana* (1970), *Le Charme discret de la bourgeoisie* (*The Discreet Charm of the Bourgeoisie*, 1972), *Le Fantôme de la liberté* (*The Phantom of Liberty*, 1974) and *Cet obscur objet du désir* (*That Obscure Object of Desire*, 1977).

19 Following the Spanish Civil War and the establishment of Franco's Fascist regime in Spain in 1939, Buñuel spent most of his life in exile, mainly in the United States, Mexico and France.

20 The ban followed making 'unauthorised' changes in his film *Leonarduv denik* (*Leonardo's Diary*, 1973).

21 The emotional power of close-ups has been known to filmmakers since D. W. Griffith. The extreme close-up amplifies their aggressiveness, suggesting the bizarre and grotesque; see Per Persson (1998) 'Towards a Psychological Theory of Close-ups', *Kinema*, 9, 24–42.

22 For example, in Borowczyk's feature *Blanche* (1971).

23 The famous big close-up of an eye being slowly sliced with a razor. The shot showing the human eye is in the last moment replaced by another with an eye of a dead animal, but the effect remains.

24 See Harald Salfellner (1988) *Franz Kafka and Prague*. Prague: Vitalis.

25 The ghetto was demolished in 1890 for 'sanitary reasons'. The little that remains, including the Old-New Synagogue and the Jewish Cemetery, has become a major tourist attraction.

26 The homey, dwarf-sized room is stuffed full of Švankmajer's Surrealist collages, Eva's ceramics and other works by committed Surrealist Group members such as Karol Baron. Czech books and periodicals are also available.

27 Most of this collection was looted by the Swedish army during the sack of Prague in 1648, the last year of the Thirty Years War. It was never returned.

28 A precursor to the well-known Expressionist masterpiece directed by Robert Wiene, *Das Kabinett des Dr Caligari* (*The Cabinet of Dr Caligari*, 1920).

29 The script for *Do pivnice* was rejected by the Prague Krátký Film Studios. The director, however, exploited personal rivalry between the Czech and Slovak studios' management. He submitted the project to the (Slovak) Bratislava Studios which accepted it. Later, the Czechoslovak authorities refused the initial request from the Oberhausen Festival organisers to enter the film into competition, but they eventually gave up. *Do pivnice* won the Oberhausen Critics' Prize in 1983.

30 Among the conference's international participants were the liberal Marxist art theoreticians Roger Garaudy and Ernst Fischer. The significance of the conference was that it

removed an ideological taboo concerning discussion of Kafka which was above all a political act. The ensuing debate between East German conservative ideologues and more open-minded critics reverberated in the media for a long time afterwards, both in Czechoslovakia and abroad.

31 Athanor is a self-feeding furnace that maintains a uniform temperature; it was used by alchemists.

32 *Kostnice* exists in two versions featuring different soundtracks. The subversive irony of the original one, using a silly commentary of a local guide, was rejected by the Communist authorities and the filmmaker was forced to replace it; he chose piano music with a girl singing (in Czech) the poem by Jacques Prévert, 'Pour faire le portrait d'un oiseau' ('How to Draw the Portrait of a Bird').

Van Norris

'INTERIOR LOGIC': THE APPROPRIATION AND INCORPORATION OF POPULAR SURREALISM INTO CLASSICAL AMERICAN ANIMATION

Even a casual observer can recognise that many themes and images commonly associated with 'Surrealism' have been a part of the popular 'cel' animation form as early as J. Stuart Blackton's primitive but definitive creative experiment, *Humorous Phases of Funny Faces*, in 1906. As with any practice so derived from painterly origins perhaps the incorporation of artistic concepts from Expressionism to Abstract anti-naturalist forms somehow appears inevitable. Approaches to design and representation that are often in the setting of the animated film, shorn of the original intellectual agenda, are placed into compressed, somewhat unsophisticated narratives. Since its flowering in the late 1920s into its perceived heyday in the 1940s and 1950s, the American short cartoon has existed as a site which has often unconsciously (and consciously) contested and worked through the very complex relationships and interrelations between high and low culture for mass audiences. Animators at work at the turn of the century, from the more expressive and challenging spatial preoccupations found within Otto Messmer's oeuvre to the more workman-like and more prescribed exponents such as Paul Terry and Walter Lantz, all revelled in the artistic and creative freedom the medium afforded them. But as the 1910s shifted into the 1920s it appeared that an artistic and narrative 'pre-requisite' or imperative within 'cel' animation became the exploration of boundaries of cinematic space. Thus the overriding ethos quickly evolved from the original impulse of simplistic replication and distortion (such as those initiated on rice paper 'cels' by Winsor McCay in 1911 with his *Little Nemo in Slumberland*) into a more a complex field of artistic inquiry.[1] Once freed from simply having to reproduce a mediated 'reality' on each frame of celluloid, artists in this fledgling form could now order and manipulate their own individually-defined universe; a continuum that existed and conformed to laws conceived within purely their own imagination. By the time the 1930s arrived the American animated 'short' had solidified into a commercially viable (albeit critically unheralded) art form, assisted by the hegemonic patterns of distribution and availability as pre-booked extensions of major studio product. Due to the leaps in technology and application it had also come to embody the generally perceived 'rules' for 'cel' animation worldwide. In this production and distribution milieu an established visual lexicon became quickly fixed. Short cartoons now formally utilised 'tableau framing' as a set principle, along with a leaning towards a limited form of naturalistic representation, personality/character-based anthropomorphic animal/emblems and emphasis on fluidity and the expressivity of movement. Within these confines the self-conscious flouting of pre-determined physical laws became part of the accepted cinematic language commonly associated with the form.

Certainly by the late 1920s the animated seven-minute 'short' had been an accepted and standard component of the mainstream American cinema bill in its role as a 'filler' between newsreels and 'A' and 'B' presentations. As a regular and prominent entertainment within mass audience theatrical consumption patterns it soon evolved also into a 'cultural barometer' of no little function and relevance. This was confirmed by Eric Smoodin as being due to the glib projections of contemporary concerns found within the shorts as 'the project of presenting the world to the audience' (1993: 45). Indeed, one might further state that the very 'success', in creative terms, of this popular art form was wholly dependent on its condensation of complex narratives, its simplification of thematics and the reduction of images in a bid to connect with a wide range of audiences on an immediate, visceral level. Thus, their placement within these cinema bills, in their make-up and within the values presented, became part of 'a means of transmitting cultural norms' (1993: 46).

As the format became an established element of mass culture, in many ways it also became one of the places where 1930s/40s America processed and evaluated much of its popular culture and reflected prevailing attitudes and consensual values; a democratic space where an 'aesthetic wholeness' could emerge (Smoodin 1993: 60). Now, while many of these 'bill-fillers' were often devoid of any *overt* intellectual and artistic drive, they have (in direct and indirect fashions) responded to and articulated a range of complex ideas. These are works that could arguably be seen as conforming to existing artistic movements infiltrating the contemporary cultural consciousness, such as Surrealism, among them. Indeed there are arguably a number of American animated shorts and bodies of work that, while not proclaimed to be directly 'Surrealist' in intent, demonstrate through connections in form, narrative and particular applications of dream imagery – as well as dialogues of subconscious and unconscious desire – that certainly one might argue would be part of *any* credible and definable Surrealist blueprint.

Thus it can be perceived for the case of this chapter that popular American animation, existing as it did in this setting as an index of proletariat tastes, absorbed many of the preoccupations outlined within the original Surrealist manifesto in a fractured and distanced fashion, and then, in turn, transmitted this corrupted information back to mass audiences in simplistic culturally and artistically modified fragments. This then precipitates the inevitable effect in this context of a 'reduction' of the original concepts surrounding the form. In doing so this shifts the Surrealist movement's original impulse into a setting that becomes merely a mode to conveniently introduce the 'bizarre' or 'fantasy into art and literature' (Rosemont 1978: 7). The popularly conceived image of the form has now become inter-linked with either the utilisation of freeform imagery or as a short cut or signpost for a 'weird moment' away from the given linear narrative of a text. This refraction and corruption has thus become cemented as a somewhat commonplace, rather 'surface', summation when discussing such subject matter. Surrealism in this current climate is now shorthand for the 'wacky', the 'out of kilter' and is used as a way of discussing conceptions away from understood indexes of our agreed 'reality'. It has become a corruption of terms that illustrates a palpable sense of removal from Breton's original desire to 'shock' and 'disturb'.

Perhaps it seems only fitting that the visual manifestation of Surrealism, with its insistence via automatism as practice on a procession and presentation of often incongruous and jarring images, should be regurgitated and recast within this form. Thus it functions not only as a pointer to the workings of consciousness but also as an expression in many ways of 'cultural memory', the 'popular', mass consciousness. To take this concept further (especially in the case of Warner Bros. films) there could be an argument made that animators were practising a kind of 'cultural automatism'; a highly mediated but still very much stream-of-consciousness register that would facilitate the accessing concepts, signs and images as cultural memory to provoke a humorous response. In doing so, what subsequently emerges in this setting is the marked impression made by Surrealist artists such as Salavador Dalí and René Magritte on the common 1930s American cultural landscape and psyche.[2]

The Surrealist movement itself of course did not coalesce into any organised concerted school of thought as such in the US in quite the same way as in Europe, as Surrealism itself did not reach the US until as late as 1931. It is this factor, along with Dalí's self-managed reputation as that of a professional eccentric, an entertaining crackpot, that point to the form's 'foulest misrepresentation' and thus Surrealism in itself being 'consistently misaligned' (Rosemont 1978: 56). Dalí's financial embrace of a *nouveau riche* market and his meticulous grasp of celebrity culture has almost certainly contributed to the uncomplicated popular conceptions of Surrealism within American mainstream culture and in its early years saw the artist inextricably linked with the form. This fragmentary perception of the movement also arguably saw a stripping away of many of the less marketable political and revolutionary aspects proposed within Breton's original manifestos. Indeed by the time art exhibitor Julian Levy's 1936 soon-to-be-standard reference work, *Surrealism* had become established in the US, Dalí's position within the movement had been so distorted as to dwarf the contributions of even the likes of Breton, Eluard, Ernst and Duchamp combined.

The animated form's reliance on humour offers another tangential relationship to the Surrealists. Indeed one could confidently argue that in many ways this adherence to an obviously vulgarist narrative has undermined the form's critical reputation for some time. However Surrealism and humour have, perhaps inevitably, always maintained close links. Breton had always stressed the significance of what he perceived to be the 'revolutionary' functions of humour in itself towards structures within society and the design against rationality itself. In offering his own affiliation and affirmations of 'morbid' and 'absurd' registers of humour Breton stated that 'black humour is *par excellence* the mortal enemy of sentimentality' (1962: 21).[3] Perhaps then with Surrealism as now a part of the American cultural psyche it seems only entirely appropriate that the first self-conscious reference to Surrealism should come not from the more literal-minded Walt Disney but from the more culturally 'savvy' Warner Bros. studio output.

Away from the 'folksy' family narratives of Disney's work many other exponents within the cartoon industry of the 1930s were undoubtedly geared more towards an adult sensibility and indeed made it a selling point, as a marked contrast, of openly referencing adult life and experiences. This fact is confirmed by Warner Bros. director/animator Chuck Jones, who asserts: 'We made pictures but for ourselves, believing that if we laughed with and at each other then others would follow' (1989: 61). This emphasis on adult subjects such as sexuality and of nudging boundaries of taste, morality and acceptability share core concerns that sit at the very heart of the Surrealist movement. The Surrealists were well aware of the inevitability of humour as a by-product of combinations of incongruous images and ideas and they recognised, as a vital aspect of our psychological make-up, the importance of humour as an incisive tool in itself. As Franklin Rosemont reinforces: 'Nor is it surprising in the films of Buster Keaton and the Marx Brothers, and in Bugs Bunny cartoons, where others were content to only see comedy or bad taste; the Surrealists would find elements of a critique of Western civilisation' (1978: 63).

Accepted critical wisdom confers that the form's primary tangible flirtation with Surrealism came with the celebrated Robert Clampett short *Porky in Wackyland* made in 1938 as part of the Warner Bros. studios' celebrated 'first wave' (1930–49). It is a work that has aided the popular misconception that this is where these two points are inaccurately perceived to have intersected. While in that film Clampett is undoubtedly seduced by the potency of the incongruity of image and contradictory dialogues associated with Surrealist practice much of his work here merely debases and diminishes Surrealism as an idea. The film offers a reduction and flattens it out in a cooly ironic, reflexive refraction of the initial concept. This (perhaps more 'palatable'?) take on Surrealism is filtered through defiantly low-brow conceptions and in this setting could (at a stretch) also be perceived in this context as something of a late/postmodernist take on Surrealism, almost acting in a Lyotardian sense of levelling out the given cultural and formal signifiers across high and low. The background layouts of the short, conferring Magritte-influenced clear skies, palm trees, crumbling Greek Doric columns and skeletal remains of indistinguishable animals, all offer surface links to an abridged, Dalí-esque take on Surrealism.[4] The landscape that thwarts 'Porky Pig' operates as the nominal representative of the everyday and is testament to Clampett's blue-collar, roughhouse 'coming to terms' with the project of modernism as well as a signpost to Dalí's overwhelming success in corralling of the visual language of the 'bizarre'. In this space away from civilisation, titled captions describe how in this '*Darkest Africa*', whilst searching for the supposedly extinct '*Dodo Bird*', the 'New Deal everyman' Porky is presented as unable to progressively master his own destiny. In this setting neither can he subvert it nor even begin to rationalise it. It could possibly be argued that revealed herein is the emphasis on an existential lack of dominion that would at least bear more than a fitting connection with Breton's own rather defensive registers of '*umour*' as a mechanism to cope with the bleak absurdities that confront us all (Balakian 1971: 46).

What we have in this particular reading of Surrealism is a statement that falls into a very typical Warner Bros.-style 'literalisation', in itself a dialogue that has consistently informed American animation practice throughout the Classical Hollywood era. It is a simplistic reading and misunderstanding of appropriating icons and visual abstractions, in this case those associated with Surrealism, clumsily inserted into a very methodical dream-like landscape. This slightly more mundane, proletariat representation and misconception of the term has become somehow fixed within the populist understanding.

In Clampett's works he demarcates the dreamscape as being a very separate location; a fixed parallel dimension, a palpable and accessible space that is a site of safe entrance and departure, dependent on the central characters' own power base within the narrative. For Clampett, who stakes much of his claim on embodying a revolutionary ethos, it seems ironic that he presents his take on Surrealism as being essentially conservative.[5] For Clampett it is more about 'escape'; a space that is to be contained and confined but can never bleed into 'reality' or present an overriding or desirable worldview. In *Porky in Wackyland*, as with other Clampett journeys such as *Tin Pan Alley Cat* (1943), *The Big Snooze* (1946) and *The Great Piggy Bank Robbery* (1949), there is an established starting point of a notional and 'agreed' universe for the central character to depart from. Clampett, like Disney, offers that the Surrealist world has to be one that is entered via a dream moment or 'portal', be it the palpable line or frontier that separates 'Wackyland' from Africa, a (tellingly) self-imposed slap in the head in *The Great Piggy Bank Robbery*, or via the ingestion of sleeping pills ('...take dese and doze...') as in *The Big Snooze*. This is also a world that is beyond any control and as a result must eventually be abandoned. Of course Clampett's stated 'real' universe is in itself more anarchic, aggressive, coarse and less controlled than the one that, say, Disney offers. But this 'reality', no matter how fractured or frenetic, is ultimately the desired place to return to. But in creating this boundary he refuses and denies a total immersion. Clampett wishes not to 'shock' and 'disturb' (and thus offering a true rebellious dialogue) but within safe boundaries he merely seeks to overwhelm the viewer with colour and movement. His animated subversions are based on parody and are depicted so in an accordant relentless energy. Any vague and neutered intent of wishing to explore images from the unconscious are constrained and tempered by the implementation of a safety apparatus. The dangerous and potentially 'shocking' process that automatism can unlock is thus avoided and carefully deactivated. By offering the viewer a sense of removal we have a border set up between us, the audience, and Clampett and his animators' deepest thought processes, detouring the audience from a space where true revelation may possibly occur.

The setting up of a 'wacky space' exists as a contract made by the animators to maintain a sense of protection and propriety, of course a process entirely bogus to the *true* Surrealist. The work still retains a subversive edge but in these explorations of a lack of formal restraint the piece remains contained within arguably strict consensual boundaries of morality and taste. So what appears to be an embrace of aspects of Bretonian discourse emerges, in actuality, as merely a bastardised version and that the darker, truly revolutionary elements that would ideally form the core to any true Surrealist text are eliminated.

It is Walt Disney, arguably, who emerges as the primary contributor in *any* discussion of the twentieth-century American animated film in terms of form, practice and often ideology, by not only his studio's immersion in Classical Hollywood narratives for feature productions but primarily in his favouring of the Romantic painters of the renaissance. His then subsequent instruction of his own artists and animators to attend art classes at night to thus implement a sense of purpose and representational logic into their work can be seen as informing and defining the way American animation approaches visual discourse (Barrier 1999: 82). Such a creative statement in itself, one could argue, could be seen as a pointer towards the inherent ideological political position that can be located within the medium. This perhaps conforms to the view offered by Trotsky who felt that Surrealism, and its attacking of perceived bourgeois principles of rationality, would *always* face something of a difficult translation to contemporary American society. He saw the 'pragmatism, empiricism' within American culture, society and psyche itself as being 'the greatest curse of American thought' (Rosemont 1978: 118). Is it then logical to assume that a more authentic embrace of Surrealism would ideally be one *not* so tied to this notion of rationality that exists at the very heart of the American project but would, in fact, reflect the romanticism found within a more pronounced European sensibility?

While American animation's disregard of narrative logic is well documented (as much down to creative negligence as artistic imperative) it is perhaps in the work of key 1930s animators the Fleischer Brothers that we can observe the form's most potent expression of a 'true' Surrealist dialogue. While the likes of the Warners Bros.' animators were presenting their own randomised collages of popular culture (via the plethora of classical Hollywood movie quotations and radio comedies within the works of Clampett, Frank Tashlin and Tex Avery), a less arch declaration of Surrealism's 'penetration' had already taken place several years earlier. It is in particular within the range of the *Betty Boop/Talkartoon* short cartoons (1930–39) that a less self-conscious application can be found. Here we see more of an adherence to a 'genuine' form of 'popular' Surrealism and one that ties in with a greater authenticity to Breton's original outline of the term.

The Fleischers' cartoons were all about expressing possibilities, technically and formally, within celluloid animation and they were, unlike Warner Bros., also concerned with the immersion of their protagonists into a markedly 'surreal' world. For the animators, this was a defined continuum governed by an unquestioning 'dream logic' and one which conforms to a narrative inclusiveness. This sense of inclusiveness is thus conferred to the audience as being a particular Surrealist universe that proceeds as a normative and 'everyday' experience for the characters within it, and exists not merely as an enclosed area to step in and out of. In the Fleischers' stories, Surrealism simply 'is'.

The 'cel' animation process was, even by the Fleischers' heyday in the 1930s, still deemed a relatively new art form. Yet despite the dispensation of the constraints of cinematically accepted conventions of 'realism' the form in its own way was being constrained by another sense of verisimilitude, that of a constant reiteration that the audience were to be reminded at every twist, punchline or risible moment that the audience was watching a cartoon and that we were to be made constantly aware of this new form's flexibility and fluid, adaptable nature. The Fleischer Brothers' own applications of Surrealism were not just a cue for animators to remind the viewer that they were privy to the possibilities of this fledgling art form. Theirs was the detailing of a world that is subject and revelatory of the internal projections of the 'id'. The Fleischers' world looks more and more, as we gain the luxury of hindsight, like a peek into the resolutely male psyche and a manifestation of unconscious and subconscious desire. The films offer tangential links to an unconscious alliance and another literalised but more subversive application of Breton's own process of automatism. Without any direct articulation many of their defining works could be argued as embodying the ideal, as expressed in 1924, of 'the dictation of thought, in the absence of all control by reason, excluding any aesthetic or moral preoccupation' (Breton 1969: 26).

A statement that possibly aids this notion of an (albeit heavily mediated) model of automatism comes in the shape of a letter between studio head Max Fleischer and one of his chief animators, Shamus Culhane. In the letter Fleischer initially expressed concerns over the hegemonic aesthetic and narrative processes that could be perceived as standardising the animation industry in the 1930s. Commenting upon the progress and 'Disneyfication' of the animation medium Fleischer made it clear that he felt that '"the animated oil painting" has taken the place of the flashiness and delightfulness of the simple cartoon', and, revealingly 'it was, and still is in my opinion, that a cartoon should represent the cartoonist's mental expression' and thus resist 'the tendency towards realism' (Culhane 1986: 62).

Max Fleischer's own appeal for a more direct artistic expression within cel animation, away from the constraints of Disney-style rationalism, also points to the disparity between both Fleischer's more European sensibilities and Disney's insistence on corralling and constraining the medium within a perceived 'folksy Republican' framework. It is a process that can be seen in some of the studio's more celebrated yet extreme pieces such as *Bimbo's Initiation* (1931), *Betty Boop M.D.* (1932), *Snow White* (1933) and *Is My Palm Read?* (1933), among many others replete with the familiar Fleischer 'dream-like atmosphere' (Barrier 1999: 186). Admittedly it would be foolish and naïve to correlate Breton's methods of automatism directly and consciously with this statement, but in many ways this statement calls for the same fundamental ideal, the call for a freedom away from the ties of naturalism and exploration of 'real' unspoken desires. A plea here is self-evident to take advantage of the form as a space for the artist to express unfettered thought; all presented here in a cinematic space where such combinations of incongruous images may, in themselves, have gained Breton's very own approval in articulating freedom from what Breton saw as 'the reign of logic' (1969: 9).

Historical conceptions surrounding Max and Dave Fleischer tend to revolve around agreed narratives that discuss their competition in the pre-war marketplace framed as a family business, as technocrats and as pioneers, in extending the animation form in a search for greater fluidity in movement and a more pronounced accepted 'realism' as a by-product.[6] As Viennese Austrian/Jewish émigrés they fused their somewhat darker sensibilities with urban, Depression-era-infused narratives. This more fanciful Middle European tradition of folklore and fantasy that informs the Fleischers' view of artistic endeavour can be seen as a key instrumental point of divergence from Disney. This more inherently cynical worldview is also filtered through tough experiences as first generation immigrants searching for and creating work in the rough, urban marketplace of early twentieth-century New York.

Their initial experiments with the reflexive, the *Out of the Inkwell* series (1919–29) (what Michael Barrier calls 'cartoons about what it was like to be a cartoon' (1999: 25)), were driven by their breakthrough 'Rotoscope' process, tracing characters over previously filmed and specifically posed 'live action' figures. History dictates that once the financial umbrella offered by John Bray collapsed in 1917 this in turn led to them setting up their own studio. By 1922 they had located themselves, on East 45th Street, as independents distributed by Margaret Sullivan and by the 1930s they were the contracted animation suppliers to the Paramount studio. From thereon they created characters who provided a somewhat saltier alternative to Disney's stable of anodyne anthropomorphic creations in the 1930s (Cabarga 1976: 18). The production duties were nominally reduced and defined as Max being organiser, technocrat and studio production head and Dave given responsibility as director and overseer of the creative aspects of the enterprise, as 'dramaturge', 'scrutinising the work of others' (Barrier 1999: 181).[7]

Several factors contributed to the eventual dissolution of their partnership: a suspicious set of legal precedents by the parent studio in 1942; the loss of several lucrative foreign markets in the fallout from the Second World War and a long-running personal feud between Max and Dave that had somewhat compromised their working relationship. But in formal terms, by the late 1930s they had retreated towards a more naturalistic and cinematic approach to animation which was marked in the shape of two financially unsuccessful feature cartoons and, arguably the studio's technical high-water mark, with the opulent *Superman* series (1941–43).

However, the two most successful series instigated by the studio were E. C. Segar's Popeye (who debuted in 1929 in a cameo but became established in his own right via *Popeye the Sailor* in 1933) and the *Betty Boop/Talkartoon* series which ran parallel throughout the 1930s. Both series tellingly feature caricatured humans rather than being solely reliant on anthropomorphic animals and displayed distorted models of masculinity and femininity. The connection that the Betty Boop character subsequently forged with audiences demonstrates that a mainly working-class demographic were more than happy to accept darker, less linear tendencies within mainstream animation.

The character itself was conceived by Max Fleischer and designed by Grim Natwick as a musical interlude in the short *Dizzy Dishes* (1930) as a singing dog-woman hybrid. Up until the last released cartoon in 1939 Betty remained a crude distillation and blatant appropriation of actress Helen Kane's 'flapper' persona. The creation also emerged through the series as a somewhat subordinate model of femininity, in part reactive to East Coast, urban-Jewish male anxieties surrounding the feminine independence that had flourished in the shifts of gender consensus just after the First World War (Kleinberg 1999: 242–3).

Under the current cultural lens the character displays an uncomfortable paedophiliac undercurrent with the combination of a coy-but-knowing sexuality and the promise of both availability and dependency. With a mismatched girlish/doll's head, overly pronounced feminine curves combined with Mae Questel's high-pitched cooing tones the character appears to offer something of a deeper resonance and suggests dialogues of objectification, control, power and sexual subjugation when allying the image to male sexual desire. 'Her films then, even in the credit sequences, create a relay of male spectorial desire in which Betty's body serves as the trademark of the series just as the Paramount mountain' (Smoodin 1993: 31).[8]

Many historians agree that the series itself can be defined as pre-and post-Hays Code intervention. In keeping in line with the major studios Max Fleischer thus capitulated to concerns raised by the Hollywood regulatory body after they had been alerted to the blatant sexual themes inherent within the cartoons. The 'lax' moral centre to the films and celebration of hedonistic drives and lifestyles that inform many of the narratives thus came under scrutiny and Betty underwent a 'substantial revision' (Maltin 1987: 105). Such was the attendant pressure placed on the Fleischer studios that Betty Boop emerged reinvented, redesigned as a somewhat chastened figure after negotiation in 1934.[9] So the sexualisation and objectification that had in fact contributed to the original success of the series was carefully removed. In these post-1934 shorts we see a move away from this refraction of the sexually independent/active archetype of 'The Flapper', a perception informed by the increasingly liberated New York-Jewish young woman of the late 1920s (again as detailed by S. J. Kleinberg) towards an altogether more homely, chaste, suburban, professional construct. Thus she becomes less a figure of adult fun and of carnal possibility and is cast in the more sexually and socially neutral roles of a single professional independent woman.[10]

But along with a more pronounced sexual dynamic what really sets the *Talkartoons* apart from other works of the period is a notable adherence to a kind of 'dream logic' as a defining feature of narrative construction. The Betty Boop films themselves willingly conform to the languid, fluid logic of a 'dream state', in reducing the contradictions and blurring the lines between the conscious and unconscious, subjective and objective register and by merging the 'rational' and the 'irrational'. The shorts in their quiet way present an actualisation of freedom from social and sexual certainty and consequence.

This sense of 'removal' is enhanced and complemented by the pronounced lack of linear plot direction and resolution. While both Michael Barrier and Paul Wells see the Surrealist elements at work as much about 'process' than any attempt to become a Bretonian 'abnegation of all mental law' (Wells 2002a: 55), Wells offers that the films in their very randomness merely aid their working through 'unspeakable' urban, emotional and sexual tensions as well as where changes in 1930s American society itself can be discussed (2002a: 53–6).

This is aided by, in industrial terms, the shorts simply being developed in a more random fashion than the Fordist production practices that typified the relatively opulent Disney output. In their crudity they were simply more 'hands on', less mediated and increasingly open to a direct transfer of the animators' own imagination and creative impulses: a factor that Barrier and latterly Wells both concede. This deficiency also leant an improvised feel to the construction of the stories of the shorts themselves. This fact is also reiterated by animator Shamus Culhane, who goes on to reinforce the impact made on the shorts by an 'unsophisticated story department' and subject matter beholden to the 'earthy humour of New York street kids' (1986: 53). The shorts absolve themselves from accepted narrative/live-action filmic constraints of resolution often with sudden, unexpected abrupt endings, and exposition is often fractured, directionless and confusing in execution.

Indeed many of the Fleischer narratives share obvious similarities. They often detail a protagonist, or protagonists, thrust into a cumulative irrational situation beyond her/his/their control. They also feature at the heart of their individual stories a procession of seemingly random and incongruous images and visual puns (often related to metamorphosis and with attendant sexual overtones). But where much of this 'dream state' is cast is in the way temporal and physical locations are undermined, abandoned and disregarded at every turn.

There are notable shifts of contradictory spatial location in between the white page, the artists' table and the street scenes of the hallucinatory *Ha! Ha! Ha!* (1934). This can be seen also in the deliberately disjointed geography of *Bimbo's Initiation* and particularly in *Is My Palm Read?* where director Dave Fleischer highlights this *laissez-faire* approach to progressive consistency in a typically 'removed' opening scene. Here he depicts a graded, shadowy representation of an off-kilter, forced perspective 'house of prediction' which is set nominally against and within an urban environment yet, tellingly, is still spatially apart. In the cartoon it is signposted by a roof-mounted neon sign detailing an outlined profiled head that very literally thumbs its nose to 'past', 'present' and 'future' ('*Prof. Bimbo reveals all...*'). It is a direct signal from the animators to the audience to prepare for a fluidity in temporal and linear plotting and a subversion of narrative expectations. Two potential suitors, Koko and Bimbo (in their dubious roles as clairvoyants) offer to Betty a fatalistic premonition. This facilitates a bizarre sequence of projected events in the cartoon which straddle prediction *and* desire. The subsequent breaking down of a hitherto quite flimsy temporal and physical location is then fully realised as the short descends into a frantic chase in the final frames where typically Fleischerian chaos takes hold. In presenting this series of premonitions which apparently become 'truth/actuality', Betty and Bimbo (Koko the Clown, originally a key aspect of the story now conveniently and illogically discarded merely for the purposes of the action) then move from the city to the projected jungle/prophecy, here merging future and present 'actuality' in one abnegating motion. There is progression but no explanation for the leap to this now-physical future space as geographical logic thus becomes discarded. For the Fleischers a linking of perceivable, definable boundaries and laws are simply of no importance to the scenario. The story starts off as a 'dream' and the landscape detailed within the narrative is that of the subconscious, the landscape of the 'dream space' itself. The short in its sloppiness and its agenda to explore formal and cinematic limits thus functions also as revealing the manifold layers of a nightmare.

Whilst the shorts in themselves exist in cinematic spaces markedly different to other animation studios of the period, the universe depicted is rendered in the same fashion in many ways as their more scrupulous counterparts: a factor which could be seen as sharing a commonality with Surrealist painterly practice in alluding to the placement of the 'incongruous' within 'photo-realistic' settings. The Fleischer works still check representational animation concepts of depth and weight, along understood ideas and agreed principles of movement and physical correlation, all depicted with a naturalistic emphasis on shadow and physicality. The shorts offer a notional drive towards 'photographic' representation yet married to moments that distort and constantly reinvent the space that the characters inhabit, a place which corresponds with a sense of 'escape' beyond the rigid constraints of logic. They work via primarily fixed long or medium compositions, with the occasional close-up detail/reaction shot, and with a stress on 'tableaux' framing (with of course approximated, 'drawn-in' camera positions.) But the sense of Surreal dislocation that we now associate with the series is compounded, as Wells notes, by an 'ambivalent composition and contradictory *mise-en-scène*' (Wells 2002b: 5). The shorts' very randomness and their arbitrary quality are heightened by factors such as central characters being marginalised, overwhelmed or undermined by the sheer fluidity of the elements within the frame and the insistence of metamorphic events dominating the events (of which more later). This in itself, despite often randomly shifting from interior to exterior locations, also adds a strange sense of claustrophobia to the cartoons, unique to the studio.

For Barrier, this sense of 'discomfort' and 'dislocation' that marks early Fleischer output away from Disney rests within several other conspicuous formal tropes. The first being the peculiar 'bouncing effect' that sees the action within the frame undulate and 'bob' in set rhythms. As Barrier himself also confirms 'interpolating bizarre gags, the rhythmic twitching into cartoons otherwise dominated by smooth, unaccented animation meant that those cartoons took on a hallucinatory quality. They were in their zombie-like pacing, their aimlessness and their arbitrary transformations, literally dreamlike' (1999: 181).[11] Along with a lethargic sense of timing (enforced by a reliance on long 'takes' and all of the action occuring within the frame itself) and a hypnotic repetition of shots and gags, what also stands out is the way that sound is deployed in the context of the shorts. In itself this is an aspect of production which reveals the Fleischers' own marked inattention to detail and which gives the films their own quite singular atmosphere.[13] Unlike the common practice of recording dialogue ahead of cartoon production itself (established by Walt Disney in 1929 and an industry standard by the 1940s), Max and Dave Fleischer had initiated a system where the voices were dubbed on by actors *after* the film was completed. Actors who thrived on improvisation, such as Questel and Jack Mercer, recorded their parts onto the track, 'post-sync'. As a result although the dialogue was specific to the somewhat loosely defined narrative in execution it was often unrehearsed and committed to celluloid with an imprecise timing. This gives the shorts a further quality of strangeness and adds an incoherent quality, an effect that appears more prominent within the technically cruder pre-Hays Code releases.[13]

As Wells also notes, the brothers placed the concept of metamorphosis prominently into their narratives as a comic device, as a mode of plot/narrative progression and as often central to the theme of the cartoons themselves. This conceit adds much to the signature fluid nature of the visuals as the Fleischers insist on ascribing solid objects a 'life' of their own. For contemporary readings this adds a layer of uncertainty and compounds dislocation and anxiety and revels in a mocking of the 'concreteness' of the corporeal world (2002a: 55), transforming and subverting the everyday objects and expectations of the 'real' world. Thus there emerges a suggestion by the Fleischers that (as with all the most vivid and disturbing dreams) this world we are in is to be read in many ways as to be just like our own but somehow 'not quite'. The world detailed in such work as *Ha! Ha! Ha!* is one where clocks, pliers, mailboxes, road bridges, cars and (in typical morbid fashion) gravestones come to life, where it is required that a typewriter splits into a laughing, mocking maw complete with teeth; all of which are commonplace events within this peculiar comic universe.

There is nothing in this continuum of walls, trees, chairs and so forth that cannot sprout limbs or suddenly animate under its own congniscence. Dependable objects that appear rooted in a traditional role of service or decoration may coalesce into a face, grow a mouth that will talk to the central characters or even reach out and constrain them at any moment. It is also entirely appropriate for a Surrealist narrative that such behaviour is nearly always motivated by a desire to possess or ensnare Betty, ascribing, in this instance, the power of our heroine to libidinise even inanimate objects.

Again in *Is My Palm Read?*, in detailing a supposedly agreed 'real' world, in the projected 'future' offered we are shown a rubberised cruise liner as it moulds itself to the mountainous surf it sails upon. And then as a referent to the unknowable power of nature itself the very waves themselves then playfully actualise fists which go on to batter the man-made construct of the ship itself. Indeed those same watery hands go on to later molest and cajole Betty once she is washed ashore on the beach of the indeterminate island after the ship has sunk. Even the jungle/island hut which is nominally represented as a 'safe space' at the midway point of the cartoon then grows extendable, disproportionate arms, a definable male face and a lascivious leer before devouring Betty in its mouth/door and subsequently imprisoning her within the home itself. This could, perhaps (very tentatively, in hindsight) be read as a direct index of the anxieties surrounding feminine independence, but also a demonstration of the wilful lampooning of 'reality', a sense of the emancipation of the imagination that entirely falls into a more subtle 'subversive' and 'revolutionary' definition than, say, the Warner Bros. examples.

The metamorphosis that informs much of the work allows the expression of prevalent fears and desires, for the revealing of a 'hidden self', the detailing of a repressed identity and desire form a common narrative thread through many of their key films. In *Betty Boop M.D.* in the guise of a travelling medicine woman, Betty offers some rural townsfolk an elixir ('*Jippo*') which in turn leads to an escalating transformation-fixated montage of repressed identities revealed once imbibed. The narrative then proceeds detailing a baby and then an old man morphing and swapping 'ages', to a skeleton leaping out of one animal/person hybrid and playing a tune on his own fleshy posterior. This then shifts to several other somewhat darker metamorphic gags culminating in another small baby whose face slowly fills the frame and turns into the Rouben Mamoulian/Frederic March incarnation of Stevenson's Mr Hyde in *Dr Jekyll and Mr Hyde* (1931).[14] This, in jarring fashion, then brings the short to an abrupt and alarming close. That image in itself, apart from being a glib cultural nod, acts out a fairly unsophisticated and graphic representation of the 'beast within' released from the perceived shell of innocence.

As the films deal with the repressive and the hidden it seems only appropriate that many of the films feature sex and desire as central narratives, an activity that is acknowledged in the films in defiantly hedonistic fashion and in somewhat similar vulgar registers. The impression the Fleischers give, in shorts such as *Betty Boop for President* (1932), *Boop-Oop-a-Doop* (1932) and certainly *Betty Boop's Big Boss* (1933), is that they are intent on portraying a very real sense of carnality that speaks of a more mature life experience. The sex represented in the films often has the tang of authentic desire and articulates genuine urges. For this alone it is notable that the animators felt it necessary to mix genders of supporting characters within narratives that depict sexual attainment and control (primarily over the virginal-but-knowing Betty).

The retreat to a dark cave arrives as a common symbolic moment in several key works as 'a place associated with sexuality' (Langer 1975: 52) from *Minnie the Moocher* (1932) through to the Fleischers' venerated *Snow White*. It seems that for these shorts the only available progression in any narrative sense is to go deeper and darker into the recesses of the psyche rather than 'forward', 'upward' or 'onward'. In *Snow White* despite the left-to-right procession of images in the Queen's subterranean cave the overriding impression offered is that the animators are merely going through the motions of formal convention to suggest to the viewer a sense of the linear; that any possible escape from the underworld dominated by the jealous Queen who terrorises Betty, Pudgy and Koko via a series of metamorphic shifts from her original form is merely a background dialogue to the main subtext, which in this case are the puns and transformative horrors that index her monstrous inner self and the containment of the protagonists within her designated space. This is where the Queen can reveal her true self and thus allow a 'parade' and 'performance' *of* those desires.

In *Snow White* the rotoscoped figure of blues/jazz/swing singer Cab Calloway metamorphosises into a phallic ghost as an on-screen representation of male power, of racial and societal 'otherness' and of, simply, desire (Wells 1998: 217). He is a force created to intimidate Betty and contain her within the highly sexualised milieu of the cave in the last third of the short. While *Snow White* in itself has been cited by Wells as on one level merely representative of the Fleischers' approach and understanding of the 'conventions of cartooning', the film does also go out of its way to highlight and depict a very knowing 'phallic environment' (1998: 74) – a setting of erect stalactites and phallic uniforms and postures throughout which can be palpably linked not only to heterosexual male drives and fixations but also can be seen as conferring sexuality with power, control and fear. This very deliberate setting could very possibly be representative of the Queen's own forbidden appetites, in wishing to subjugate the chaste, heterosexual Betty and creating another layer of cross-sexual tension. This is further highlighted by the fact that such a predatory role in the narrative is generally only saved only for older, masculine enemies such as the rapacious, priapic ringmaster in *Boop-Oop-a-Doop*, for example.

The theme of denial of sex or of a 'sexual self' forms the basis for a number of their films, especially in shorts like *Minnie the Moocher* and in particular *Bimbo's Initiation*. Of a film described as the very manifestation of a 'bad dream' (Cabarga 1976: 44), an experiential reality which discusses the travails suffered by Betty's suitor Bimbo when in the process of denying his own sexual identity by refusing to answer the chorus line mantra of 'wanna be a member?', Mark Langer offers a Freudian/castration reading of the piece in stating that 'Bimbo is drawn a long vaginal corridor lined with knives' [*sic*] (1975: 52) but the denial of sex as binding social force and as a release is undoubtedly featured strongly in the primary narrative. This ties in with Langer's assertion that more effective Fleischer films were concerned solely with 'sex and death' and indeed holds water. The 'death drive' (in being linked to sexual activity) as isolated by Langer, informs not only the short unofficial series of three films starring Cab Calloway – *Minnie the Moocher*, *Snow White* and *The Old Man of the Mountain* (1933) – but is a recurrent theme that can also be isolated in one extreme sequence in *Betty Boop M.D.* as the old man who cheerfully welcomes death in. This is a character who rolls out his *own* grave and submerges himself beneath a singing gravestone and an animated singing flower, something which extends to the very familiar Fleischian phallic ghosts that infiltrate the arbitrary representation of the 'present' in *Is My Palm Read?* Typically sexualised spirits emerge via the conduit of the crystal ball from the fatalistic future predicted and controlled by Betty's (resolutely male) co-stars/acolytes. These rampaging priapic monsters are representative here as a commonsensical Fleischerian statement on what they view as the unstoppable male sexual urge. These on-screen actualisations and flirtations with death images and the adherence to supernatural totems affirm the fears and concerns in our make-up that cross boundaries of class, gender, culture and race, thus allowing the Fleischers to speak to the broadest possible demographic. Escape and confrontation of repressed anxieties surrounding mortality and destiny can be found in any number of the early 1930s shorts.[15]

The cartoon format has continually propagated this restatement of Surrealism as somehow being that of the 'wacky' and the 'weird' merely for its own sake. This refraction process via low-brow forms has undoubtedly been one of the many visual art forms, from comic books to advertising to mainstream film, that have contributed to this dilution of the ideas central to Surrealist practice. Yet Surrealism in its purest form as a rejection of bourgeois ideology and as an expression of the possibilities for life, thought and art *does* seem entirely in keeping with the animation form – an art form that is borne from low-brow, commercial settings but one that dovetails perfectly into Franklin Rosemont's definition of an 'unrelenting revolt against a civilisation that reduces all human aspiration to market values, religious impostures, universal boredom and misery' (1978: 1). A creative vehicle that in hindsight and as part of the increasingly fixed historical and commerce-defined narrative that seems to have shaped our understandings of classical American animation is a direct index of proletariat experience and taste. While Breton felt that no bourgeois artist could accurately depict or translate the aspirations of the 'pre-revolutionary' working classes it seems only fitting (and perhaps surely he would take some pleasure in knowing) that such a proletariat expression could take on his ideals and incorporate them (however clumsily) into their stories.

The sense of non-conformity, the free play of images, corresponds to this. The freedom desired by the artists wishing to explore the form almost could be seen as an idealism of the concept. Yet while Breton always refuted the establishment of 'conventional Surrealist patterns' (Breton 1978a: 40) what we *can* determine is that in the free-associative work of Max and Dave Fleischer (and their animators) we have a less constrained expression of Surrealism in a resolutely populist setting, while with the Clampett examples we have merely a colourful exploration of possibilities within the form and a profound lack of confidence in expressing a *true* Surrealist dialogue. Clampett, in his Warner Bros. work, is often questioning and mocking of the 1930s American consensus: the background message to his work is ultimately that despite it all he inherently believes in the notion of society and in that conception of structure (even if that structure is there to be rebelled against and still set within definable moral confines). He is more concerned with (pop) culture than with art. Perhaps that is why Surrealism in its purest form could never really flourish within such a truly Americanised art form and why readings of the movement err towards surface appropriation and quotation rather than a true embrace of the 'revolutionary'. While as close as the Fleischers are in this compromised and expedient setting in actualising the project of Surrealism with their more fatalistic European sensibilities they too fall short of a true expression of Bretonian purity. Thus what emerges in the wake of the American cultural imperialism of twentieth-century art and cinema is a populist definition that has now successfully overtaken the original statement.

Notes

1   The popular animation form in itself is perhaps a testament to the 'power of the image'; a concept that at a stretch could be seen as very much in line with André Breton and Pierre Reverdy's celebration of the 'image' as a construct of pure imagination (Breton 1969: 20). Uneasy alliances between avant-garde art traditions and this populist medium have littered the form's historical narrative, from the modernist layout designs found in Disney's 'Baby Weems' section of *The Reluctant Dragon* (1941) to Chuck Jones' incorporation of expressionism into his 1943 works, *The Aristo Cat* and *Wakiki Rabbit*. Of course the United Productions of America studios' work of the early 1950s offered perhaps the most apparent formal embrace of a 'painterly' Surrealism to be found within the remarkable Expressionist/Surrealist hybrid short designed by Paul Julian and directed by Ted Parmalee, *The Tell Tale Heart* (1953).

2   An indicator towards not only the complex fragmentation and perceptions of twentieth-century culture but also towards the shifts in the political paradigms of this early twenty-first century now far removed from Surrealism's politicised conception and origins.

3   Breton's somewhat imprecisely defined term, '*l'humour noir*' or '*umour*' is discussed and actualised within his 1940 '*Anthologie de l'humour noir*' (re-published 1972). As the likes of Simon Critchley (2002) suggest the process of humour in undermining social ritual, in expressing and playing out of aggression and managing inhibitions and taboo subjects all also hold a place within established Freudian dialogues. The emphasis on 'black humour', within not only Surrealist settings but arguably within the adult narratives and sensibilities of 1930s cartoons, relates closely to many pivotal Freudian ideas on 'tendentious jokes' rather than models of the more 'innocent' non-confrontational joke. This darker, 'black humour' and approach can be seen as managing aspects of 'hostility' and 'sexuality', as Freud himself explains, working to 'liberat[e] pleasure by

lifting inhibitions' (1963: 134). However *l'humour noir* in the Bretonian sense and in its relation to Freudian notions of the tendentious joke can be allied more to 'hostile' registers than to merely 'smutty' types of humour.

4   The chequerboard warped backgrounds and the narrative framework of the short itself can be clearly identified as beholden to the dark whimsy of the Breton-endorsed Lewis Carroll (Grant 2001: 55), and a factor which offers tangential, but altogether appropriate, links in tone and desired effect to Breton. Carroll's own 'sense of revolt' has been long admired by Breton himself (Balakian 1971: 236). The opening credit titles of the 1948 frame-for-frame remake, *Dough for the Dodo* (supervised by Friz Freleng) even goes as far to outline the Warner Bros. agenda by depicting the suspension of melted clocks hanging out to dry on a washing line, a move that offers reclamation, referencing and mocking all in equal measures.

5   This 'stepping into a different space' is part of an ongoing definable, traceable animation lineage. We can point to the celebrated 'Elephants on Parade' sequence from *Dumbo* (1941) as an example of this, where animators are given a sense of free reign to push the boundaries of the form in terms of design and movement. This became a minor tradition throughout Disney's mainstream feature-length productions where a series of inter-linked dream/fantasy images away from the main story are passed off as a harmless drunken interlude or magical episode (Leslie 2002: 187–91).

6   Max Fleischer, as with Disney, held great stock in what Mark Langer defines as an 'ideology of progress' (1992: 355) and their parallel West Coast/East Coast competitiveness has been observed as being fuelled by a drive towards photographic 'realism' and up until 1942 as an 'unbroken march towards mimesis' (1992: 347). Another emergent irony is that while the Fleischers' natural urge was to express a series of gags as an uninterrupted train of thought (tangentially based on formal rules of naturalism) they were, in industrial and in product presentation terms, arch rationalists.

7   Michael Barrier, Mark Langer and Leslie Cabarga among others all note the fluidity of these roles and the importance of collaborations from key animators, designers and directors such as Seymour Kneitel, Grim Natwick, Shamus Culhane and Dan Gordon, among others.

8   An unmistakable dynamic is made uncomfortably explicit within the narrative of *Is My Palm Read?* when we are encouraged to view a hat stand animate momentarily to slap the behind of a disturbingly infantilised, yet still objectified, Betty.

9   A more elongated body shape became incorporated into the design of the character with less emphasis on exaggerated feminine curves along with a more modest, all-covering attire. Forged in the links to Betty Boop's canine origins (and often a source of anxiety over subtexts of 'bestiality' and 'sexual availability'), the dog/boy character of Bimbo was thus also removed, as was the masculine/suitor clown-figure Koko. Less problematic replacements were then inserted, such as the de-sexualised presence of the decrepit Grampy figure and the sidekick dog, Pudgy, who are both situated as harmless foils for this new incarnation. This rationalisation process also sees the Surrealist aesthetic (which dominates the Fleischers' more individual work) diminish in proportion

with the reduction of the more overt subversive elements in the narratives themselves.

10 Betty, in shorts such as *The Swing School* (1938) and *Musical Mountaineers* (1939), not only offers a progressive bridge between classes (rather than pointed social comment), she also conforms entirely to the model of autonomous, career-minded womanhood that Maureen Honey outlines as a staple of literature and cinema in her 1984 book *Creating Rosie the Rivetter* (noted in Smoodin 1993: 36–7).

11 As animator Myron Waldman states in interview with Barrier, this was beholden to Dave Fleischer's wish to not have 'any characters "held" on screen' and as a move to ally the films to synchronised musical soundtracks (1999: 179).

12 The desire to replicate corresponding naturalist sounds in such a universe here is name checked as a nominal expectation within the animated form at this historical juncture. So intent on providing a serious riposte to Disney's ongoing project of technological progression the common aim with most studios at this time would be to provide as close as possible an index of pre-recorded sound effect to rendered image. In doing so this would be seen as approximating the conventions and expectations of 'live' film and maintaining a desired verisimilitude.

13 A practice that perhaps forges tangible links to the way that contemporary cinematic Surrealist David Lynch utilises incongruous background/foreground sounds, pop songs and disjointed dialogue within such works as *Eraserhead* (1977) and *Blue Velvet* (1985).

14 The Fleischers, like Warner Bros. who followed, often stressed links with popular culture as ways to register humour and audience identification, often nodding to cinematic genres and ideas directly and indirectly and to other forms of contemporary relevance, such as jazz music, including musicians like Cab Calloway, Louis Armstrong and Don Redman in stories.

15 *Snow White* casts Calloway as index of the bestial and the forbidden. His presence is usually offered as a signpost or as entry to an 'underworld' and to then delineate a more heightened depiction of the 'supernatural', in a setting already very far removed from the 'everyday', perhaps in line with the Flesichers' own acknowledgement of the singer's dark subject matters of drugs, sex and death and the sense of social transgression that comes when detailing these within mainstream settings.

Graham Roberts

SOLUBLE FISH: HOW SURREALISM SAVED DOCUMENTARY FROM JOHN GRIERSON

The cinema? Three cheers for darkened rooms.
    – André Breton

True realism consists in revealing the surprising things which habit keeps covered
and prevents us from seeing.
    – Jean Cocteau

Documentary is a term as ill-used and ill-defined as Surrealism itself. 'Documentary'
was coined in a 1926 *New York Sun* review of Robert J. Flaherty's *Moana* (1926) by
John Grierson. Grierson, born in 1898, was the son of a Scottish village schoolmaster
and brought up in the driest of Calvinist households. After active service in the First
World War he graduated in Philosophy and headed to the University of Chicago in
1924.

Grierson was a frequent contributor to scholarly periodicals, writing on problems of education and public information. He specialised in the psychological impact of propaganda and made a study of the development of newspapers and the ever
more popular cinema. In America he read Walter Lippmann's *Public Opinion* (1922).
Lippmann argued that democracy was deteriorating because the citizens could no
longer understand public issues. The general public, aware that they could neither understand nor control events, were growing apathetic. Grierson dedicated his life to
helping the citizens to learn. Thus his life's work was entirely praiseworthy – but utterly
condescending and potentially profoundly dull.

Grierson's solution to Lippman's democratic deficit problem was the documentary film – 'the creative interpretation of reality' as he called it in 'The Documentary Producer' in *Cinema Quarterly* in 1933. Grierson consistently stressed that the
creative urges should be kept in careful check. As he put it in the *Fortnightly Review*

'The documentary was an essentially British development. It's characteristic was the idea of social use ... It permitted the national talent for understatement' (in Higson 1986: 72).

When Grierson went home to Britain he set about learning how to engineer finance in order to make 'documentary' films. His first patron was the Empire Marketing Board (EMB) which promoted British products and British workers. In 1928 he secured EMB funding for *Drifters*, about 'the ardour and bravery of common labour' or - more accurately - the herring fishing industry. Grierson spends a lot of (screen) time on machinery and engines. He seems happier with inanimate objects or fish than people. The innovative 'underwater' shots were achieved at the Plymouth Marine Biological Research Station - a close viewing reveals the reflection of the camera in the tank's glass.

Grierson's twin aims of education and glorying in the ordinary led to two interlinked problems. The films he oversaw tend towards a didacticism that can teeter into strident hectoring. They also launched a tendency for glorying in the dull and prosaic rather than revealing the extraordinary. In his own words: 'The basic force behind [documentary] was social and not aesthetic. It was a desire to make a drama out of the ordinary, to set against the prevailing drama of the extraordinary: a desire to bring the citizen's eye in from the ends of the earth to the story, his own story, of what was happening under his nose' (in Hardy 1966: 112).

For the next decade Grierson dominated the 'British Documentary Movement' at the EMB and later the General Post Office Film Unit. Thus, at least in the Anglophone world, documentary became a genre rather damned by the stolid and humourless image of the man himself. As producer, Grierson steered the films of Robert Flaherty (*Industrial Britain*, 1931) and Alberto Cavalcanti (*Coal Face*, 1935) into a most solid and stolid cul-de-sac.

In 1935, he founded the Film Centre in London, a central organisation for the financing and direction of documentary film units. He also founded and published *World Film News*. Having become the pervasive authority of British documentary Grierson spread his influence across the Atlantic. On the invitation of the Canadian Government he travelled to Canada in 1938 to survey and report upon film work and possibilities and helped to draft the National Film Act of 1939. In October of that year he was appointed Government Film Commissioner and became head of the National Film Board (NFB). In 1945 Grierson stepped down from the NFB to take on the job of Director of UNESCO's Mass Communications in Paris. From 1948 to 1950 he was Controller of Films at the Central Office of Information in London. Then, in 1951, together with John Baxter, he took charge of the National Film Finance Corporation's Group 3, designed to develop the talents of young feature filmmakers. Grierson turned to television in 1957, conducting for many years his own programme *This Wonderful World* for Scottish television.

Grierson is an iconic figure in the history of documentary - but of a particular history of a particular type: the prosaic. David Thomson - in a less than flattering portrait in the *New Biographical Dictionary of Film* – writes of Grierson as a 'harsh, restrictive enthusiast ... essentially bigoted and unintelligent and isolated by history' (2003: 359). Thomson is over-strident in the first part of this denunciation and simply wrong in the second. Grierson's influence for good or ill lingers over much of British television and cinema and the majority of documentary output in the English-speaking world.

In the Griersonian documentary along with a rather dry 'realism' the faint whiff of voyeurism is never far away – neither is the vicarious pleasure of *schadenfreude*. His – often less able – progeny have taken these tendencies to the limit with the miserablist realism of Ken Loach or Mike Leigh, or the televisual equivalent of bear-baiting which is so much of reality TV. Through no fault of his Grierson can be positioned as a key player in the development of the 'social porn' (see Taylor 2005) which has permeated our visual culture.

Another perhaps richer tradition touched by a Surrealist viewpoint exists alongside the worthy, unvarnished (but tarnished) verisimilitude of Griersonian documentary. A recent (commercially and critically successful) example of this continuing tradition is *Être et avoir* (2002). This French film, which investigates the goings-on in a one-class school in rural France, begins with a black screen and the sound of wind. The first image is of cows being herded in the snow. We are shown the storm through a window followed by the classroom ... and the tortoises. In this surreal early scene one tortoise crawls across a classroom floor, followed by another. It is a full four minutes before the film gets to the school bus. Within a simple story a host of small details – like the stuffed donkey on the window ledge in the train carriage during the school trip – add to the dream-like atmosphere of the film which develops at a most sleepy pace.

The director, Nicolas Philibert has made his (contra-Grierson) approach clear in an interview with Nick Walker (on the DVD issue of the film): 'My work turns its back on the traditional forms of documentary, which is often this didactical, journalistic approach '; 'I don't make documentaries ... with the desire to give a speech ... instead, I try to tell a story and bring out emotions ... [a documentary] is not a photocopy of reality'; 'Sometimes these decisions have to be made very quickly ... and sometimes you don't have much time to think about it ... it's often quite instinctive ... we deny [documentary] all poetic, metaphoric capacity.' Philibert sums up his aims with: 'The film is very open, it gives everyone the possibility of projecting into it what they wish, their own memories of childhood.' In this statement we can identify echoes of Buñuel: 'You have to begin to lose your memory, if only in bits and pieces, to realise that memory is what makes our lives. Life without memory is no life at all, just as an intelligence without the possibility of expression is not really an intelligence. Our memory is our coherence, our reason, our feeling, even our action. Without it, we are nothing' (in Anon. 2004).

Philibert's work has often focused on the internal logic of institutions (in the grand tradition of 'direct cinema', for example Frederick Wiseman's *Titicut Follies* (1967) and *High School* (1968)). His first documentary feature, *La Ville Louvre* (1990), dwells on the bizarre world of that great museum as it prepares to construct a giant glass pyramid. *Un animal, des animaux* (1994) wanders the Paris Natural History Museum taking in a paint-job on an elephant.

The tradition of dream-like reverie and making strange by juxtaposition is alive and well in documentary. It goes beyond the dry observation of Grierson's fish in *Drifters* and taps into the rather more intriguing tradition of André Breton's *Soluble Fish* (1924). This early piece of Surrealist writing is full of acute observations – juxtaposed in strange and disturbing ways but each with its own internal logic – many of which have echoes in the documentaries of such as Philibert and (as we shall see) Humphrey Jennings, Dziga Vertov and Chris Marker.

Breton's *First Surrealist Manifesto* (1924) begins with reality (and discovering meaning by making strange):

> So strong is the belief in life, in what is most fragile in life – real life. I mean – that in the end this belief is lost ... If [man] still retains a certain lucidity, all he can do is turn his back toward his childhood which, however his guides and mentors may have botched it, still strikes him as somehow charming ... now he is only interested in the fleeting, the extreme facility of everything. (1969: 3)

The images exposed in Surrealist works are of course as confusing and startling as those of dreams. Thus it is perfectly acceptable for Surrealist works to be presented in a realistic (if irrational) style. Surrealists could search for juxtapositions that were (in Lautréamont's phrase which became their slogan) 'beautiful, like the chance meeting of a sewing machine and an umbrella on a dissecting table' (in Gould 1976: 24). Many Surrealists were drawn to the audio-visual media in imaginative ways, from Man Ray's photographs to Luis Buñuel's short films *Un chien andalou* (*An Andalusian Dog*, 1929) and *L'Âge d'or* (*The Golden Age*, 1930).

Jeffrey Rouff has turned an anthropologist's eye on Buñuel's major 'documentary' work *Tierra sin pan* aka *Las Hurdes* (*Land Without Bread*, 1932): 'No anthropological film from the 1930s provides such a comparable, almost encyclopedic, portrait of a given region or demonstrates such a subtle understanding of ethnographic film style' (1998: 45). Rouff notes that 'the Surrealist movement in poetry, literature and film overlapped with the emerging discipline of modern anthropology in France' (ibid.). He also notes that James Clifford has coined the term 'ethnographic Surrealism' to describe the intersection of anthropology and art in Paris in the 1920s and 1930s. Unlike traditional anthropological discourses, which strive to make the unfamiliar comprehensible, ethnographic Surrealism, Clifford writes: 'attacks the familiar, provoking the irruption of otherness – the unexpected' (1986: 145).

Rouff sees *Tierra sin pan* as a parody of non-fiction film:

> *Land Without Bread* brilliantly and perversely combines objective detail and illogical continuity ... Documentary is supposed to be a serious, even educational, genre. It prompts sincere readings. Still today many critics take *Land Without Bread* at

face-value, seeing it as a straightforward work of social-issue documentary. (1998: 55)

When Buñuel's film went into commercial release in 1937, the British film director and arch-Griersonian Basil Wright praised it as an important work of non-fiction. Then he went on to criticise the inappropriate voice-over commentary and poor choice of music. He concludes his 1937 review of *Tierra sin pan* with the following comment: 'Unfortunately, someone (presumably not Buñuel) has added to the film a wearisome American commentary, plus the better part of a Brahms' symphony. As a result, picture and sound never coalesce' (in Wright 1971: 146).

Wright has simply failed to read the film in Surrealist terms. He defines *Tierra sin pan* as a 'complete volte-face' by a director who 'had hitherto specialised in shots of dead donkeys ensconced in a grand piano' (ibid.). He manages to deny not only the subversive role of sound in the documentary but also Buñuel's parody of accepted cinematic techniques, such as the point-of-view shot, in his earlier works. In addition, Wright fails to notice that *Tierra sin pan* actually does include a shot of a dead donkey. Rouff points to the fact that Buñuel's work is

> foreign to Wright's understanding of the social role of the documentary. Simply put, satire is not serious and therefore has no place in non-fiction. We can measure the distance between our world and Wright's by recognising how we value those features he sought to disavow: contradiction, doubt, carnivalesque inversions, deliberate incongruities. Within the field of anthropology, some sixty years after the commercial release of Buñuel's film in Paris, it is time to recognise *Land Without Bread* as a parody of ethnographic film. (1998: 56)

Michael S. Bell (2004) has put forward the view that there were/are two distinct trends of Surrealism with marked differences. 'The Automatists' leaned towards the suppression of consciousness in favour of the subconscious, focused on feeling and were less analytical than the 'Veristic Surrealists'. This group, on the other hand, were keen on allowing the images of the subconscious to surface undisturbed so that their meaning could then be deciphered. They wanted to faithfully represent these images as a link between the abstract spiritual realities and the real forms of the material world. Through metaphor the concrete world could be understood, not by looking at the objects but by looking into them.

In crude terms, the Surrealist documentarists are veristic. The most famous of filmic Surrealists – Buñuel – was not. The Surreal documentarists are rather more realists than Buñuel. Nonetheless they are magic realists. The Surrealist edge that regularly rejuvenates documentary can be traced through the work (and influence) of three key documentarists: Jennings, Vertov and Marker.

Humphrey Jennings (1907–50) was twelve years younger than John Grierson. To be fair he benefited greatly from Grierson's aptitude for choosing talented filmmakers, focusing their energies and organising the money to support them. Nonetheless Jennings' vision could not be constrained by the already well entrenched 'Griersonian tradition.' As well as being a filmmaker, Jennings was also a poet, a painter, an intellectual and an anthropologist. He began his intellectual life at Cambridge as part of *Encounter* magazine – a journal dedicated to science and history as well as the arts.

Jennings is Britain's most obvious link between documentary and Surrealism in that he was personally and explicitly involved in both. He took a leading role, with Eluard and Breton, in staging the first Surrealist exhibition in Britain. He also exhibited his own Surrealist paintings and photos.

Since he began painting as a young man, Jennings' work had always been figurative and modernist. However, he visited Paris and met Surrealists including Breton. It was not until June 1936, when the first International Surrealist Exhibition was held in the New Burlington Galleries in London that a British Surrealist group was officially formed. Jennings was a member of the exhibition's selection committee.

As left-wingers debated their ignorance of the 'masses' in the *New Statesman*, Charles Madge wrote a letter to the journal saying that the public reaction to the recent abdication of Edward VIII needed to be studied by 'mass observations'. Tom Harrisson had a poem printed in the *New Statesman* – on the same page as Madge's letter. He had had a similar idea as to how to find out about working people, and contacted Madge. In 1937, Harrisson, Madge and Jennings teamed up and founded Mass Observation with a view to 'investigating public opinion qualitatively and quantatively by the direct observation of behaviour in public places and above all by listening to people's conversations ... a form of loosely organised visual and aural eavesdropping' (in Lovell & Hillier 1972: 64).

Their aim was also to look at British society as the new discipline of anthropology applied to non-Western cultures. The movement collated reports from observers across the country on such things as the number of people with beards, and the different types of hat worn going to the theatre. The picture they painted of Britain had Surreal roots.

Mass Observation pioneered a method which involved making precise observations of what people did during their daily routines. As well as helping to edit some of the first volumes of Mass Observation reports, Jennings also designed the covers. The project exhibits connections with the experimental writing of Breton particularly in the bizarre facts unearthed (in Bolton a 'tough' man in a pub suddenly took a tortoise out of his coat), odd questions asked and observations made; it looked at how many people wore bowler hats in pubs, how often spittoons were used, how people behaved at war memorials and who told what kind of dirty joke.

Jennings continued his project of the close observation of life. He achieved dissemination of his vision through, rather than within, the confines of the British documentary institutions of the General Post Office, the Ministry of Information and the Crown Film Unit. These epitomes of the British bureaucratic system were not designed to encourage original vision. Yet Jennings (at least in part informed by a Surrealist attitude) set out on a body of work outstanding in the rather dull history which is British cinema. As Lindsay Anderson (another rare British visionary) put it: 'He sought therefore for a public imagery, a public poetry' (1954: 181).

Jennings' film work started in 1934 editing *Post Haste* for the General Post Office film unit. He joined the unit and was involved in numerous productions, including co-directing *The Birth of the Robot* with Len Lye in 1936. Right from the beginning of his documentary work with *Spare Time* (1939) Jennings and his collaborators moved away from the British documentaries that had gone before.

It is true that films such as Edgar Anstey and Arthur Elton's *Housing Problems* (1935) chose to describe the problems of its subjects in their own words. But *Housing Problems* takes us on a trip through other people's misery in a world of dereliction. The faint whiff of voyeurism is never far away. We are guided by a 'voice of God'-style narration. This middle-class voice presents a dichotomy with the working-class dialect of the film's subjects, providing a point of association for the intended middle-class audience. Andrew Higson suggests it also acts to separate the subject from the viewer: 'that voice intervenes between the spectator and the diegesis, keeping us at a distance from the working-class victims of the film' (1986: 79). The narrator acts as our guide, introducing all the early images with a description of the contents: 'here are some pictures...', 'here are examples...', 'here's a typical interior of a decayed house...' and 'now for the people who have to live here...'. The effect is akin to watching a slide-show presentation with a speaker providing the link between alien visuals and the viewer.

Spare Time is Jennings' 'Mass Observation' film, and is set within the heart of the industries and towns affected by the Industrial Revolution. It is a look at Britain's leisure life in three industrial centres – cotton production in Manchester, the steel industry in Sheffield and coal mining in Pontypridd. The film has a very personal observational tone.

Jennings continued his attempts to break away from the 'show and tell' tradition of Grierson's typical audio-visual and developed a more reflective style through his work with Donald Watt (*London Can Take It*, 1940) and with Stuart MacAllister (*Listen to Britain*, 1942). The latter is a compilation documentary in the tradition of Russian documentarists such as Vertov and Esfir Shub and is Jennings' greatest film. In *Listen to Britain* narration and interview is abandoned in favour of a seamless flow of images, sound and music. With neither interview nor voice-over to present a narrative, Jennings uses a continuous juxtaposition of images and sound spanning all ages and class in both rural and urban Britain.

Jennings then went on to his sole-directed war-time movies: *Fires Were Started* (1943), *The Silent Village* (1945) and *A Diary for Timothy* (1945). As Thomson puts it in the *New Biographical Dictionary of Film* Jennings became 'a true war artist in the way that Henry Moore's drawings of the underground and Evelyn Waugh's *Sword of Honour* trilogy transcend war and reassert the intimacy of human imagination' (2003: 440). Jennings' films are imbued with symbolism: 'Although he used public images, these images had associations and connotations which were not usually accessible to the public at large. Most people would not consciously associate the locomotive with the tarot pack, the horse, the Industrial Revolution' (Lovell & Hillier 1972: 68). No wonder Grierson damned Jennings as 'an intellectual dilettante' (ibid.). Nonetheless, the viewer will search in vain for a consistently Surrealist approach in any of Jennings' films. He is above all else a documentarist if undoubtedly a Surrealist documentarist. His work is notable for its lack of explanation and dream-like atmosphere of juxtaposition. He can certainly be seen as a precursor of the radical cinema movement of the Third Cinema as conceived in the late 1960s by the Argentine filmmakers Fernando Solanas and Octavio Getino. Another way of looking at Humphrey Jennings is as the British Dziga Vertov, the Russian filmmaker doing strikingly similar work which prefigures Jennings by a decade.

Vertov was born Denis Kaufman in 1896 in the Polish territories of the Russian empire. His studies in music were cut short when the family moved to Moscow at the outbreak of the Great War. There he took the name of Dziga Vertov. Vertov has its origins in the verb that means to spin or rotate (as well as obvious connotations of 'truth'). His first name was derived from the repetitive sound that a camera crank emits as it turns and derives from the Russian word for gypsy. The young Vertov took to experiments in recording sound and then pictures whilst posing ostentatiously in his aviator's helmet.

A meeting with a newsreel cameraman in 1917 sparked Vertov's interest in motion pictures. In 1918 he joined the Bolshevik regime's newly-established film unit, learning his craft on the job during the Civil War. He took collected un-coordinated footage of the new Soviet state and worked it into a powerful propaganda format. Vertov rode mobile studio/cinemas, agit-trains and agit-boats across the Bolshevik-held territories.

Vertov, like his Surrealist contemporary Breton, became an issuer of manifestos. There are other odd (surreal) parallels. Vertov's earliest experiment in filmmaking involved faking a 'jump' from a roof-top. He simply spliced together a shot of him on the roof with one of him on the ground to produce a startling image. Shortly after Breton would write: 'What you must know is that beneath all the windows you may take a notion to jump out of, amiable imps hold out the sad sheet of love' (1969: 109).

In 1919 Vertov formed the Kinoks ('kino-oki', meaning cinema-eyes). The Kinoks (including his editor Elizaveta Svilova and his brother, the cameraman Mikhail Kaufman) rejected 'staged' cinema with its stars, plots, props and studio shooting. They insisted that the cinema of the future be the cinema of fact: newsreels recording the real world, as 'life caught unawares'. Vertov proclaimed the primacy of the camera itself – the 'kino-eye' – over the human eye. The camera was a powerful, innocent machine – working much as the unconscious could do for Breton.

Thus whilst proclaiming himself a constructivist his 'Surrealist' phase predated that of Jennings. Vlada Petric (1987), who situates Vertov firmly within a constructivist tradition, spends much of his seminal book discussing the oneiric in the director's work. Vertov's concept of the 'kino-eye' predates mass observation and the early feature-length films contain elements of surreal detail, juxtaposition and atmosphere. In *Kinoglaz* (1924), made the same year as the first Surrealist Manifesto and *Soluble Fish*, the kino-eye 'moves time backwards' (according to an intertitle in the film). At another point the audience is entertained by a bizarre interlude: 'The stately progress of an elephant through the streets of Moscow.'

Kinoglaz, like many of Vertov's early features, equates process and production with magic (and vice versa). Vertov is presenting a rather more complex view of the world than that contained in Marxist-Leninist dialectical materialism. *Shagay Sovet!* (*Stride Soviet*, 1926), *Shestaya chast mira* (*The Sixth Part of the World*, 1926) and *Odinnadt-satyy* (*The Eleventh Year*, 1928) mixed images of different fragments of Soviet society to reveal how they were all connected and supported each other. His fragmented allusive connections came in for much criticism from documentarists including friends like Esfir Shub as well as foes such as critic Viktor Shklovsky.

Vertov believed that a textile worker ought to see a factory worker making a machine essential to the textile worker. The worker at the machine tool plant ought to see the miner who gives his factory its essential fuel. The coal miner ought to see the peasant who produces the bread essential to him. As such Vertov aimed at 'the communist decoding of the world' rather more in line with the Second Surrealist Manifesto than the first. Nonetheless Vertov's decoding was achieved through editing which involved a deep understanding of the material. It was not enough to show bits of truth on the screen. The organisation process followed a lyrical sequence based on a model which Vertov had developed during his earlier sound experiments. The *kinoki* shot unscripted scenes in which the people being filmed appear unaware of the filming process. These 'film facts' were stored away in Vertov and Svilova's archive and could be used for any project at any time.

By 1927 Vertov's clashes with his colleagues and employers in the film community caused the state film studio in Moscow to fire him. He was then hired by the Ukraine's state studio where he produced his finest film, *Chelovek s kino-apparatom* (*Man with the Movie Camera*, 1929). This work is, in fact, a study in film truth on a philosophical level. It presents a swirl of events (mostly mundane) across the Soviet Union. There is little attempt to label these events in terms of specific geography or time; they are all grist to the mill of a construction of a day in the life of a cameraman – Mikhail Kaufman. Vertov's brother climbs smokestacks and bridges, sets up a trick shot of a train running him over and rides in many types of transportation. Scenes of the documentary are intercut with the production of the documentary. Through the lens, we see a person walking by and realise he is being photographed. From the opposite angle – his perspective – we see the camera with his reflected image on the surface of the lens. In other more subtle sequences the shadow of the camera is permitted to loom into the frame. Unlike in *Drifters* this is not a technical mistake.

Throughout the film Vertov and Svilova deal with unreality. They explore the dichotomy of the sense that human perception is not real – compared to machines. Rather more surreally they deal with the unreality of the oneiric: 'subconscious' images are intercut with or superimposed on 'characters' within the diegesis as the whole action of the 'day' is framed by a dreaming woman. Grierson reacted badly:

> With Dziga Vertov's *Man with the Movie Camera* we are at last initiated into the philosophy of the Kino-Eye. Some of us have been hearing a great deal about the Kino-Eye and it has worried us considerably. Only the younger high-brows seem to know anything about it … Now that Vertov has turned up in the original it is easier to see why intelligent students of cinema were betrayed into their extremity … Vertov, however, has pushed the argument to a point at which it becomes ridiculous. The camera observes in its own bright way, and he is prepared to give it its head. *Man with the Movie Camera* is in consequence not a film at all: it is a snapshot album. (in Hardy 1966: 155)

Fortunately for the health of documentary cinema Vertov's influence has been pervasive – at least away from the mainstream of Griersonian hegemony. Within six years of his death, the French documentary filmmakers Jean Rouch and Edgar Morin adopted Vertov's theory and practice into their *cinéma vérité*.

It is not too ridiculous to state that Vertov's mixture of voyeurism and making strange has influenced everybody (directly or indirectly) from Godard to the networks of webcams such as www.camcentral.com and the rather less salubrious variations of 'Janeycam' as well as other websites which subvert and play with voyeurism rather than simply reinforcing socialised pornography.

In Russia itself Vertov's tradition has been carried on through Maria Goldovskaia, whose films *Povezlo roditsia v Rossii* (*Lucky to Be Born in Russia*, 1994) and *The Prince is Back* (1999) gain their Surrealist edge from their subject matter, and especially through Alexander Sokurov. Sokurov's documentaries have a dream-like quality which go even further into Surrealism than his feature films such as *Molokh* (*Moloch*, 1999) and *Russkiy kovcheg* (*Russian Ark*, 2002). Films like the 'Elegy' series of 1986–2001 and *Hubert Robert, Schastlivaya zhizn* (*Hubert Robert, A Fortunate Life*, 1996) include long passages of reverie often containing strange uncontextualised detail. Sokurov's style of presentation is clearly influenced by, and serves as a reminder of, arguably the greatest of all docu-Surrealists Chris Marker.

Marker was born Christian François Bouche-Villeneuve on 29 July 1921 in Neuilly-sur-Seine, France – or possibly not as he is keen to mythologise his own life. He may have been born in Mongolia. When asked for a photograph he sends one of a cat:

> When Mikkel Aaland, an artist and web designer who wrote about meeting with Marker during the early 1990s (while the filmmaker was working on *Immemory*, an interactive CD-ROM that explores the concepts of memory and understanding), wanted to record on tape his talks with the multimedia artist, he was told, 'no interviews. Instead, if you must write something, use your imagination. Place us on a boat on the Nile. We are drunk. It's your story.' (Christley 2004)

In the 1950s Marker turned to documentary filmmaking. After *Olympia* (1952) he worked with Alain Resnais on *Les Statues meurent aussi* (*Statues Also Die*, 1953) and *Nuit et brouillard* (*Night and Fog*, 1955). His solo-directed work continued with *Lettre de Sibérie* (*Letter from Siberia*, 1957) and *¡Cuba sí!* (1961). In the 1960s and 1970s he was actively involved with the Societe pour le Lancement des Oeuvres Nouvelles (SLON), a filmmaking collective, including Jean-Luc Godard, dedicated to activist production. Marker returned to make films under his own name again in 1977 with *Le Fond de l'air est rouge* (*Grin Without a Cat*), a film-essay on the worldwide political struggles of the 1960s and 1970s and the fate of the New Left. However overtly political his work, Marker always takes care to present ideas and images in interesting juxtapositions. His use of striking, allusive imagery in his political work is surely due to the influence of the Soviet masters, particularly Vertov and Alexander Medvedkin.

Marker went on to make several films on other filmmakers including, naturally, Medvedkin (*Le Tombeau d'Alexandre/The Last Bolshevik*, 1997) and Andrei Tarkovsky (*Cinéma de notre temps: une journée d'Andrei Arsenevitch/One Day in the Life of Andrei Arsenevich*, 2002). The former followed on from his own film *Le Train en Marche...* (1977) which captured Medvedkin's reminiscences of his career on the agit-train of the 1930s (his own tribute to the Vertov of the 1920s).

For the Surrealist documentary canon the key Marker film is *Sans soleil* (*Sunless*, 1983). David Thomson labels it thus: 'a documentary that leads into a reverie on Japan, technology and the conjunction of different times and peoples in the world' (2003: 566). The key term here is 'reverie'. Much as with Vertov's *Chelovek s kino-apparatom* the film is presented in a dream-like manner as a woman's voice intones on the subject of a (presumably) imaginary correspondence with a photographer. This is not the dry distancing voice-over of the British documentary movement. This photographer is clearly a modern-day embodiment of the *kinoki* peripatetically capturing reality in all its complexity. Many of the images: eyes, showroom dummies, the orchestral metaphor, echo *Chelovek s kino-apparatom*. *Sans soleil* is a hymn to the fleeting impermanence of things and the nature of memory. The cameraman reflects on a visit to Tokyo: 'I spent my first day in front of my TV set – that memory box ... The commercial: a kind of haiku to the eye ... Not understanding obviously adds to the pleasure.' He remembers: 'The (metro) train inhabited by sleeping people puts together all the fragments of dreams, makes a single film of them, the ultimate film ... he wrote me that only one film had been capable of portraying impossible memory, insane memory...' – naturally that film is Alfred Hitchcock's *Vertigo* (1958). The spiral in the title sequences contains the eye – echoing the eye within the lens of *Chelovek s kino-apparatom*. *Vertigo* in itself contains echoes of Vertov as well as the vertiginous spirals of falling into dream. The central psychological obsession of Madeline (played by Kim Novak) echoes the Proustian madeleine of Marker's obsession with memory. The Chris Marker website quotes: 'I claim for the image, the humility and the powers of a Madeleine' (Miles 1995).

This hyper-complex sequence of *Sans soleil* ends with a plan for a science fiction movie with future inhabitants full of 'unhappiness and memory'. The film will be 'sunless' (after the Mussorgsky songs). *Sans soleil* ends with footage (filmed in 1970) of the volcano which had destroyed the area, filmed in 1965 for the sequence that had started the film: 'the first image he told me about was of three children on a road in Iceland … He said that for him it was the image of happiness' (*Happiness* is the title of a deeply Surreal comedy made by Medvedkin in 1932).

Marker has been described as a 'writer, filmmaker, photographer, scholar, poet, traveller, explorer, researcher, collector of images, producer of texts – a zone of conversation between individual and collective memories' (Roth & Bellour 1997: 7). This epithet could describe all the filmmakers celebrated in this chapter and the fellow travellers who have joined them in the struggle against documentary as prosaic, narrow, drab and ultimately pessimistic and restricting. We should exult in the Surreal documentarists (or documentary Surrealists) who have celebrated the nature of, and attempted to capture, the uncapturable of life as it is lived; that most elusive of creatures: soluble fish.

As Breton put it: 'I believe in the pure Surrealist joy of the man who, forewarned that all others before him have failed, refuses to admit defeat, sets off from whatever point he chooses' (1969: 46).

Andrew Spicer

AN OCCASIONAL ECCENTRICITY: THE STRANGE COURSE OF SURREALISM IN BRITISH CINEMA

The deep-rooted British tradition of surreal fantasy

There was a clearly identifiable Surrealist grouping in art and literature in Britain in the 1930s, and a major exhibition in London in 1936, but this had little direct influence on the cinema except in the work of the documentarists Len Lye and Humphrey Jennings (see Ray 1971; Remy 1999). However, if British feature filmmakers were resistant to the aesthetic experimentation and formal ideology of Continental Surrealism (and to Modernism in general), this does not mean that they were necessarily impervious to Surrealist ideas. Indeed, those ideas were deeply ingrained in English culture, going back at least to the nonsense genre in the mid-Victorian period, part of a rich fantasy tradition that had its origins in Gothic fiction and the Romantic poets. It was a tradition admired by the Surrealists themselves, celebrating strangeness, eccentricity, madness, the extraordinary and the bizarre, and using dreams, visions and the creation of other worlds to contest the emphasis on order, coherence and rationality that was the cornerstone of the nineteenth-century realistic novel (Prickett 1979: xiii–xvi, 1–37). What could be more surreal than the moment in Lewis Carroll's *Through the Looking-Glass* (1887) when Tweedledum and Tweedledee urge Alice not to disturb the Red King because he is dreaming about her: '"Well, it's no use your talking about waking him", said Tweedledum, "when you're only one of the things in his dream. You know very well you're not real." "I am real!" said Alice, and began to cry' (1993: 156).

This alternative fantasy tradition has proved to be a pervasive and significant influence on British cinema, but the dominance of the social realist tradition deriving from the nineteenth-century novel, together with the British tradition of quirky individualism rather than adherence to a systematic body of ideas, has meant that it has manifested itself as an occasional eccentricity rather than a coherent body of films. Indeed, Surrealism in British cinema rarely manifests itself explicitly; rather it forms an element within particular films.[1] As David Pirie argues in his seminal *A Heritage of Horror*, British Gothic horror films often contain Surrealist elements, but these 'were not rationalised according to any dialectical schema' (1973: 21). The tradition of British 'madcap' comedy, whose true homes were the music hall and later radio and television, has also created a disparate body of films which contain surreal moments, often derived from the whimsical and absurd humour of Victorian fantasy. A third strand is represented by the films of maverick *auteurs* – notably Michael Powell and Emeric Pressburger, Ken Russell and Derek Jarman – whose obvious differences should not obscure their shared indebtedness to this highly British tradition of quirky eccentricity that draws upon Surrealist notions as part of a wide-ranging eclecticism. Each has, I would argue, a genuinely Surrealist cast of mind, unlike other candidates for inclusion such as Lindsay Anderson, Nicolas Roeg and even Peter Greenaway, who has remarked that his films 'perhaps relate to an English literary tradition that includes Edward Lear and Lewis Carroll' (in Hacker & Price 1991: 212). Within the space of a single chapter it is impossible to do full justice to the full range and richness of the Surrealist elements of this alternative tradition in British cinema. As this is, to my knowledge, the first discussion of the topic, it attempts an overview of these three strands, rather than analysing examples in depth, and concentrates on popular or influential feature films rather than documentaries or the avant-garde.[2]

Surrealism in British horror films

The Surrealists valued tales of 'terror' – with a particular admiration for English Gothic fiction (Buñuel wanted to make a film of M. G. Lewis's *The Monk*)[3] – because they were capable of evoking the marvellous and depicted the presence of unsuspected and irrational forces, including sexual desire, which lay beneath appearances and that threatened to overwhelm reason and social order (Matthews 1971: 21–8). As already noted, David Pirie argues that British horror incorporates Surrealist elements within a 'robust' Gothic tradition that eschewed the overt Freudian and intellectual qualities of Continental horror, and was indebted to the English tradition of rational eccentricity found in Lewis Carroll, Wilkie Collins or Arthur Conan Doyle. Pirie contends: 'If there had been a full-scale Surrealist movement in Britain then I would speculate that the comparative naivety and spontaneity of the British approach to horror would be impossible. It may be that Hammer-type horror film is one of the more welcome by-products of the English reluctance to embrace artistic systems' (1973: 21). It is worth noting that Hammer horror films readily attracted the interest of French critics who admired their Surreal qualities, in contradistinction to British critics who tended to regard them as vulgar and devoid of artistic or intellectual interest.

However, British horror is not co-extensive with Hammer or the Gothic tradition, and one of the most thoroughly surreal examples, *Dead of Night* (1945), which uses the very English form of the ghost story, came from Ealing Studios, of all places. Ian Aitken has convincingly argued that the formative influence on *Dead of Night* was the Brazilian-born Alberto Cavalcanti, whose cinematic education took place in the Parisian avant-garde where he gained an extensive knowledge of Surrealism that permeated into many of his films (2000: 12–41, 155–60). The two most impressive episodes of the four stories that compose *Dead of Night* – Robert Hamer's 'The Haunted Mirror' and Cavalcanti's 'The Ventriloquist's Dummy' – are disturbing tales of morbid sexuality and dark emotions that draw on Surrealist tropes, but these manifest themselves most powerfully within the framing story in which an architect, Walter Craig (Mervyn Johns), who has been troubled by recurring nightmares, is shocked to discover the same people who populate his dreams present when he arrives at Pilgrim's Farm, whose owner has commissioned Craig to draw up plans for some alterations. At the conclusion of the fourth story ('The Ventriloquist's Dummy'), narrated by the psychologist Dr Van Straaten (Frederick Valk) who represents sceptical rationalism, Craig, against his rational judgement, strangles Van Straaten. This murder plunges him into a rapid montage of scenes from the previous stories as he tries to escape the consequences of his act. At the culminating moment he is ushered into a cell where the ventriloquist's dummy, Hugo – now clearly animate – attempts to strangle him. At this point Craig wakes up, which suggests that it was all a nightmare. However, in the final frames we see him arriving 'back' at Pilgrim's Farm, in a cyclical movement that is now laden with dread as the nightmare appears to be about to come true. Thus the most disturbing aspect of *Dead of Night* is its blurring of the boundaries between the real and the dream world, the normal and the abnormal, the rational and the irrational, which, in true Surrealist manner, merge and become confused. However, *Dead of Night* was an isolated film, unwelcome within Balcon's reconstructive ethos at Ealing and producing no imitators or cycle at that point. British horror was stillborn until Hammer's *The Curse of Frankenstein* (1957).

Hammer horror consistently depicts a dualistic world in which rationality and irrationality are starkly opposed. In John Gilling's *The Plague of the Zombies* (1965), a representative example characteristically set in the nineteenth century, the irrational and evil figure is the squire (John Carson) of a small Cornish village (a typically enclosed, powerless community) who has returned from the West Indies with knowledge of voodoo, and turns the local inhabitants who are unwilling to work in his tin mine into zombies. He is opposed by the rational man of science, Sir James Forbes (André Morell), professor of medicine, summoned by his former pupil the local doctor Peter Tompson (Brook Williams), to help him investigate the seemingly inexplicable deaths. When the doctor's wife dies, they watch over her grave and witness her resurrection as a zombie, whereupon Forbes decapitates her. Tompson collapses in shock, and the screen dissolves to a panorama of the whole churchyard in which he sees other graves gradually open as the zombies churn their way up through the soil to crowd in upon him, before he wakes up with a shriek of terror. Arthur Grant's accomplished photography, using tilted angles, green filters and spectral mist, makes this surreal scene – ambiguously both real and a nightmare – both shocking and oddly beautiful, capturing the dual pull of desire and fear that is the heart of horror's appeal. As in all of

Hammer's most accomplished films, this ambiguity complicates the ethical dualism, a Surrealist understanding that rationality and irrationality are inseparable and that monstrous forces, cloaked like the squire by the 'charm of evil', are constantly poised to take possession of the weak and the unwary.

As the horror cycle developed and younger filmmakers, including writer Christopher Wicking, became attracted to Gothic horror as a genuinely creative space in which to work, there was a vigorous period of revisionism in which the genre was rethought and redefined, both visually and thematically. Through this it became more knowing, self-reflexive and occasionally overtly intellectual in its use of surreal elements. A striking example, which Pirie considers a 'surreal masterpiece' (1973: 159) was *Murders in the Rue Morgue* (1971), written by Wicking and directed by Gordon Hessler.[4] Madeleine (Christine Kaufman) is an actress in a play based on Edgar Allan Poe's famous story. The script alternates ambiguously between the play, the circumstances of Madeleine's everyday life and her recurring nightmares where she is pursued by a masked man wielding an axe, the same figure who later falls from a great height. In another nightmare, she discovers a coffin in which her darkly-attired self beckons to her and then changes into a skeleton. Madeleine's life has been blighted by the violent murder of her mother by her lover Marot (Herbert Lom). Marot, supposedly dead, has returned to enact a series of grisly revenge murders, culminating in that of Cesar Charron (Jason Robards), the leader of the troupe who has married Madeleine, who confesses that he killed her mother when she rejected him, triggering Madeleine's dream in which she remembers having witnessed her mother's murder. After Marot himself finally dies, falling from the rafters of the theatre when Madeleine cuts the ropes that support him, the police inspector tells Madeleine that her nightmares will be over. But in the final scene she wakes from another dream only to find Marot's companion, a dwarf who seems to exist both in her dreams and her waking life, entering her bedroom to present her with an orchid with Marot's face superimposed behind him. With its convoluted and baffling plot that deliberately mingles past, present and future, *Murders in the Rue Morgue* explores the confusion of the erotic and the monstrous, the real and the imaginary, dreams and waking life, a thoroughly Surreal conceit.

The main Gothic horror cycle was over by the mid-1970s, but there were several isolated examples in the 1980s that dealt with the interpenetration of dreams and reality, including the uneven *Dream Demon* (1987) with a script by Wicking, and Bernard Rose's accomplished *Paperhouse* (1988). However, the key film of the decade was Neil Jordan's *The Company of Wolves* (1984), based on two stories from Angela Carter's *The Bloody Chamber* (1979), who co-wrote the screenplay with Jordan. It retells the seminal fairytale 'Little Red Riding Hood' in order to make its Freudian elements – the fascination with and also repulsion from sex – explicit. It showed a profound debt to Jean Cocteau's *La Belle et la bête* (1946). More generally, as Jordan himself has commented, *The Company of Wolves* was 'quite simply about human dreams and nightmares' (in Park 1984: 90) and in a Surrealist manner explores liminal spaces – between childhood and adulthood, man and beast, fantasy and reality – as well as the nature of perception in its ambiguous and fluid diegesis, organised as a series of dream vignettes within a dream. Unlike conventional fairytales, it refuses to endorse conventional morality: in the final sequence the central character Rosaleen (Sarah Patterson) is transformed into a wolf, an expression of her commitment to fulfilling her desires, however dangerous, which fulfils the Surrealists' nostrum that the 'terror' film should unsettle rather than reassure.

Surrealism in British 'madcap' comedy

The Surrealists recognised the potential of American popular comedians to disrupt the ordinary rules and controls of society and offer glimpses of the marvellous irrationality of true being. Robert Desnos praised Mack Sennett as a '*libérateur du cinéma*' because of the 'madness presiding over his scripts ... the madness of fairytales and of those dreamers whom the world holds in contempt, and to whom the world owes what is delightful in life' (in Matthews 1971: 29). In Britain this madcap comic tradition derived from the music hall. Although the 'respectability' of cinema tended to curb the more outrageous aspects of many of the comedians who made the transition – including Arthur Askey, George Formby, Will Hay, Arthur Lucan (who performed in drag as Old Mother Riley), Frank Randle and Tommy Trinder – there was always the potential for their films to create anarchic situations in which the world is turned upside-down and bizarre happenings occur.

The surreal potential of this tradition is best exemplified by the Crazy Gang, often thought to be an English version of the Marx Brothers' unpredictable lunacy, which was actually composed of three separate double acts: Charlie Naughton and Jimmy Gold, Jimmy Nervo and Teddy Knox and Bud Flanagan and Chesney Allen. In the 1930s they made, for Gainsborough Pictures, a series of freewheeling knockabout films whose episodic structure and liberal use of dream and fantasy sequences allows the Gang's anarchic talents fairly free rein. The bizarre linguistic flights of Flanagan and Allen's cross-talk are a verbally surreal element, but the Gang's comedy was primarily visual as in the fantastic transformations in *Alf's Button Afloat* (1938), based on W. A. Darlington's famous farce, when Alf (Flanagan) unleashes a literal-minded genie (Alastair Sim) by rubbing a magic button on his naval uniform. As Sue Harper remarks, the gang's humour is highly allusive, celebrating the energy of popular culture and undermining the status of high art forms (1997: 87–8). For example in *The Frozen Limits* (1939), where the Gang seek their fortune in the Yukon having read a 40-year-old advertisement for the Gold Rush, they enact a parody of a nineteenth-century drama ('Sir Marmalade's Hair'), lampoon D. W. Griffith's parallel editing techniques in the bathetic climax and, in the most surreal moment, perform a wonderful burlesque of *Snow White and the Seven Dwarfs* as they prepare for bed. As their films always begin by emphasising the Gang's low status as outcasts or unemployed, their zany antics give a voice to the socially marginalised, celebrating a surreal anarchy and irrationality rather than order and decorum.

The anarchic energies of popular comedy were curbed during the Second World War by the need to raise morale. They suffered a further setback after the war when there was a concerted critical attack on the vulgarities and aesthetic crudity of the music hall tradition, with only an occasional surreal eccentricity erupting in the films of Sid Field, Norman Wisdom and, especially, Charlie Drake. However, it was radio (later television) that proved to be more hospitable to madcap comedy, especially *The Goon Show*, which ran from 1951 to 1960. The Goons (Michael Bentine, Spike Milligan, Harry Secombe and Peter Sellers), whose early name was 'The Junior Crazy Gang', made only one film, *Down Among the Z Men* (1952), an attack on National Service and Cold War paranoia, but the influence of their radio programmes was profound and far-reaching. The driving force was Milligan who defined 'Goonery' as 'critical comedy. Its starting point is one man shouting gibberish in the face of authority and proving by fabricated insanity that nothing could be as mad as what passes for ordinary living' (in Foster & Furst 1996: 144). This attack on the madness of everyday life influenced films such as *One-Way Pendulum* (1964), adapted by N. F. Simpson from his play, where suburban clerk Arthur Groomkirby (Eric Sykes) sets up a dream court in his home in which his son (Jonathan Miller), who spends his time teaching speak-your-weight machines to sing the *Hallelujah!* chorus, is placed on trial for multiple murder, having struck each one of his 43 victims on the head with an iron bar after telling them a joke. In another room his wife's aunt (Mona Washbourne) thinks she has boarded the wrong train and is stuck in the Outer Hebrides waiting to get back to St Pancras. It also inspired *Morgan: A Suitable Case for Treatment* (1966), adapted by David Mercer from his television play, which overlays Goonery with R. D. Laing's then fashionable philosophy that insanity was the only legitimate defence against the oppressive stranglehold of 'normality'. Its anti-hero, Morgan Delt (David Warner), a working-class artist unable to espouse his parents' hard-Left ideology, nor accept the middle-class world of his wife Leonie (Vanessa Redgrave), becomes increasingly schizophrenic. In a memorably surreal moment he wakes in a gorilla suit (his disguise to gatecrash Leonie's remarriage) on a rubbish tip next to Battersea Power Station and hallucinates that he is being hoisted in a straitjacket by one of the cranes working on the site and is about to be'shot by a firing squad, which includes Leonie dressed as a Cossack.

However, the most important legacy of the Goons came, paradoxically, through the films of an American, Richard Lester. Lester's first film, *The Running, Jumping & Standing Still Film* (1959), an 11-minute Surrealist short made on a couple of Sundays for £70 to test a 16mm camera that Peter Sellers had bought, is a light-hearted Goonian celebration of English eccentricity, with the ubiquitous Mrs Mopp vigorously scrubbing a field, or a long-sighted violinist reading his score through a telescope and then cycling across to the music stand to turn the pages (see Sinyard 1985: 1–4). However, its playfulness is underscored by the theme that was to preoccupy Lester: Britain's post-imperial status where traditional authority figures have atrophied and decayed leaving an ideological vacuum.

Lester's *The Bed Sitting Room* (1969), derived from the play by Spike Milligan and John Antrobus, and with Milligan and Secombe playing important roles, develops this concern through its depiction of a devastated world three years after a nuclear war that has reduced the population of Britain to twenty. The survivors, drawn from all strata of British society, struggle to make sense of their lives amidst the wreckage and decay, clinging desperately to their old mental and social habits. The upper classes are represented by Captain Bules-Martin (Michael Hordern), late of the household cavalry and first seen on a huge mound of old shoes searching for a matching pair amid hills of grey-blue slag, and ex-Minister Lord Fortnum (Ralph Richardson), convinced he is turning into a bed-sitting room and desperate to 'find Belgravia before I turn' and thus avoid social disaster. The ordinary lower-middle-class family are trapped on the one remaining Circle Line train. Father (Arthur Lowe) finds comfort in being selected as Prime Minister by his (erroneous) inside leg measurement, before changing into a parrot, while Mother (Mona Washbourne) accepts that she must be taken away as she has been officially certified as dead even though she is palpably alive and eventually metamorphoses into a cupboard. Their daughter Penelope (Rita Tushingham), seventeen months pregnant, is much less tractable. When Alan (Richard Warwick), her boyfriend and father of their child, tells her that they must keep going because they are British, she replies: 'British. What a lot of use that is. We don't know who's won the war. We've run out of food. We've no medicine and we're eating our parents. *British.*' Other characters represent institutions. Marty Feldman in nurse's uniform embodies the Health Service, wanting to wallpaper wombs so that babies will not want to leave, while Frank Thornton, representing the BBC, wanders around delivering news broadcasts through hollow television sets on any subject the viewer requests. In a Morris Minor suspended under a hot-air balloon, Peter Cook and Dudley Moore are the Police, barking pointless orders through a megaphone. These odd characters, the strange metamorphoses and the frequently bizarre exchanges between the characters, are complemented by the bleak, eerie beauty of the visual style and the surreal art direction which creates a collage of disturbingly juxtaposed images: a devastated motorway with the skeleton of a toy dog nodding back and forth on the back window of one wrecked car; a wrought-iron bedstead stationary by a parking meter on a deserted beach which is strewn with reels and reels of tangled film instead of seaweed; endless sets of false teeth being fished out of a polluted stream; the dome of St Paul's sinking into a stagnant lake, an evocative image of Britain's decay. *The Bed Sitting Room* is a thoroughly surreal masterpiece, which has not had the recognition it deserves.

The influence of Lester and Goonery extended into the 1970s as in Peter Sellers' *The Magic Christian* (1970) and Marty Feldman's *Every Home Should Have One* (1970), which use Surrealist devices to critique rampant consumerism. However, the real heir of this tradition was Monty Python (Graham Chapman, John Cleese, Terry Gilliam, Eric Idle, Terry Jones and Michael Palin). The first Python film, *And Now for Something Completely Different* (1971) simply transferred their television sketches to the big screen. *Monty Python and the Holy Grail* (1974) was altogether more ambitious and remains their best film, even if the final scene of *Monty Python's Life of Brian* (1979) in which the crucified figures sing 'Bright Side of Life' is the most memorably surreal moment. In *Monty Python and the Holy Grail*, co-directors Gilliam and Jones managed to unite their obsession with the actualities of life in the Middle Ages and an epic narrative with the surreal, anarchic wit that had characterised the television sketches and Gilliam's animations. King Arthur's quest for the Grail is punctuated by robust denunciations from recalcitrant peasantry who question the whole ethical structure of monarchy preferring their own anarcho-syndicalist commune, or bizarre figures such as the giant knights who say 'Ni', whose burning desire is to have an ornamental shrubbery. When Arthur (Graham Chapman) and his knights seek the Grail in a French occupied castle, they are verbally abused by the Captain of the Guard (John Cleese doing an impersonation of Salvador Dalí) – 'Your mother was a hamster and your father smelt of elderberries' – before being pelted with stuffed cows, wooden rabbits and other animals. At the climactic moment when the Grail castle has been reached, Arthur and his knights are arrested for the murder of a famous historian much earlier in the film and taken away in a police van. Python's iconoclasm is invested with the whimsical Surrealism of the Victorian nonsense tradition and is more eccentric and madcap than overtly political, but their work continued a critique of a moribund British Establishment (especially the military), and was a powerful component in helping to dismantle the English tradition of deference to authority. Their legacy was Terry Gilliam's films, financed by American studios (see McCabe 1999), Vivian Stanshall's *Sir Henry at Rawlinson's End* (1980) and the films of Bruce Robinson – including *How to Get Ahead in Advertising* (1989) in which successful advertising executive (Richard E. Grant) is attacked by a talking boil on his neck, a surreal motif that spouts the ideology of Thatcherism – but most importantly 'alternative comedy' which has become such a significant presence in contemporary television (see Thompson 2004).

Surrealist auteurs: the British romantic tradition

Each of the filmmakers discussed in this section – Powell and Pressburger, Russell and Jarman – has a highly personal style, eclectic and wide-ranging, in which Surrealism is one element in a complex engagement with Romanticism. Although their politics may differ significantly, all are at odds with the dominant social realism of British cinema, and have been highly controversial figures, subject to widely divergent valuations. As Romantics, their work exhibits an overriding concern with dreams, fantasies, imaginary worlds, time (the co-presence of past, present and future) and irrational forms of consciousness, with a concomitant exploration of the role of the artist. Each accords a high place for passionate romantic love – in keeping with the Surrealist claim that such love gives access to the marvellous and defies rationality and ordinary constraints – but this love may be tragic, corrupted or, in Jarman's case, same sex.

The films of Powell and Pressburger were clearly part of a neo-romantic revival that emerged during the Second World War, and blended an English mysticism with

European high culture (Mellor 1987). Powell referred to Buñuel as 'my master, the only filmmaker I would defer to … he has known from the beginning what most of us have only learnt in brief moments of vision and clarity' (1992: 123). As part of Rank's elite corps of Individual Producers, they were able to make a series of increasingly complex and ambitious films during the latter part of the war that were at odds with the social realism of the 'documentary boys'. *The Life and Death of Colonel Blimp* (1943) was the story of a transcendent love amidst vanishing values; *A Canterbury Tale* (1944) combines a mystical Englishness, modern pilgrims following in Chaucer's footsteps and sexual repression. The most ambitious, however, was *A Matter of Life and Death* (1946), which is, in the words of the opening caption, 'a story of two worlds – the one we know and another which exists only in the mind of a young airman whose life and imagination have been violently shaped by war'. The two worlds that that Squadron Leader Peter Carter (David Niven) experiences, his ordinary life and Heaven where he is overdue having baled out of his stricken plane without a parachute but was missed in the fog by his celestial 'conductor', are connected by the surreal trope of a gigantic escalator. In keeping with the playfulness of what Pressburger conceived as 'a real fantasy with supernatural beings' that had 'a kind of Surrealism' (in Christie 2000: 12), the ordinary world is shot in Technicolor, Heaven in monochrome. Throughout the story there is an emphasis on the power of reason with the neurologist Dr Reeves (Roger Livesey) offering a scientific explanation for Peter's hallucinations and the whole apparatus of a celestial trial where his fate is decided is invoked because, logically, Heaven must have laws and therefore a right of appeal. But these rationalisations are insisted upon only to be overturned in the final scene when it is the irrational power of love that triumphs as June (Kim Hunter), the American wireless operator whom Peter had fallen in love with as his plane crashed, offers to take his place – a sacrifice that wins his case in order to enjoy a further time on Earth with her.

After the war, Powell and Pressburger's films became more overtly imaginary: 'the end was to go out into the real world and turn it into a romantic fantasy where anything could happen' (Powell 1992: 653). *The Red Shoes* (1948) deliberately adopts a broadly realistic approach until the moment when Vicky (Moira Shearer) dances in the premiere of 'The Red Shoes' ballet. Once she puts on the red shoes we leave the real theatre space and enter a surreal fantasy where the camerawork, Hein Heckroth's set designs, special effects and editing combine to create an authentically cinematic work of art that synthesises music, dialogue, sound effects and images in order to demonstrate the transcendent power of creation itself. It is also the moment that seals her fate, as the terrible logic of this fairytale world requires her death. The logical outcome of this aesthetic was *The Tales of Hoffman* (1951), structured as a series of bizarre tales of disappointed love told by Hoffmann himself (Robert Rouseville), where imagination and reality become interchangeable.

In a very different mode is the Surrealism of excess of Ken Russell. Russell's neoromanticism is informed by his Catholicism, which fuels his interest in violent imagery, sexual repression, the grotesque and mysticism. In his more successful films, Russell creates a Surrealist dialectic between the fantasies of the central characters that are prey to irrational forces, and an objective presentation of their situation. This is realised in a very distinctive visual style that combines a highly wrought *mise-en-scène* filmed from multiple set-ups which create abrupt shifts in perspective, mood and tempo with startling and incongruous juxtapositions created by very abrupt cuts, 'shock editing' designed to create unexpected connections that would stimulate thought. This clearly Surrealist technique is deployed in Russell's finest film, *The Devils* (1971), where Urbain Grandier (Oliver Reed), a flawed hero, opposed to the tyranny of Cardinal Richelieu, is also the object of the masochistic sexual fantasies of the hunchbacked Sister Jeanne (Vanessa Redgrave). She imagines herself as Mary Magdalene with Grandier as Jesus walking on the water towards her, but as she wipes his feet with her hair, her dress is blown back to reveal her deformity and the faces of the nuns in her charge distorted in laughter. In a later fantasy, Grandier descends from the cross to have his wounds licked by her before their bodies intertwine, an ecstatic scene ended when Jeanne realises she is bleeding profusely from the end of the crucifix that she has ground into her palm. These fantasies reveal the depths of her repressed sexuality, her horror at her deformity and her frustration explains her collusion in Grandier's downfall. In the dream-like concluding scene, after he has been burnt at the stake, his wife Madeleine (Gemma Jones) watches his ashes being blown by the winds, before climbing over the rubble of Loudun's torn-down walls. As she leaves the city, the colour drains from the image, and the perspective shifts as the camera cranes upwards to show her walking along a road lined with Protestant corpses suspended on wheels, a memorably haunting image which evokes Bruegel's *The Triumph of Death* (Gómez 1976: 161).

The Devils is somewhat atypical in that the majority of Russell's films are surreal biographies of artists which, as he remarked, 'evolve through a stream of consciousness in which the man and the myth, the music and its meaning, time, place, dream and fact all flow and blend into the mainstream of the film itself' (in Gómez 1976: 96). Like Powell, Russell wanted to create films that were total works of art in which dance and music are the controlling elements. *Tommy* (1975), Russell's version of the Who's rock opera, dispenses with dialogue, telling its story through song, music, mime, dance and the play of visual images in which reality and fantasy are deliberately confused. Russell thought *Tommy* was 'about a modern messiah, a possible messiah, who might have been a messiah but was totally exploited and commercialised' (in Gómez 1976: 195). This is exemplified in the scene where Tommy's mother (Ann-Margaret), guiltily enjoying the luxury that the exploitation of her son as the 'pinball wizard' has brought, sings 'Today it Rained Champagne' as the television blares out adverts for baked beans, chocolates and detergents. At the climax of the song she throws her champagne bottle at the set, which splinters, releasing a huge tide of detergent, baked beans and liquid chocolate in which she luxuriates in a kind of sexual ecstasy. This surreal image is bizarre, memorable, shocking and functional within the film's argument, but it teeters on the edge of banality and vulgarity, the twin weaknesses of Russell's imagination which vitiate his later work including his excursions into Gothic horror: *Gothic* (1986) and

The Lair of the White Worm (1988). Increasingly, the films' fantasies are not located in a particular character's perception, and therefore it is unclear what they represent, and the dialectic that is essential to Surrealism is lost.

Another maverick filmmaker, Derek Jarman's films are highly personal – their basis in home-movies made for friends followed a Surrealist tradition – yet they can be located, as Michael O'Pray has argued, in a long line of English romantic radicals who have embraced a romantic conservatism, a tradition that includes William Blake and William Morris, as well as Powell and Pressburger whom Jarman admired, and Ken Russell for whom he worked as the set designer on *The Devils* (1996: 8–9, 12). Jarman remarked: 'I really believe that the cinema should dream. The films that are constructed out of the imagination and explore interior worlds are the valuable ones' (in Park 1984: 82). But these 'dreams' should provide both a radical scepticism that questioned all forms of authority and a vision, albeit a fractured, fragmented one, of an idealised world. *Jubilee* (1978), for instance, is structured between a violent and tawdry present and the more vibrant world of Elizabethan England, 'our cultural Arcadia'. In order to realise his vision, which lies beyond the realm of reason and systematic thought, Jarman needed to evolve an eclectic, multi-layered style which drew on oppositional gay imagery, alchemy and occult philosophies, the legacy of 1960s counter-culture and radical student politics, as well as European art cinema. For the most part, his films abandon narrative cohesion and psychological explanation in favour of an eclectic vocabulary of image, symbolism, colour, sound and dream-like associational structures that is his principal debt to Surrealism.

This style is most effective in Jarman's masterpiece *The Last of England* (1987) which begins, in black and white, in Jarman's own study, and attacks the moral, cultural and spiritual bankruptcy of contemporary Britain. In what he called a 'dream allegory', Jarman abandons dialogue and sequential narrative altogether, deliberately mixing documentary (including old family home-movies) and fictional sequences from an imaginary feature film so that the two forms 'are confused and coalesce' (O'Pray 1996: 161). The rapid-fire editing creates many bitter and disturbing juxtapositions, which are interspersed with the sounds of Hitler's speeches, boots stomping on watery ground and football chants. The focus is on anonymous, neurotic or despairing individuals who pick their way through the debris of a blighted landscape, a rapidly approaching future in which the military rule England with callous violence. Some of Jarman's memorably surreal figures include a naked man tearing a cauliflower apart, a stooped man pushing a pram through a night slum while holding on high a burning torch and a woman (Tilda Swinton) shown cutting, ripping and devouring her wedding dress in an increasingly desperate frenzy.

The Garden (1990) was a more intimate film, a complex recounting of Christ's passion precipitated by Jarman's knowledge of his own impending death through AIDS. It contains often hideously violent images, but is pervaded by a strong sense of redemption in what appears to be Jarman's own dream: in the first scene he falls asleep as water drips on a crucifix and at other points he is shown huddled on a bed in shallow coastline waters. It was filmed in and around his home, Prospect Cottage, on Dungeness, with its surreal incongruity, the garden of Elizabethan flowers, stones and driftwood in the shadow of a huge nuclear power station. *The Garden* ends with a coda depicting a disparate grouping, a kind of Last Supper, presided over by Swinton as a Madonna figure dispensing Amaretti whose wrappers rise up in the wind: a joyous, beautiful and poignantly elegiac image. Jarman was linked to the 1980s' 'New Romantics' including his disciple, John Maybury, whose Surrealist *Love is the Devil* (1998), was an exploration of the life of the iconoclastic painter Francis Bacon.

Surrealism in contemporary British cinema: beyond Social Realism

A memorably surreal moment occurs in Danny Boyle's *Trainspotting* (1996) when Renton (Ewan McGregor) dives down into the fetid bowl of 'the worst toilet in Scotland' in order to rescue the two heroin suppositories he has just defecated. He emerges into a sun-kissed, translucent tropical pool in which he swims like a pearl diver and retrieves the suppositories. It was a moment in which the constrictions of the social realist tradition were deliberately abandoned in favour of a more vibrant, outrageous and provocative visual style that could represent the linguistic flights and black humour of Irvine Welsh's novel. As the most influential British film of the 1990s, *Trainspotting* encouraged other filmmakers to incorporate surreal elements into a wide variety of different types of film, notably innovative crime thrillers including Paul Sarossy's *Mr In-Between* (2001); Marc Evans' psychological melodrama *Trauma* (2004); black comedies such as Justin Kerrigan's *Human Traffic* (1999), a fantastical documentary about Cardiff's club culture; Paul Tickell's *Christie Malry's Own Double-Entry* (2000), based on B. S. Johnson's surreal novel; and Nick Hamm's psychological horror *The Hole* (2001). There is even an ambiguously surreal ending to Lynne Ramsay's *Ratcatcher* (1999) – does the central character drown or is his fantasy of his family's move to a new home about to come true? – which adds a new dimension to its conventional social realism. Surrealism has become a diffused and widely dispersed presence in an eclectic, postmodern British cinema, used to startle audiences into a new perception of the multifaceted nature of experience, the interpenetration of reality and fantasy.

Conclusion: Surrealist influences, not a Surrealist cinema

These films contain moments of Surrealism, or elements of a Surrealist style, rather than being Surrealist films and they therefore exemplify the occasional eccentricity that I have suggested characterises British cinema's engagement with Surrealism. I would argue that there is only one fully Surrealist film in British cinema, Richard Lester's *The Bed Sitting Room*, and even that can be located, as has been demonstrated, within powerful and deep-rooted cultural traditions that are specifically British. However, as I hope this chapter has shown, if the course of Surrealism in British cinema has been fitful, it has contributed to the production of a number of challenging and memorable films that have created a complex dialectic between ordinariness and fantasy, reality and dreams, the rational and the irrational, opening up a space for an exploration of the forces that are repressed or excluded by social realism. It is an achievement that needs to be recognised and celebrated.

Notes

1 As a representative example of the British distrust of Continental Surrealism see Tony Hancock's *The Rebel* (1961), a brilliant debunking of the pretensions of Surrealist art and a paean to eccentric individualism.

2 The Surrealist influence on British documentaries is discussed elsewhere in this volume; Jarman's work admittedly straddles the shifting divide between avant-garde and commercial cinema. I have also not been able to include films that have important surreal elements but which are one-offs, notably Albert Lewin's *Pandora and the Flying Dutchman* (1950), Jack Clayton's *The Innocents* (1961), Roman Polanski's *Repulsion* (1965) and Michaelangelo Antonioni's *Blow-Up* (1966).

3 Buñuel co-wrote (with Jean-Claude Carrière) the screenplay for *Le Moine* (1973), a version of *The Monk*, directed by Adonis Kyrou.

4 *Murders in the Rue Morgue* was butchered by its distributors, American International Pictures, which coloured the fantasy sequences red thereby losing the ambiguity. Fortunately a copy of the original version was preserved by Hessler and has been released on DVD, MGM Home Entertainment, 4004352 (2003).

Barbara Creed

THE UNTAMED EYE AND THE DARK SIDE OF SURREALISM: HITCHCOCK, LYNCH AND CRONENBERG

A sliced eyeball, scorpions fighting to the death, ants crawling from a hole in a hand, delirious lovers – these images, designed to delight and shock, capture the essence of the Parisian Surrealist movement of the 1920s and 1930s. The continuing influence of early or classic Surrealist filmmaking on popular, commercial filmmakers of the latter part of the twentieth century is evidenced by a different but equally disturbing set of Surrealist signature images: a severed ear lying on a country lane, a woman falling twice to her death from a bell tower, an exploding head and a man disappearing into the parted lips of a television screen. There is no doubt that early Surrealists were in love with the image and its power to move the viewer. The Surrealists, however, did not extol the power of the image *per se*; rather they were drawn to the art of montage, that is, the way images could be edited together to create shocking and fantastic associations in order to affect the viewer emotionally. Contemporary filmmakers such as American director David Lynch and Canadian David Cronenberg are similarly fascinated by the power of Surrealism and shock montage to open up the imagination. The British director Alfred Hitchcock, who made a series of Surrealist masterpieces in Hollywood in the 1950s and 1960s, was the first popular director to work in the Surrealist mode. The horror film, of course, has for decades drawn, tongue-in-cheek, on the dark jittery side of Surrealism.

Surrealism, as a revolutionary art movement, was and still is concerned with creating a specific emotional response, one that challenges the viewer to embrace the world of the marvellous, the dream, the abject and the irrational. Surrealism is first and foremost an attitude of mind, a desire to liberate the unconscious, to create room for the imagination, to confront the abject, to change the conditions of ordinary mundane reality. Film with its unique ability to yoke together disparate images and to obliterate the distinction between oppositions – particularly dream and reality, life and death, man and woman – is perfectly suited to the Surrealist project of expanding the imagination.

Given its defamiliarising and uncanny power, cinema, it is argued, is ontologically sur-real (Charney & Schwartz 1998: 124–8).

In discussing the aims of the early Surrealist movement, C. W. E. Bigsby argues that it is essential to distinguish between style and philosophy.

> Surrealism is not simply the striking image, the irrational phrase or the dream-like texture. These are methods. It is essentially concerned with liberating the imagination and with expanding the definition of reality. (1972: 78)

The Surrealist movement of the 1920s was short-lived, but it continued to exert a marked influence on artistic practice and popular culture. Bigsby argues that the 'influence of Surrealism has been considerable not only in France but throughout the world' (1972: 77). He sees its impact on 'pop art's concern with the object' (ibid.) on the importance given to 'improvisation and spontaneity' (ibid.) in the theatre, on the 'nature and tone of popular culture' (ibid.) To those intent on 'changing consciousness as altering the structure of society, the ethos of Surrealism, humane, iconoclastic, imaginative and international, seems more relevant and attractive than ever' (ibid.).

Bigsby defines Surrealism primarily in terms of André Breton's vision, that is, as a movement of love and liberation. Viewed from the eyes of Breton – regarded as the founder of the movement – Surrealism has been defined as an artistic practice whose central aim was an encounter with the marvellous which Breton, in the 'First Surrealist Manifesto', defined as an encounter with the beautiful: 'the Marvellous is always beautiful, everything marvellous is beautiful' (in Waldberg 1966: 70). Yet there is another side to Surrealism which is not incompatible with the definition above, but which focuses on what Hal Foster terms its darker side. It is this area of Surrealist thought that has primarily influenced later directors such as Hitchcock, Cronenberg and Lynch.

Foster claims that this crucial area of Surrealism underwent a repression and in recent decades, particularly the 1980s, a recovery. He argues that 'no given categories, aesthetic *or* Surrealist, could comprehend Surrealism conceptually – could account for its heterogeneous practices or address its quintessential concerns with psychic conflict and social contradiction' (1993: xvi). He argues that there is one term that comprehends Surrealism – the uncanny. A psychoanalytic concept developed by Sigmund Freud, the uncanny explores events 'in which repressed material returns in ways that disrupt unitary identity, aesthetic norms and social order' (1993: xvii). Foster argues that many of the Surrealists, particularly Georges Bataille, were drawn to the uncanny, and 'the return of the repressed', the basis of the uncanny, which is central to Surrealist notions of 'the marvellous, convulsive beauty and objective chance'. Foster examines Surrealism from its darker side: as an art devoted not just to love and liberation but also to sadism and masochism, desire and death. He encapsulates this division as one caught between the competing visions of Breton and Bataille.

It seems clear that the Bataillean vision of Surrealism has strongly influenced the contemporary cinema of primarily independent directors such as Lynch, Cronenberg and the Coen Brothers, whose films abound with images relating to the uncanny, doubling, the abject body, sadism, desire and death. We can also trace the influence of Surrealism on popular Hollywood genres such as horror and fantasy. In Clive Barker's view, the horror film as a genre embodies the major aesthetic qualities of Surrealism, that it is in fact 'still the last refuge of the surreal' (in Wells 2000: 20–1). Horror films such as the *Nightmare on Elm Street* series (1984–2003) explore a dream-world in which it is impossible to distinguish reality from fantasy; the werewolf genre revels in human/animal metamorphoses much beloved by Bataille; vampire films excite with their unabashed eroticism linked to sex and death; and the figure of Hannibal Lecter epitomises a surreal monster, one both sympathetic and repulsive, a man of learning and refined appetites whose desire to cannibalise representatives of bourgeoise mediocrity and hypocrisy is deliciously surreal. In addition, there are no doubt many films which, as J. H. Matthews argues in relation to *King Kong* (1933) – a film revered by the Surrealists – reveal 'involuntary surrealist elements' (1971: 17). Hollywood films which explored the world of the dream or which created a strange dreamlike quality throughout, such as *Peter Ibbetson* (1935), *Laura* (1944) and *Pandora and the Flying Dutchman* (1951) were endorsed by the Surrealists.

In his important study of the original Surrealist movement and its relationship to Dada, Steven Kovács raises some concerns about an ahistorical approach to the question of influences. He agrees that 'the Parisian Surrealist movement quickly spread all over the world' (1980: 11) and that since then Surrealism has left an indelible mark on world cinema, both experimental and commercial. However, he is critical of an ahistorical approach that would either search for the 'traces' of Surrealism in motion pictures or try to 'isolate its many offspring'. Specifically interested in the historical conditions that produced Surrealism in different periods, Kovács advocates a 'historical approach to the evolution of Surrealist cinema in order to rediscover the fundamental sources and salient features' (ibid.) which gave birth to the films in question. He also sees genre criticism as ahistorical because it is 'based on a formalistic, idealistic conception of art, which addresses the hows rather than the whys, and which is more interested in the evolution of a type over generations or even centuries than in the actual historical conditions of production of those works' (ibid.).

While I support the importance of a historical approach, I do not agree that a generic or auteurist approach is necessarily ahistorical. Both can and ideally should take into account historical, social and cultural factors as well as individual and even psychological factors. Just as it is possible to trace the effects of the First World War on early Dada and Surrealist writers and artists, it is also possible to see the influence of the Second World War and the horrors of the Holocaust on later Surrealist filmmakers, as well as the influence of the Vietnam War on directors of the 1970s and 1980s horror film. These momentous events have helped to shape the iconography, choice of images and narrative patterns of later Surrealist filmmakers.

As I have argued contemporary filmmakers are not so much attracted to the Bretonian vision of Surrealism but rather drawn to what Foster has termed as the darker side of Surrealism, that is, its fascination with the uncanny, the dream, desire and death. In relation to this, it is interesting to note how so much of what the early Surrealists said about the cinema supports Foster's position. They appear drawn to the cinema because of its power to depict the dark side of life. They emphasised the nature of film as dream, asserted that film should speak to the 'untamed eye', defined the status of film as conscious hallucination and applauded its power to express strong emotions and to portray taboo themes such as sexual perversion, sadism and death. Their views are worth exploring in more detail.

Jean Cocteau once said that all films are surreal. In a sense he is correct; the cinematic image and the form of 'reality' created by its seamless and mechanical projection is very different from the flow of events in the real world. Film has much more in common with a dream where there is no logical relation between signifier and signified, and events do not necessarily unfold in a credible, logical or realistic manner. Many of the early Surrealists (Luis Buñuel, André Breton, Jean Goudal, Ado Kyrou, Jean Ferry and others) fell in love with the fledgling cinema and its power to disorientate, to disturb and to follow the movements of the dream-world.[1] They did not, however, produce a comprehensive document – as they did with painting – which set down the views about film. Georges Sadoul wrote that 'Surrealism did not have, properly speaking, a cinematographic doctrine' (in Matthews 1971: 11). Instead, the Surrealists wrote short personal statements about the cinema. The most significant of these appear in an important collection edited by Paul Hammond, *The Shadow and Its Shadow* (1978). A detailed discussion of this collection – and other sources – is outside the scope of this chapter; it is possible, however, to convey enough of what the Surrealists thought about the cinema as a basis for further discussion of how Surrealism of the 1920s has influenced contemporary cinema. It is relevant to note how much their views lend themselves to the creation of films about the dark side of Surrealism.

The Surrealists were drawn to film that challenged and upset the viewer, films that in Robert Desnos' terms were 'frenetic' rather than 'academic' (in Matthews 1971: 13). Matthews describes the Surrealist approach perfectly when he says: 'the first Surrealists viewed with distrust any attempt to tame the eye' (ibid.). The famous eye-slicing scene in Luis Buñuel's and Salvador Dalí's *Un chien andalou* explores this proposition. The film begins with the classic fairytale line 'Once upon a time...' and a young man (Buñuel himself) stands casually by a window. A cigarette hangs from the side of his mouth as he carefully sharpens a large razor. He watches the full moon and a solitary cloud in the night sky. A young woman stares ahead into the eye of the camera. As a cloud cuts across the moon the razor slices her eye. In an unexpected extreme close-up the jelly-like contents of the slivered eye spill forward.

Subsequent viewings fail to ameliorate the shocking impact of that image. When Buñuel learnt that critics had described the film as avant-garde and poetic he was appalled; rather, he saw the film as 'a desperate appeal to murder' (quoted in Aranda 1985: 63). His intention was to provoke his audience into radical action. Although Buñuel and Dalí argued that their film defied interpretation, it is tempting to see the slashed eye as a warning that everything which was to follow would speak not to actual vision but only to the mind's inner or unconscious eye. From 1929 to the present the Surrealists' slivered eye has continued to haunt the cinema – from the giant close-up of Norman Bates' voyeuristic eye in *Psycho* (1960) to the inhuman eyes of the cyborg in *The Terminator* (1984) and the terrified eyes of the citizens under surveillance in *Minority Report* (2002).

The Surrealists praised the way the cinematic image unfolded to approximate the workings of the imagination and the dream-state. The Surrealists' untamed eye is first and foremost an inner eye. Of central importance to their views on the cinema is the relationship between the viewing of a film and the act of dreaming. To them watching a film unfolding in a darkened cinema embodied the closest thing to a dream. Jean Goudal described the cinema as a 'conscious hallucination' – even more powerful than literature:

> The cinema, then, constitutes a conscious hallucination, and utilises this fusion of dream and consciousness which Surrealism would like to see realised in the literary domain. These moving images delude us, by leaving us with a confused awareness of our own personality and by allowing us to evoke, if necessary, the resources of our memory. (In Hammond 1978: 52–3)

Dreaming and viewing both take place in the dark; the subject is not in control of the flow of images which in both contexts seem to originate from a point outside the conscious control of the individual. Goudal argued that the physical conditions of film viewing enhanced the dream-state. The darkness of the auditorium closed out distracting images from the real world while the music shut out any sounds. The dream-state was further intensified by the way that the images unfolded, not in accordance with rules of logic but in terms of their own logic. Even when a film narrated a logical story the images continued to obey their own logic, even moving from present to past and future and often with such speed that the spectator is forced to surrender to the logic of the filmic world. David Lynch is particularly attuned to the power of film to collapse dream and reality and to operate according to dream logic.

Thus film was able to express powerful emotions – always of crucial importance to the Surrealists – and open up, for the viewer, an encounter with the surreal or extraordinary. Powerful emotions were created through a range of scenarios, particularly those which dealt with an overwhelming desire for a beautiful or mysterious woman, or created psychological terror, or explored themes of love and death, chance and fate. These themes are central to Hitchcock's films, particularly *Notorious* (1946), *Vertigo* (1958) and *North by Northwest* (1959).

Breton developed the concept of 'deracination' to describe the way film could express powerful emotions. In deracination the spectator begins to identify so strongly with what is taking place on the screen that she or he is transported into another realm; thus the viewer experiences the events and emotions in an act of transcendence:

The temptation is so great to make this disorientation [deracination] last and to increase it to an impossible degree that it has been able to tempt my friends and me along the path to paradoxical attitudes. To be precise, it is a question of *going beyond* the bounds of what is 'allowed', which, in the cinema as nowhere else, prepares me to invite in the 'forbidden'. (1978c: 44)

The Surrealists were very much interested in those experiences outside the boundaries of acceptable behaviour, such as the forbidden and the taboo, particularly in relation to desire. Through its power to stimulate the imagination film offered another experience much valued by the Surrealists – an encounter with the erotic. The Surrealists argued for the importance of films showing sex and violence but without any moralising. Ado Kyrou spoke strongly against 'love films' that only succeeded in creating a sense of moral order and tranquility. Instead he called for films about love, sex and eroticism: 'I would like it if we could or would forget all prohibitions, all previously acquired conceptions, all advice, to make films in which love, seen normally and sanely, would no longer be conditioned by bourgeois mores' (1978: 126). He called for films which depicted love 'purged of the terrible notion of sin' and in which the 'magic of the encounter' and the 'splendid grandeur of the sexual act' could be shown: 'This love will be pleasure, knowledge and a call to revolt, it will change the world' (ibid.). In his controversial film *Crash* (1996) Cronenberg sets out to confront sexual taboos without moralising.

The Surrealists also defended the elevation of the popular in the cinema. Louis Aragon called for a full understanding of the way the cinema presented beauty in signs of the popular and commercial, the ordinary and everyday. He argued that 'cinematic *décor* [is] the adequate setting of modern beauty' (1978: 29):

All our emotion exists for those dear old American adventure films that speak of daily life and manage to raise to a dramatic level a banknote on which our attention is rivetted, a table with a revolver on it, a bottle that on occasion becomes a weapon.

It is not surprising to learn that the Surrealists loved a great many of the popular Hollywood genres, particularly films belonging to the horror, comedy and the love story (Matthews 1971). In particular the Surrealists liked to interpret popular film irrationally – they applied Salvador Dalí's paranoiac-critical method to probe beneath the surface features of the film in order to stage an encounter with the surreal. Dalí's approach involved a 'spontaneous method of *irrational knowledge* based upon the critical and systematic objectification of delirious associations and interpretations' (Matthews 1971: 50). Given his stated disdain for critics, and his fascination with the unconscious, Alfred Hitchcock would no doubt have approved thoroughly of Dalí's paranoiac-critical methodology.

The popularity of directors such as Cronenberg and Lynch, who explore themes of horror, doubling and the uncanny, the abject body, madness, death and desire demonstrates the continuing power and attraction that the dark side of Surrealism holds for contemporary audiences. This power was perhaps best understood and most effectively utilised by one of the modern cinema's greatest directors, Alfred Hitchcock. It was arguably Hitchcock who was the first popular director to explore consciously the Surrealists' ideas about the cinema in his films. Setting the scene for more recent directors such as Cronenberg and Lynch, Hitchcock has exerted a profound influence on the direction of contemporary film in relation to Surrealism. Cronenberg has developed Hitchcock's interest (and of course that of the early Surrealists) in horror and the abject body; Lynch in the double, the dream and the theme of *l'amour fou*.

Alfred Hitchcock

Hitchcock dreamed in broad daylight. His razor-sharp, fantastical imagery – he himself said he sought to achieve these effects – was Surrealist.
– Nathalie Bondil-Poupard (2001: 170)

Alfred Hitchcock is one of the cinema's great popular Surrealists. His personal interest in the early Surrealists (who were his contemporaries) as well as his fascination with the irrational, sexual desire and the dream-state, combined with the potent forces of modernity, all helped to shape his Surrealist aesthetic. Hitchcock did not simply adopt a Surrealist style for its own sake; he was an unconventional thinker whose aim was to challenge complacency and liberate the darker side of the imagination, particularly through the aesthetics of shock.

Famous as 'the master of suspense', Hitchcock's enduring legacy owes more to his rarely discussed fascination with the surreal and the power with which he captured the dark side of Surrealism in some of his most widely applauded films: *Vertigo, North by Northwest, Psycho, Spellbound* (1945), *The Birds* (1963), *Marnie* (1964). It is my contention that these films reveal Hitchcock's commitment to the Surrealist aesthetic which in some (*Spellbound, The Birds, Vertigo*) is very apparent and in others (*North by Northwest, Marnie*) is perhaps less obvious, but nonetheless central. They also reveal his desire to challenge complacency and conformity and to awaken the viewer to a different understanding of her/his own nature and subjectivity, particularly the individual's capacity for acts of sadism, masochism and murder.

As a member of the London Film Society in the 1920s Hitchcock saw the great early Dada and Surrealist films whose influence he acknowledged. Given his love of art and interest in Surrealism he no doubt attended, or read about, the great Surrealist exhibition in 1936, held at the Royal Academy.[2] In his short essay 'Why I am Afraid of the Dark', published in June 1960, Hitchcock talked about his discovery of the stories of Edgar Allan Poe when he was sixteen and of the later influence of Poe's work on his suspense films. He also writes that Surrealism was indebted to Poe and that his own work was influenced by the French Surrealists:

And Surrealism? … This literary school certainly had a great influence on cinema, especially around 1926–30, when Surrealism was transposed onto the screen by Buñuel with *L'Âge d'or* and *Un chien andalou*, by René Clair with *Entr'acte*, by Jean Epstein with *The Fall of the House of Usher*, and by your French academician Jean Cocteau with *The Blood of a Poet*. An influence that I experienced myself, if only in the dream sequences and the sequences of the unreal in a certain number of my films. (1997b: 144)

In his autobiography, *My Last Breath*, Buñuel makes an interesting comment. In 1972 Buñuel and a small group, including Hitchcock, met at George Cukor's house for dinner. Buñuel wrote:

At one point during our conversation, we heard footsteps shuffling behind us, and when I turned around, there was Alfred Hitchcock, round and rosy cheeked, his arms held out in my direction. I'd never met him, either, but knew that he'd sung my praises from time to time. He sat down on the other side of me, and, one arm around my shoulders, he proceeded to talk nonstop about his wine cellar, his diet, and the amputated leg in *Tristana*. 'Ah, that leg … that leg,' he sighed, more than once. (1985: 195)

That Hitchcock would link female beauty (Tristana was played by Catherine Deneuve) with wine, amputation, fetishism and longing in one conversation is typically surreal.

In a fascinating essay on *Vertigo*, Peter Wollen analyses Hitchcock's Surrealism, concluding that he is 'a closet Surrealist' (1977: 17); but in my view there is nothing 'hidden' about his Surrealist concerns. Emil Stern has suggested, in an eloquent essay on *Marnie* as a Surrealist text, that because Hitchcock imbeds his 'Surrealist elements and concerns in a conventional enough framework' his films are 'perhaps incompatible with the deepest aims of the Surrealists' (2000: 43). On the contrary, Hitchcock is a great *popular* Surrealist whose Surrealist style and subject matter is designed to entertain as well as unleash the power of the imagination through shock. Using a 'conventional framework' – a classic narrative form which ultimately seeks to resolve the main narrative enigma – does not necessarily make one's aims 'incompatible with the deepest aims of Surrealism' if these are to shock and disorient the viewer in order to bring about an altered state of consciousness. In fact, it is debatable that Hitchcock employs a conventional framework in films such as *Vertigo*, *Psycho* and *The Birds* where narrative closure – such as it is – leaves more questions unanswered than resolved. When the shocking is aligned with the ordinary or everyday, the effect is potentially even more surreal as evidenced by the horror of the famous shower-scene murder in *Psycho* or the inexplicable attack of the birds on the inhabitants of a small seaside town.

Drawn to the dark side of Surrealism, Hitchcock expressed his interest in it through style, *mise-en-scène*, imagery, motifs, symbolism, jokes and his own persona which – like Dalí – he manufactured or staged as a surreal event. Hitchcock was not simply influenced by the Surrealists, figures such as Dalí, Magritte, de Chirico and Buñuel, rather he was committed to and pursued Surrealist themes and stylistic structures in many of his most admired and important films. Hitchcock's films take as their subject matter themes of murder, transgressive sexual desires, voyeurism, sadism, cannibalism, necrophilia, the compulsion to repeat, death and the uncanny. He aimed to change or alter the consciousness of the viewer, to open the viewer up to the dark side of the self. His films resonate with Magritte's slightly menacing images of doubles and lost lovers, Ernst's drawings of uncanny human/creatures, Man Ray's spirals, the eerie urban landscapes of de Chirico, the traumatic scenes of Hans Bellmer and the nightmare worlds of Dalí. In what might seem a contradictory gesture, Hitchcock also embraced Breton's belief in the power of love to liberate the individual from fear of betrayal as in *Notorious*, *North by Northwest* and *Marnie*.

Hitchcock, like the Surrealists, responded in similar ways to the new tropes of modernity including a disregard for classical realism (Hitchcock's love of rear projection and painted backdrops); fascination with narratives about love and the failure of desire; an interest in the uncanny and the death drive and an exploration of the workings of repression and the unconscious. It is the direct and confronting way in which Hitchcock and later filmmakers, such as Lynch and Cronenberg, have presented their Surrealist concerns that helps to explain their dramatic and enduring popular appeal. Surrealism is the artistic movement of the twentieth century *par excellence*.

Bretonian Surrealism focuses on the marvellous but Breton also stated that Surrealism would introduce one to death – an arena explored by Buñuel, Dalí, Magritte, Ernst, Bellmer and Bataille. Images of abjection – death, murder, torture, rape – are central to modernity. With the rise of a new mass media, from newspapers to television, it became possible to view the most horrific images in one's home. The once external public world of horror has become domesticated in an unprecedented manner. Hitchcock was very much attracted to the dark side of modernity and domesticity. One of the most important ways in which Hitchcock's films can be seen to inhabit a modernist and surreal landscape is in relation to his use of images, the manner in which he thinks through images, editing images in such a way that the audience produces the meaning, which is invariably related to the dark side of existence – death, perversion, murder.

In an essay, Hitchcock discusses influences on his filmmaking, one is a specifically Surreal concept which he traces back to Poe's influence – that of a 'hallucinatory logic':

Without wanting to seem immodest, I can't help but compare what I try to put in my films with what Poe put in his stories: a perfectly unbelievable story recounted to readers with such a hallucinatory logic that one has the impression that this same story can happen to you tomorrow. (1997b: 143)

Hitchcock sets out to shock his audiences into a hallucinatory state in which they realise – in Hitchcock's words – 'that this same story can happen to you tomorrow'.

Hitchcock's urbane sophisticated protagonists, who are very much products of modernity – not unlike the modern business man of Magritte's paintings – suddenly find themselves plunged into a nightmarish world of terror. These figures are not unlike the bourgeoisie whom the Surrealists also wanted to shock into an encounter with the world of the imagination, terror and the sublime. In Hitchcock's films, however, this transformation is almost always brought about by an encounter with death. Although Breton wrote that 'Surrealism will introduce you to death' (1966: 70), he was ultimately more interested in the 'marvellous as beauty' than was Hitchcock. In drawing on the power of film to shock and disorient through editing, Hitchcock went further than the Surrealists in his encounter with death. Three areas of particular interest to the early Surrealists and Hitchcock were the distinction between real and imaginary, the dynamics of *l'amour fou* and the aesthetics of shock.

In 'The First Surrealist Manifesto' Breton discusses a number of contradictory or oppositional states – real/imaginary, life/death, high/low. He believed Surrealism had the power to resolve these contradictions. This was its main aim. 'I believe in the future resolution of these two states – outwardly so contradictory – which are dream and reality, into a sort of absolute reality, a *surreality*' (ibid.). This was one of the central tenets of Surrealism – dream and reality are one.

Hitchcock was particularly interested in the states of dream and reality and the relationship between the two. In his interviews with François Truffaut, Hitchcock talks about his desire to make films in which the two worlds are indistinguishable. In discussing the dream sequences of *Downhill* (1927) he said:

> At one point I wanted to show that the young man was having hallucinations. In those days dreams were always dissolves and they were always blurred. Though it was difficult, I tried to embody the dream in the reality, in solid, unblurred images. (in Truffaut 1984: 57–8)

Hitchcock did not want to signal to his audience that they were moving from the real world into the dream world – he wanted one to inhabit the other. The new inventions of modernity, specifically the movie camera, suddenly made it possible to blur this distinction in a way never before experienced. In all of his suspense thrillers his characters – ordinary everyday people – suddenly find themselves in an imaginary, nightmarish world of suspense and terror. Hitchcock's Surrealism resides in his unfailing power to render the 'dream in reality' in solid, sharp images. He achieves this not only through his creation of a dream-world but also through the way in which he explores the dark side of the dream – the nightmare. Known as a 'master of suspense', Hitchcock is also accurately described as a 'master of the surreal'.

Psycho could be interpreted as a sustained nightmare in which dream and reality are indistinguishable, in which the narrative itself seems to follow the bizarre logic of the dream. When Marion Crane (Janet Leigh) begins her flight into the unknown, Hitchcock draws on images which suck us deeper and deeper into the imaginary: images of bloody water swirling down into a drain; the close-up of an eye superimposed over a plughole; a car containing a dead body being sucked into a bog; a mummified skeleton in a cellar. In *Psycho* we are sucked into the imaginary through images of descent and falling. The same is true of *Vertigo*. Scotty (James Stewart) lives completely in a nightmarish dream world into which he draws the woman he desires (played by Kim Novak); in the end she is sucked into the vortex of death in place of the male. Emil Stern (one of the few critics to write about a Hitchcock film as embodying the surreal) analyses the Surrealist elements of that film in its 'blurring or removal of the distinction between the imaginary and the real' (2000: 40). He hesitates to describe *Marnie* as encapsulating Surrealism but in my view there is no doubt. With her glazed expression, Marnie (Tippi Hedren) moves through the film as if in a dream, caught up by her nightmare hallucinations triggered by the colour red. In some sequences Hitchcock simply cuts from Marnie to a red screen. There is no sign that we are entering the world of unreality – real and imaginary fuse to create a truly surreal world.

With its surreal dream sequence, designed by Dali, *Spellbound* is sometimes referred to as staging the surreal in an artificial manner. Yet if one attends to the context of the dream sequence, it becomes evident that the events surrounding this sequence are even more surreal than the nightmare. This is because the scene in which the Gregory Peck character who descends the staircase in a sleepwalking state refers directly to *Un chien andalou* and the power of the camera to merge dream with reality. The camera focuses on a razor that the man holds in his hand, evoking the razor sequence from Bunuel and Dali's film which emphasised the crucial role of the internal eye, the mind's eye, in viewing film. The events that follow the razor sequence in *Spellbound* gradually become more and more bizarre.

Like the Surrealists Hitchcock was fascinated with the art of illusion; this is most evident in his use of rear projection. Rear projection enables an exterior scene to be projected onto a translucent screen to appear as the background for live action filmed in a studio. By using rear projection Hitchcock was able to play with the audience, to trick the eye into imagining it has seen the 'real thing'. However the deception is only momentary as it is easy for an audience to recognise rear projection. In fact, Hitchcock did not appear at all concerned about concealing its use which suggests that he wanted to give a painterly, even artificial, look to his frame much as Magritte does in his use of the frame within a frame. Rear projection also reminds the viewer they are watching a film, an illusory world, because it introduces an 'unreal' feeling – even a dreamlike sense – into the supposedly 'real' scene before them. Hitchcock used transparencies to create a false reality or a 'surreal real' to great effect in his Surrealist masterpieces, particularly *The Birds* (the attack in the schoolyard), *Marnie* (the horse-riding sequences, the ship at the end of the mother's street), *North by Northwest* (the car chase around the cliffs), *Vertigo* (Scotty's fall from the roof) and *Psycho* (Arbogast's murder and fall on the staircase). Hitchcock's decision to continue to use rear projection – even after the technology had been superceded through the introduction of the travelling matte

– points to his greater concern with aesthetic pursuits than with the benefits of new technology. The frequency and consistency with which he used rear projection points to his obsessive love of illusion.[3]

One central aspect of the Hitchcockian text is its representation of fatal love, of the male/female relationship and its impossibility. The Cuban novelist and critic Cabrera Infante praised *Vertigo* as the 'first great Surrealist film' particularly in relation to its 'fainting theme of love' (quoted in Mogg 2006: 88). Here, of course, he is referring to the Surrealists' fascination with *l'amour fou*. In *Vertigo*, Scotty kills the woman with whom he is obsessed – the woman who signifies death itself. Like the clergyman in Dulac's *La coquille et le clergyman* (*The Seashell and the Clergyman*, 1928), Scotty in *Vertigo* pursues the woman as if in a trance, finding and losing her as she transforms from one state to another. In *Psycho*, Norman murders all of the women to whom he is sexually attracted. Mark Rutfield in *Marnie* pursues a woman who lives in a trance-world and who is sexually frigid. In *The Birds*, the woman (Tippi Hedren) – traumatised with fear – returns to the embrace of the mother not the son. There is a profound sense of incommensurability and loss in Hitchcock's films – a sense that there can be no reconciliation between the sexes – the oppositions of male/female.

These moments are frequently expressed in Hitchcock's films when the male protagonist embraces the woman but she is not emotionally a part of that embrace. She either looks ahead or elsewhere (knowing she will have to betray the man as in *North by Northwest* and *Vertigo*) or gazes ahead as if in a trance as in *The Birds* and *Marnie*. These moments, which express the impossibility of the sexual relationship, are also central to Surrealist art. In particular I am thinking of the paintings of Dalí and Magritte (*The Threatened Assassin* (1926), *The Lovers* (1928), *The Rape* (1934), *Collective Invention* (1935) and *The Forbidden Universe* (1943)).

Hitchcock's heroines are frequently discussed in the context of the 'ice blonde'. Hitchcock's representation of woman as unobtainable relates to the theme of *l'amour fou*. He uses the figures of the icy blonde and the paranoid obsessive male – both existing on different planes, forever circling each other (as in *Notorious*, *North by Northwest*, *Vertigo*, *Marnie*) but forever unable to meet – to represent the impossibility of a union between the sexes. In his frustrated pursuit of compulsive beauty as a sexual union, a moment of shock and transformation, Hitchcock is his most surreal.

Modernity created an environment of sensation, shock, distraction and fleeting impressions. Walter Benjamin argued that the best way of representing the moment was through an image because he believed images provided the most effective way of capturing an immediate perception. Hitchcock used film images to capture the moment that shocked. In his 1936 essay entitled 'Why "Thrillers" Thrive' Hitchcock carefully distinguishes between horror films which 'exploit sadism, perversion, bestiality, and deformity' in order to 'create *unnatural* excitement' in 'a neurotic section of the public' (1997a: 111) and the thriller which use techniques of shock – even 'terrific shock' – to create an emotional response resulting in an ultimately 'beneficial' or therapeutic experience (ibid.).

Like the Surrealists, Hitchcock wanted to use shocking images to bring about a specific effect in his audience. The farmer whose eyes have been pecked out leaving black sockets in *The Birds*; Marion's smooth wet skin ripped by a knife; Norman Bates' 'sweet old' mother transforming into a grinning death's head. His aim was to shock his audience from a world of comforting modernity into a world of horror where there are no secure footholds. Hence the images of falling in his films – characters hanging from roof tops, cliff edges, falling backwards down steep staircases, about to fall into the vortex or abyss. All of his great films contain images of falling. The Surrealists were also fascinated with the spiral, the vortex. *Vertigo* is specifically about fear of falling – of falling in love, of falling into the grave. The ill-fated heroine wears her hair in a bun shaped like a vortex.

Like the Surrealists Hitchcock has also been criticised for his misogynistic fetishisation of woman's body (Kuenzli 1990). Hitchcock fetishises woman's body in the context of shock; it is woman's body (not man's) as an image that is made to bear the outward signs of dislocation and shock, to act as the film's emotional register for the man and the audience. The scenes of Marion's murder in the shower, one of the most shocking in the history of the cinema; of Madeleine falling twice to her death from the bell tower; of Melanie's attack/rape by the birds – these all focus on woman, not man, as the one who is subjected to the most horrifying ordeals. While it is clear that Hitchcock's heroines are resilient and feisty, their ultimate bravery does not ameliorate the shocking nature of the images that convey their vulnerability and degradation.

The Birds, Hitchcock's most obviously surreal film, is an exercise in shock montage. Based on a short story by Daphne du Maurier, it tells of a small seaside town in which birds, without any explanation (and none is ever given) suddenly turn on the human inhabitants, attacking and killing them. Carl Belz argues that the hallmarks of Surrealist art – 'emotional shock', 'psychological chaos', 'unabashed eroticism' and 'a disturbing "aura" surrounding characters' – are all present in *The Birds* (1972: 145). In particular he explores the way in which Hitchcock takes an ordinary everyday situation ('boy meets girl') and transforms it into an unreal, surreal one. He is struck by the way Hitchcock uses tensions and ambiguities, contradictions and absurd logic to produce 'an encounter with the fantastic' (1972: 148).

Camille Paglia similarly sees *The Birds* as surreal, concentrating more on the surreal quality of the images. In her discussion she draws on a number of classic Surrealist texts and techniques – *Un chien andalou*, Dalí's melting watches, the Dadaesque transformation of everyday objects, the Surrealist use of puns and symbols. Paglia, like Stern, also picks up on the surreal quality of the Hitchcockian image. In her discussion of the sequence where Melanie sails her boat towards Mitch's (Rod Taylor) house she writes: 'A woman in a fur coat with a bird cage in a rowboat: it could be a Surrealist painting by Dalí or Magritte' (1998: 33).

Ken Mogg discusses *The Birds* in the context of Mitch's remark to Melanie about what it is like 'to be on the other end of a gag' – the gag or joke of course is central to

Surrealist art. Mogg, who discusses the libido as 'prankish' in relation to Hitchcock's silent film *Champagne* (1928), argues that the whole of *The Birds* 'pivots' on Mitch's remark 'to be on the other end of a gag' (1999: 163). Similarly, Norman Bates' throwaway line, 'mother's not herself today', signifies a black joke that runs throughout the film. Mother is not herself on any day; she is her son, Norman.

Other surreal contexts in Hitchcock films are: the device of the red flashes which cover the entire screen in *Marnie*; the uncanny images, black humour and sexual disguise of *Psycho*; the hallucinatory dream sequence, the uncanny play on doubling, the conscious exploration of image and representation, the surreal urban landscape (reminiscent of de Chirico – see Gould 1976: 104) in *Vertigo*; the bizarre Mount Rushmore sequence from *North by Northwest* in which the world becomes surreal through the play with size and scale. Hitchcock's fascination with motifs such as eyes and windows – central to Surrealism – is apparent throughout his oeuvre. For instance, *Rear Window*'s (1954) multiple images of windows also recall the Surrealists fascination with windows represented as a frame: Duchamp's *Fresh Window* (1920) and Magritte's many paintings of windows positioned as a frame within a frame – *The Human Condition* (1933), *The Domain of Arnheim* (1949), *Evening Falls* (1964).

Even his carefully constructed public persona (the outlandish publicity photographs, appearances in drag, his signature cartoon, his black, punning humour) invokes a Surrealist mode of being. The jokey presence of his own cartoonish body in his films reminds us of the Surrealists similar play with their own images in photographs and paintings. Think of Dalí's painting in which Mary spanks the baby Jesus while the Surrealists watch from above through an open window. Many of Hitchcock's films share common motifs, artistic aims and aesthetic techniques of the Surrealist movement. His disregard for classic realism; his representation of everything as image; his desire to shock his audience into the dark surreal; his desire to merge dream and reality; his fascination with themes of doubling; *l'amour fou*; perversity; the compulsion to repeat; the uncanny; death; jokes and self-reflexivity – all of these mark Hitchcock out as the cinema's first great popular Surrealist.

David Lynch

David Lynch is too committed to the principles of Surrealism to pitch for true thriller suspense: he'd rather catch its shadow after it's passed.
– Marina Warner (1977: 8)

David Lynch is regarded as the most prominent and successful Surrealist director currently working in American cinema. His films are remarkable for their depiction of disturbing dream-like worlds, macabre characters, hallucinogenic states of mind and explorations of the dark side of the human psyche. Lynch is particularly interested in the horror that lies beneath the seemingly normal surfaces of everyday suburban life. He draws on motifs much beloved of the classic Surrealists: doubles, identity loss, the bizarre and unexpected, doomed lovers, the dream, the uncanny, decay and death. Lynch believes that life does not make sense and that this knowledge makes people uncomfortable. He has an unequalléd ability to create the uncanny and disturbing atmosphere of the dream-world and of psychological states of madness.

Like the early Surrealists Lynch is fascinated by the world of disrupted narrative; hence he feels no obligation to follow events in a linear or logical manner. Events appear to be following a clear narrative trajectory when abruptly Lynch will move in a completely different direction, one that seemingly has no links with what went before. As in the great Surrealist classic *Un chien andalou*, Lynch frequently seems to use the principles of disassociation as a rationale for narrative movement and montage. In this way he creates a sense of dream logic which characterises all of his work. Lynch has been described as 'a Surrealist in the tradition of the great Spanish filmmaker, Luis Buñuel' (Rodley 1997: jacket). David G. Imber sees Lynch as 'the most orthodox proponent of Surrealism working in contemporary cinema' (1999).

His Surrealism is very different from that of Hitchcock's in that he depicts Surrealist states of mind in direct and confronting ways, blurring the boundary between dream and reality, adopting non-linear and narrative forms, presenting the world as weird and incomprehensible and refusing to provide any 'answers' let alone closure to his narrative enigmas. Hitchcock embedded his Surrealist techniques more formally, and unobtrusively, into the *mise-en-scène*. Hitchcock was drawn to the aesthetic qualities of Surrealism as a means of intensifying the emotional states of his characters, and his audience, whereas Lynch's Surrealism represents more a response to what he sees as the bizarre and nonsensical nature of everyday life. Hitchcock uses Surrealism to encourage his audiences to examine their own psychological states whereas Lynch seems more concerned to force the audience into a confrontation with the strange and the irrational.

His films (such as *Eraserhead* (1977), *Blue Velvet* (1986), *Lost Highway* (1997), *Mulholland Dr.* (2001) and *Inland Empire* (2006)) are surreal, not so much because of their power to shock – at which they are very effective – but because of their power to disrupt conventional boundaries between reality and dream, creating their own weird sense of dream logic. One of his most disturbing films, *Blue Velvet*, begins and ends with an image of a bodily organ – not an eye, a favourite Surrealist image – an ear which suggests that everything that happened in between was a dream. (The severed ear, crawling with ants, also recalls the sliced eyeball and ants of *Un chien andalou*.) In the opening sequences, a young man (Karl MacLachlan) discovers a severed ear as he walks along a country lane; this discovery delivers the hero into a dark world of murder, kidnapping and sado-masochism. In the final scene there is a shot in which the camera, having focused in close-up on the hero's own ear as he sleeps, pulls back into a wide shot, suggesting that the events in between belong to a dream-world. The penultimate shot of a mechanical robin sitting jauntily on the window ledge only confirms this suggestion. Lynch's Surrealist vision is most clear in his fascination with the dark side of the dreams and is evident in all of his films.

In *Lost Highway* Lynch explores a nightmare world of identity loss, doubles, demonic possession and alternative realities. The film plays with a dilemma it never resolves: did the male protagonist brutally murder his wife or was he 'swapped' for someone else? In homage to Buñuel's *Cet obscur objet du désir* (*That Obscure Object of Desire*, 1977) Lynch has the same actress (Patricia Arquette) play the twin roles of wife and lover: Buñuel used two different actresses to play the role of the lover. The doubling of the wife/lover character combined with the film's disrupted narrative contribute to the way the film seems to operate according to the logic of dreams.

Mulholland Dr. again creates the bizarre dream-world of identity loss, amnesia, desire and death. It presents a troubling and deeply moving tale of romantic loss. Drawing on the structures of narrative disruption, Lynch presents a classic tale of *l'amour fou*, or fatal love, which was a favourite form of the Surrealists. This time the tale of *l'amour fou* is between two women (Laura Harring and Naomi Watts), two Hollywood actresses, one famous, the other a newcomer to the dream factory. As one attempts to help the other recover her memory, the couple become involved in a whirlpool of betrayal, jealousy and murder. Lynch draws parallels between their doomed love affair and the power of Hollywood to drive the female actor into a destructive and hallucinatory world of self-deception. There are clear references in *Mulholland Dr.* to the classic noir film *Sunset Boulevard* (1950) in that both explore Hollywood as a dream factory and both are narrated by a main protagonist who is dead. *Mulholland Dr.* also explores the possibility of alternate worlds when the heroine, Betty, falls into a mysterious blue box that recalls Buñuel's surreal boxes of *Un chien andalou* and *Belle de jour* (1967). *Mulholland Dr.* is a moody, claustrophobic film about sexual awakening, passion and corruption that recalls the surreal nightmarish quality of *Blue Velvet*. As in all of Lynch's surreal films, including his recent digital video work *Inland Empire*, the boundaries between dream, reality and nightmare merge, creating a disturbing world which is both bizarre and uncanny.

David Cronenberg

> Cronenberg's films have a dream-like quality, an irrational logic which associates them, quite broadly, with a Surrealist tendency to be found in the horror genre at its best.
> – Michael O'Pray (1984: 48–9)

David Cronenberg's horror films explore a Surrealist vision of the body. Whereas Lynch is fascinated by mental states, alternate realities and dream logic, Cronenberg is drawn to the body – its vulnerability, transformations and weird assemblages. Like Lynch, Cronenberg has forged his own vision of Surrealism which is similar to but different from classical Surrealism in a number of important ways. Cronenberg's appropriation of Surrealism excludes the Bretonian domain of the poetic and the marvellous. In Cronenberg the dream-like quality of classic Surrealism is swamped by the abject horror of the nightmare. As with many of the Surrealists (Ernst, Dalí, Lautreamont, Hannah Hoch) Cronenberg explores surreal states of bodily transformation and couplings with other life forms. Lautréamont encapsulated the Surrealists' interest in the beauty of bizarre couplings with his famous statement: 'Beautiful, like the chance meeting of a sewing machine and an umbrella on a dissecting table' (in Gould 1976: 24).

Cronenberg's vision is associated with the motto of the 'New Flesh' which he first explored in *Videodrome* (1983), the film which firmly established Cronenberg's reputation as the creator of a weird, surreal universe solely of his own making. *Videodrome* explores an alternate reality of sex-and-death TV signals, eroticism, sado-masochism and snuff movies. He had touched on a similar theme about expanded consciousness in *Scanners* (1981) in which the main character who has telepathic powers is unable to turn off the sounds of other people's thoughts inside his head. He becomes involved with the 'scanners', other individuals with telepathic powers who are able to take over other minds and destroy them by causing the victim's head to explode. The reference to Magritte's *The Pleasure Principle* (1937) in which a man's head appears to explode with an excess of pleasure is darkly ironic. In *Videodrome*, Cronenberg creates a hallucinogenic world in which the body transforms into a kind of VCR of the flesh and a repository of pornographic imagery. In an uncanny reversal the television set metamorphoses into a living fleshy mass. Disturbing in the extreme, *Videodrome* depicts its main character, Max Renn (James Woods) in an erotic relationship with a huge pair of lips on a television screen while his stomach develops a secret pouch/vagina in which he hides his gun. New Flesh represents a postmodern melding of human and machine although Cronenberg casts his net wider, also exploring the melding of human and insect as in *The Fly* (1986). In both *Scanners* and *Videodrome* – and later in *eXistenZ* (1999) – Cronenberg draws upon the early Surrealists' belief in the supreme power of the imagination, and creates strange worlds in which characters experience the potentially deadly effects of mind expansion and alternate mental states.

In *The Fly* Cronenberg pushes the horror film's fascination with the abject body to new limits. An over-ambitious scientist, Dr Seth Brundle (Jeff Goldblum), accidentally fuses his body with that of a housefly, giving himself strange new powers and a ravenous sexual appetite. Exhilarated, he denounces society's 'fear of the flesh'. 'I've become free, I've been released' he cries out, but his delirium is short-lived. Gradually, as the insect genes begin to dominate and destroy the human, the doctor's body sheds its appendages such as its teeth, fingernails and genitals. In this brave new world of 'Brundleflesh' reproductive organs and sexual desire are rendered obsolete. The film's exploration of the dark side of Surrealism (the uncanny, desire and death) in the end retreat completely from the virtues of 'New Flesh', settling instead for a much more pessimistic view of the possibilities for the free play of the libido and sexual desire.

Cronenberg's films adopt a Surrealist style to explore the dark side of the imagination, the nature of desire and human fears of mutation, metamorphosis and bodily transformation. Based on the William Burroughs' novel of the same name, *The Naked Lunch* (1991) explores the 'New Flesh' in dreamy, hallucinogenic worlds that encapsulate the irrational logic of Surrealism. Peter Weller plays William Lee, a pest exterminator who lives with his wife, Joan (Judy Davis), in a world of drugs and delirium. When Lee accidentally shoots Joan he is unable to prevent a headlong fall into a hallucinogenic world, called Interzone. Interzone is inhabited by a talking asshole typewriter, cockroaches, insects, Mugwumps and a string of sexually ambiguous characters – including Joan in a different role – who also appear to share Lee's hallucinations. Sex scenes are accompanied by fears of mutation and metamorphosis. In classic Surrealist style, it is impossible (even at the film's bizarre ending) to distinguish the dream-world from reality.

In *Crash* Cronenberg looks at the erotic appeal of car accidents. Cronenberg depicts a perverse primal scene in which his protagonists develop a sexual fetish over car crashes and accident victims. They join together in a perverse band, dedicated to re-enacting the road accidents of the famous (James Dean, Jane Mansfield, Albert Camus), they read books on pathology and view test-crash videos. Characters are aroused by the melding of flesh and metal as well as the leather and steel of prosthetic devices. *Crash* created public outrage in the UK and a censorship controversy that would have earned Cronenberg applause from the early Surrealists who delighted in public scandal (see Barker *et al.* 2001). Cronenberg seems to revel in shattering taboos but he is not an iconoclast without a mission. His aims are Surrealist in that his films attempt to expand the viewer's consciousness and awareness of the intimate relationship between mind and body, the influence of one on the other and the bodily transmutations that are possible in the postmodern world of cloning, genetics and the Internet. He places the body in surreal contexts in order to push his argument to its limits.

Cronenberg has inherited Hitchcock's fascination with the abject body but he explores its ramifications in a science fiction/horror context. Many of his images are shocking and focus on the female reproductive system as a source of abject horror which points to a misogynistic point of view in a number of his classic films.[4] The heroine of *Rabid* (1977) grows a penis inside her armpit; the heroine of *The Brood* (1979) gives birth to non-human creatures (they have no navel) from an external sac attached to her body; the heroine of *Dead Ringers* (1988) has a triple uterus; and the lost souls of *Crash* enjoy sex inside the wounds of a (female) accident victim. These images are just as outrageous and shocking as the scenes in *Un chien andalou* where a man watches ants crawl from a hole in his hand and a young girl prods a severed hand along the road with a stick. As the first expressions of the Surrealists' fascination with the surreal body these scenes from *Un chien andalou* shocked and scandalised audiences in the late 1920s. As part of a long tradition of filmic body horror, to which contemporary audiences have become accustomed, Cronenberg's images still have the power to invoke shock and incredility.

The films of Hitchcock, Lynch and Cronenberg reveal that there is no such thing as a uniform style of popular cinematic Surrealism. All three directors have focused on different areas of Surrealist concerns. Hitchcock was particularly interested in themes of *l'amour fou*, abjection, hallucinatory logic, the double, the uncanny. Lynch's cinema is distinguished by a concern with the nature of desire, alternate realities, the logic of the dream-world, death and the double. Cronenberg has developed his own style of Surrealist filmmaking in order to explore the world of dream and hallucination, the abject body, bodily metamorphosis, bizarre couplings, desire and death. The one thing that all share in common is a fascination with the dark side of Surrealism – in particular desire, abjection, the uncanny and death.

Notes

1 Steven Kovács presents a fascinating analysis of their views in his book *From Enchantment to Rage* (1980) in which he explores the Surrealist movement of the 1920s in relation to Surrealist films of that period, particularly *Un chien andalou* (*An Andalusian Dog*, 1929) and *L'Âge d'or* (*The Golden Age*, 1930), Germaine Dulac's *La coquille et le clergyman* (*The Seashell and the Clergyman*, 1928), Man Ray's *Le Retour à la raison* (1923) and *L'Etoile de mer* (1928).

2 Hitchcock himself attended art school as a young man, and owned a significant art collection which included works by a number of modernist and Surrealist artists: Milton Avery, Jean Dubuffet, Raoul Dufy, Paul Klee, Georges Rouault, August Rodin, and Salvador Dalí. Dalí of course designed the dream sequence for Hitchcock's *Spellbound*. Hitchcock once said he found Dalí interesting but his unconscious more so. Hitchcock also greatly admired the work of Magritte, de Chirico and Edward Hopper.

3 For a fascinating discussion of illusion and Surrealist cinema see Michael Gould (1976) *Surrealism and the Cinema*, London: Tantivy Press.

4 For an important discussion of misogyny and Surrealism, see Rudolf Kuenzli's 1990 essay 'Surrealism and Misogyny'.

Mark Schilling

JAPANISING THE DARK SIDE: SURREALISM IN JAPANESE FILM

The Japanese film industry has hardly been reluctant to borrow from abroad. The list begins at the beginning, when the Japanese were importing everything from films to projectors and cameras in the last years of the nineteenth century, continues through the middle years of the twentieth century, when Yasujiro Ozu was applying lessons learned from Ernst Lubitsch, to the present, when producer Chihiro Kameyama studied *Star Wars* (1977) and *Toy Story* (1995) to produce Japan's highest-grossing live-action film, *Odoru daisosasen the movie 2: Rainbow bridge wo fusaseyo!* (*Bayside Shakedown 2*, 2003). But Surrealism, in its original European incarnation, had little visible impact on Japanese films of the period. By contrast, Surrealist theories spread quickly among Japanese artists and writers and had a significant influence on their work, beginning in the 1910s. The one large exception was Teinosuke Kinugasa's *Kurutta ippeji* (*A Page Out of Order*, 1926) a film about a former sailor who becomes a caretaker in a lunatic asylum where his wife is a patient. Kinugasa claimed that the film's fragmented, hallucinatory style was inspired by Robert Weine's *Das kabinett des Doktor Caligari* (*The Cabinet of Dr Caligari*, 1920), Abel Gance's *La Roue* (1923) and an unnamed Universal Bluebird film by Rupert Julian.

James Peterson has suggested other, literary influences, particularly a school of Japanese writers called New Impressionists who were avid followers of European modernists, the Surrealists among them. Be that as it may, Kinugasa, a former Kabuki and Shimpa actor who had played women's roles in early silents, soon reverted to more traditional forms in his films. Others attempted similar experiments – but an experimental film movement was slow to emerge.

By the time Luis Buñuel made *Un chien andalou* (*An Andalusian Dog*, 1929) and *L'Âge d'or* (*The Golden Age*, 1930), Japan's political climate was shifting from the short-lived flirtation with liberal democracy of the Taisho Period (1912–26) toward the militarism that, starting in 1931 with the Manchurian Incident, was to lead Japan into war in Asia. Challenges to authority, Surrealist or not, were becoming more difficult in any medium, but particularly the public one of film, which Japanese officialdom had long regarded as a potential subverter of public order and decency – and regulated accordingly.

In an era when kissing scenes in foreign films were routinely scissored and Lewis Milestone's *All Quiet On the Western Front* (1930) was butchered (300 cuts, or nearly 20 per cent of its running time) for its offences against the martial spirit, a Japanese film attempting to replicate the cinematic outrages of a Dalí or Buñuel would have never survived the first screening by the censors. (Whether its maker would have survived his first interrogation by the police is another matter.)

Not all Japanese filmmakers marched to the militarists' drumbeat, but their resistance took other forms, from the *keiko-eiga* or 'tendency films' of the late 1920s and early 1930s that drew attention to social conditions, to the *bungei-eiga* or 'literary films' that used the cover of classic literature to question the status quo.

Meanwhile, Japanese critics such as Tai Kanbara and Sakutaro Hagiwara were deriding literary Surrealists as dilettantes playing superficial aesthetic games while ignoring dark political realities. For Hagiwara, writing in 1931, Japanese Surrealism was little more than 'rhetoric exaggerated through cleverness' that had all the content of advertising copy (Sas 2001: 45).

Whether or not Japanese Surrealists 'mistranslated' the rebellious spirit of their European models, as their critics insisted, their work did not much resonate with Japanese filmmakers, even of the dilettantish or aesthetically adventurous sort. Then, as the militarist grip on power tightened and the war spread beyond China, the film industry, resisters included, had to fall in line – or at least give the appearance of doing so – with films that were 'authentically' Japanese, if not outright propaganda.

The post-war period brought a new freedom to Japanese filmmakers, albeit under the watchful eye of Occupation censors, who frowned on anything hinting at 'feudal' (that is, wartime) values or attitudes. Also, for the first time in nearly a decade Japanese audiences had access to films from former enemies and their allies, including Jean Cocteau's *La Belle et la bête* (*Beauty and the Beast*, 1946), a signature Surrealist film that was to become a much-revived classic.

The appetite for entertainment – pent up for years by wartime restrictions and privations – was huge and the films were one of the few forms the masses could afford. Despite strikes and other disruptions, the Japanese film industry grew into the second largest in the world in the decade and a half following the end of the war. In 1952, the first year for which Eiren (the Motion Picture Producers Association of Japan) began compiling figures, the industry released 278 domestic films on 4,109 screens. By 1960 these numbers had risen to 547 and 7,457, respectively – the former an all-time high.

Opportunities for filmmakers abounded as long as they wanted to work for the studios, which by the mid-1950s included Toho, Shin Toho, Shochiku, Toei, Nikkatsu and Daiei. The number of independent productions was tiny: five in 1952, two in 1960. This does not count the large numbers of instructional, industrial and other films made for non-theatrical distribution, but few filmmakers of any kind were making feature films outside the industry structure. Among them was Kaneto Shindo, a director and scriptwriter who co-founded Kindai Eiga Kyokai, postwar Japan's first independent production company, in 1951, and director Tadashi Imai, who released Japan's first independently produced film, *Dokkoi ikiteru* (*And Yet We Live*), under the Kindai banner that same year. Both, however, were leftist filmmakers more inspired by the Italian neorealists than Cocteau.

At the major studios realism prevailed at the box office, with Hollywood codes a strong, if not always dominant, influence. (More Japanese still flocked to samurai swashbucklers than to westerns.) Even master directors given latitude to depart from studio formulas tended to contextualise their innovations in ways the mass audience could understand and accept. In Kenji Mizoguchi's *Ugetsu monogatari* (*Tales of Ugetsu*, 1950) the potter hero may have been lured into the world of the dead, but Mizoguchi's view of that world was closer in spirit to familiar *kaidan* (Japanese ghost stories) than Cocteau-esque visions of the supernatural.

Meanwhile, freed from wartime controls, Japanese painters, poets, dancers and playwrights produced modernist works in abundance. Among them were Tatsumi Hijikata (1928–86), Min Tanaka and Kazuo Ono, whose Ankoku Butoh school of dance was not only inspired by the theories and practices of European Surrealism, but used its texts as source material. At the same time, Butoh was unlike much Western modern dance in its low postures, slow movements and focus on the Stygian depths of the unconscious, while the pronouncements of its founders reflected native philosophies as well as Western ideas.

Filmmakers influenced by Surrealism and other modernist currents also began to emerge in mid-decade, though the real flowering of the experimental film movement came, together with so many other changes in Japanese arts and society, in the 1960s. Like the founders of Butoh, these filmmakers were not just aping foreign models, but stirring them into a Japanese pot, with ingredients derived from sources both ancient and contemporary, personal and social.

Among the early leaders of this movement was Donald Richie, an American-born writer and critic who had first come to Japan in 1947 and started making experimental films while a student in New York as a self-proclaimed disciple of Buñuel, Cocteau and Maya Deren. Richie transgressed in approved Surrealist style in such films as *Wargames* (1962) (animal sacrifice by children), *Boy With Cat* (1966) (masturbation) and *Dead Youth* (1967) (masturbation again, this time in front of a tombstone), *Five Philosophical Fables* (1967) (with a blackly humorous look at cannibalism) and *Cybelle* (1968) (an all-nude gangbang set to the music of the baroque).

The last film caused a disturbance, not in Japan, where it was shown only once, but in Germany, where, as Richie later reminisced, 'everybody was saying it was about the slaughter at Auschwitz – all those naked bleeding bodies. I thought it was a feminist statement: up with the girls' (in Schilling 2001). Another influential experimentalist was Shuji Terayama (1935–83), who was at various times a poet prodigy, amateur boxer, horse-racing aficionado, scriptwriter, drama troupe leader and, starting in 1960 with the 16mm short *Catology*, film director. Terayama was also a co-founder, in 1961, of Art Theatre Guild (ATG), a company that, for the next quarter of a century, underwrote and screened films by independent filmmakers including Shohei Imamura, Nagisa Oshima and Masahiro Shinoda.

Terayama's own filmmaking career, however, did not truly take off until *Tomato kecchappu kôtei* (*Emperor Tomato Ketchup*, 1970), a notorious 16mm short about an imaginary empire of children, with scenes of simulated child/adult sex. His first 35mm feature, *Sho o suteyo machi e deyou* (*Throw Away Your Books, Rally in the Streets*, 1971), was a coming-of-age film about a youth living with his eccentric family (dad is a dissolute small-time criminal; grandma, a kleptomaniac; sister, a rabbit lover) in a ramshackle flat. The hero has a mortifying first-time sexual encounter with a blowsy prostitute who has serviced his entire soccer team. Later his sister is raped in the team locker room, while he stands helplessly by. He fantasises about flying away from his woes, but is brought back to earth – and his nightmare existence – again and again.

There is little in the way of plot, but much energy, invention and strangeness in the individual images, which range from nostalgic glances at childhood to hand-held-camera reels through Tokyo streets, with graffiti and J. A. Seazer's potpourri of a score (protest songs mixed with nursery rhymes) commenting sardonically on the action. The film exemplified not only Terayama's autobiographical preoccupations, but the era's excesses and experiments, now at the point of exhaustion. A druggie movie, in other words, but one reminiscent of a nasty, jagged come down.

More narratively coherent – it was based on the Oedipus legend – if bolder in its taboo-shattering examination of gay sex, love and death in 1960s Tokyo was Toshio Matsumoto's *Bara no soretsu* (*Funeral Parade of Roses*, 1969). The first explicitly gay film made in Japan, *Bara no soretsu* was also innovative in its treatment, a melange of the semi-documentary and the surreal. Set in a transvestite bar and revolving around the rivalry between a pretty young hostess and the bar's mama-san for the affections of the bar's studly manager, the film swings between winking, if knowing, glimpses of gay life, from shopping exhibitions to pot parties, to flashes of hallucination and memory, acts of lust and violence.

Although Matsumoto, like Terayama, challenged conventional definitions of cinematic reality in the best surreal manner, both finally had little faith in the era's rebellions against bourgeois politics and culture. But whereas Terayama's title, *Sho o suteyo machi e deyou*, is ironic – street protests had long since peaked by the time of the film's release – Matsumoto's, *Bara no soretsu*, is more straightforward. Instead of being satisfied with campy celebration, the film takes a darker, more classically stoic turn: beauty and love are fleeting, it says – but tragedy is ever with us, even if the hero ends up sleeping with his father instead of, like Oedipus, his mother.

Toward the end of the 1960s the social and political currents that had driven the experimental film movement subsided and the audience began to drift away. 'The people who had been looking at my films all started working for Parco,' Richie commented (in Schilling 2001). He stopped making experimental films in 1968. Meanwhile, the mainstream industry, under severe pressure from the rising medium of television, searched frantically for new formulas during the decade. One that proved successful, starting in 1963 with Tadashi Sawashima's *Jinsei Gekijo: Hishakaku* (*Theatre of Life: Hishakaku*), was the so-called *ninkyo eiga*, which was the gang picture set in the post-feudal to prewar past, using *giri-ninjo* story lines (that is, a gangster hero battles evil rivals out of an obligation to a good-but-weak boss) and all-against-one climaxes common to old samurai swashbucklers.

The first director to become well-known abroad for his films in this sub-genre, Seijun Suzuki, was the also the one to most thoroughly subvert it. His style was a mix of Kabuki theatrics, Taisho-era flamboyance, 1960s go-go excess and his own freewheeling personality. His work for the Nikkatsu studio, even more than that of his colleagues in the experimental scene, challenged industry conventions and social norms, including commonly accepted definitions of sanity.

His ultimate cinematic rejection of genre expectations was *Koroshi no rakuin* (*Branded to Kill*, 1967), a film that even his fans found hard to follow and the Nikkatsu president famously found incomprehensible. Suzuki lost his job as a Nikkatsu contract director and did not make another feature for nearly a decade. Beginning with *Tsigoineruwaizen* (also known as *Zigeunerweisen* or *Gypsy Ways*) in 1980, he filmed what came to be known as his 'Taisho' trilogy – independent films set in his favorite era, between the borders of fantasy and reality, life and death.

Suzuki is tight-lipped about his Nikkatsu experiments. ('I didn't want people to say I was making only the same thing', was his explanation; in Schilling 2003a: 101). They began, however, as attempts to add visual or comic flair to what would have otherwise been standard genre product. In *Tokyo nagaremono* (*Tokyo Drifter*, 1966), Tetsuya Watari's gangster hero whistles the title tune throughout. This in itself was not unusual – the heroes of Nikkatsu action films often broke into song to better sell records. But after being left for dead in a barroom brawl – a parody of similar dust-ups seen in countless westerns – he opens his eyes and starts whistling. The effect, at once cool and absurd, is quintessentially Suzuki.

It was in *Koroshi no rakuin*, however, that Suzuki finally let out all the Surrealist stops, plunging his hitman hero, Hanada (Jo Shishido) into a nightmare of omnipresent danger from which he never awakens. Hired by a sultry half-Japanese, half-Indian woman with a death wish (symbolised by the dead bird hanging from the rearview mirror of her sports car), he is about to pull the trigger when a butterfly lands on his rifle scope, making him botch the shot and kill the wrong person.

He spends much the rest of the film alternately pursuing his employer, with whom he has become hopelessly infatuated, and fending off mysterious forces bent on killing him for his mistake. His chief nemesis, however, is Number One (Koji Nambara), the head of the hitman hierarchy he had once hoped to climb. They finally meet – and handcuff themselves together in a bizarre test of wills. The scenes of these two answering the door, sitting down in a restaurant and going to the men's room in lockstep go beyond genre parody into a realm in which all bets are off and all rules, cinematic and otherwise, cease to apply.

There is also an undercurrent of menace that Hanada, for all his macho posturing, cannot ignore or abide. Fear eats away at him, until he would rather throw himself suicidally at its source than live with it. Suzuki's mix of black humour and dread would later find its echo in the work of David Lynch and Jim Jarmusch, including the homage to assassination by water pipe in *Koroshi no rakuin* in the latter's *Ghost Dog: The Way of the Samurai* (1999).

One of Suzuki's contemporaries, Teruo Ishii, was taking his films in a similarly surreal direction at the rival Toei studio – but being rewarded instead of punished for it. Born in 1924 in Tokyo, Ishii had made everything from space monster movies (the Super Giants series) to sophisticated caper movies (most notably the *Line* series for Shin Toho) before finally finding his niche as a director of contemporary gang films for Toei, beginning with the 1961 hit *Hana to arashi to gang* (*Flower and Storm and Gang*).

Starting in 1968 Ishii made a series of eight *ero-guro* (a Japanese-English term meaning 'erotic and grotesque') films, most of which purported to 'educate' audiences on the sex and torture practices of the feudal era, using an omnibus format. Unlike Suzuki, Ishii did not have to sneak his fascination with the flamboyant and bizarre into his films – it helped to sell their main product: sex. Fortunately for Ishii, studio boss Shigeru Okada not only approved, but had green-lighted the series in the first place.

The oddest entry, by any standard, was *Edogawa rampo zenshu: kyofu kikei ningen* (*Horror of a Deformed Man*, 1969). Based on stories by Edogawa Ranpo (Taro Hirai, 1894–1965) – who borrowed his name and aesthetics from Edgar Allan Poe – the film is occasionally revived in Japan. It is not, however, available on video – distributor Toei does not want to deal with the protests that would surely greet its appearances on the shelves. 'Certain groups object to its depiction of disabled people,' explained one Toei executive (in Schilling 2003a: 112). The film, however, is less the Japanese companion to Tod Browning's *Freaks* (1932) than Ishii's interpretation of Edogawa's eccentric vision, aided by Butoh founder Tatsumi Hijikata, creating in his first screen role the most brilliantly 'deformed' of the film's creatures.

It begins as an offbeat murder mystery. Hirosuke (Teruo Yoshida), a medical student working at a mental hospital, learns that Hatsuyo (Teruko Yumi), a girl circus performer of his acquaintance, has been killed. Determined to find the murderer, he takes a train to her home in the Hokuriku region, by the Sea of Japan. On the way he learns about another death, this time of a close friend. Meanwhile, the friend's father, Saigoro Komoda (Hijikata), has left for an uninhabited island, supposedly to hide the shame of his webbed fingers. Posing as the friend, Hirosuke enters the Komoda house. Oddly, Genzaburo's wife, daughter and steward all accept him as the real thing. Then the wife is killed and Hirosuke escapes with the daughter and servants to the island. At the beach they are met by Saigoro, who leads them into a seemingly endless cave. There they encounter Hideko (Teruko Yumi, in a double role), a creature who looks uncannily like the dead wife, but is no longer quite human. This, they soon learn to their horror, is only one of many such revelations.

With his scraggly beard, long tangled hair and flowing robe, Hijikata as Saigoro looks like the mad prophet of an unholy religion. Moving across the rocks of his island kingdom with an angular grace and crab-like resolve, he obscures the divide between the real and the unreal, the human and inhuman. He not only knows more than he is telling, but more than we want to imagine.

Together Hijikata and Ishii created a new, domestic definition of Surrealism, that accepted its origin in popular literature and its setting in exploitation cinema, while transcending both. The film's world may have been transported directly from the stage – with costumes looking like costumes, props like props – but its inhabitants were hostile to humanity the way the island was itself, with its wildness, harshness and dark secret places.

In the mid-1970s the audience for Ishii's *ero-guro* entertainments began to fade and in 1979 he stopped making feature films altogether. He did not return to the screen until 1993 with *Tsuge yoshiharu world: gensenkan shujin* (*Gensenkan Inn*), an omnibus film based on the manga of Yoshiharu Tsuge. Japan's nearest equivalent to Robert Crumb, Tsuge drew semi-autobiographical comics about lonely young men exploring obscure corners of Japan where everyday reality has fled – or never existed in the first place. The hero of the film's title segment stays at a countryside inn managed by the sexually voracious widow of a man the village crones contend is his doppelgänger. He falls under her spell and is about to start a new life as the inn's master – when the doppelgänger returns.

Both Suzuki and Ishii responded to the upheavals of their youth – militarism, war and Westernisation among them – by escaping into a freer, more human-centred past (the Taisho era for Suzuki, the Edo for Ishii) while reordering the present to their own playful, anarchic specifications. Their Surrealism was less borrowed from foreign sources than derived from native roots and personal obsessions.

The generation of directors who came up in the 1980s and 1990s found their inspiration less from Edo-era ancestors, more in the postwar popular culture, particularly the anime (animation) and manga that made the surreal familiarly Japanese. Their concerns tended to be more personal than social, while their films often catered more to narrow segments, including foreign cultists, than the mass audience.

Among the avatars of this Baby Boomer cohort was Shinya Tsukamoto. Born in 1960 in Tokyo and raised in a middle-class family (his father was a designer for an advertising agency, his mother a housewife), Tsukamoto was a boyhood fan of the television series *Urutora Q* (*Ultra-Q*) and began making his own Super-8 movies at the age of 14. Graduating from the Fine Arts Department of Nihon University, he worked for a production house making TV commercials. In 1985 he left to start his own theatre troupe, Phantom Theatre. He also made experimental films and in 1989 released his first feature, *Tetsuo* (*Tetsuo: The Iron Man*). Shot in black-and-white and set to a punk metal score by Chu Ishikawa, *Tetsuo* was a sustained assault on the senses that may have been inspired by the work of David Lynch (*Eraserhead*) and David Cronenberg (*The Fly*) but exceeded both in its extremity of vision. A metal fetishist, played by

Tsukamoto himself, has an insane desire to transform himself into machinery, amidst a bleak, chaotic industrial landscape. Botching an 'operation' to insert a metal rod in his leg, he runs into the street – and is hit by a passing car. The driver (Tomoro Taguchi) becomes 'infected' by the metal virus and watches with horror as metal extrudes through his cheeks and his penis becomes a whirling, menacing drill. He has violent sex with his girlfriend in a manic apotheosis, as the last vestiges of his flesh-and-blood humanity fall away. Then, his transformation into a moving junk pile complete, he fights a duel with the fetishist, now an iron man himself.

Unlike an earlier generation of Japanese Surrealists, who at least genuflected towards genre convention and audience expectations while committing their outrages, Tsukamoto seemed to be wrestling with inner demons, in a style that bore the same relation to traditional Japanese film aesthetics that a jackhammer does to a wind chime. ('I don't like the decorative and the artificially embellished ... Instead I find beauty in things that are made for a purpose, like steel pipes' he later wrote; 2003: 172). The film's aggressive, almost autistic strangeness divided audiences into loathers and lovers – the latter quickly elevating Tsukamoto to international cult status. (Even today, he is more feted abroad than in Japan.) Tsukamoto continued to explore the outer limits of violence in *Tetsuo II: Body Hammer* (1992) and subsequent films, with better technical tools and more narrative coherence, but without surpassing the raw shock of *Tetsuo*.

Equally extreme, but in a quite different context, was Takashi Miike, who was born the same year as Tsukamoto, but in a working-class Osaka neighbourhood. As a teenager Miike's main interests were racing motorbikes, playing pachinko and listening to rock music – studying was far down on the list. After high school, he applied to Shohei Imamura's film school in Yokohama, now called the Japan Academy of Moving Images, more out of a desire to escape real work than any serious interest in filmmaking. After sliding through his film education while barely showing his face in the classroom, Miike spent nearly a decade crewing for television dramas, while working on the occasional feature film, including Imamura's *Zegen* (1987) and *Kuroi ame* (*Black Rain*, 1989).

In the early 1990s the demand for straight-to-video films, called 'original videos' or OV in Japanese, exploded, giving Miike his first opportunity to direct, with the OV actioner *Toppuu! Minipato tai – Aikyacchi Jankushon* (*Eyecatch Junction*, 1991). Over the next decade and a half, Miike ground out more than fifty films, mainly set in the Japanese and Asian underworld. Much of his work trafficked in the perverse, depraved and borderline psychotic for the amusement of bored men living alone in rented rooms, but it also had a crazed energy, untamed invention and bad-boy black humour. Where Tsukamoto's visual and aural assaults often left audiences feeling battered (or abused), Miike's plunges into prop blood and gore were more likely to leave the more delicately minded staring at the screen stony-eyed with disgust (or heading for the nearest exit). Also, where Tsukamoto meticulously integrated various elements into a unified, if unrelentingly violent, whole, Miike was more likely to suddenly plunge from hyper semi-comic action into scenes of grotesque horror. One often-quoted example is the opening sequence of *Dead or Alive: Hanzaisha* (*Dead or Alive*, 1999) that hurls through a tour of sex and violence in Shinjuku's Kabukicho District to a pounding rock score, ending with two gangsters shooting up a Chinese restaurant. One patron, who has been shown gobbling noodles, is hit in the back, causing the contents of his full stomach to explode – and spray over the floor in a white stringy fan. The detective hero then enters, picks up a noodle with a pair of chopsticks and carefully examines it, as though preparing to bite. Does one laugh at the visual punchline – or stifle the urge to retch? Either way, the film soon settles into a standard thriller groove – only to rev up again at the end with a showdown between the hero and his gangster nemesis that resembles a worlds-colliding Dragonball cartoon.

Miike's most sustained attempt to create an alternative universe was *Koroshiya Ichi* (*Ichi the Killer*, 2001). Based on a comic by Hideo Yamamoto, the film depicts the adventures of a wimpy coffee-shop waiter (Nao Omori) who is transformed by a Svengali-like gangster (Shinya Tsukamoto) into a deadly fighting machine. Called Ichi, he slices his victims from stem to stern with a blade concealed in his boot. He cries as he rages and climaxes as he kills. After a Shinjuku gang boss and his girlfriend are spattered from floor to ceiling and disappeared by a gangster clean-up crew, the boss's lieutenant, Kakihara (Tadanobu Asano), goes on the hunt for the perpetrators. A violent psychotic whose mouth splits into a horrific rictus when he loosens the pins that hold its corners, Kakihara conducts his search with an eerie calm, punctuated by eruptions of fiendish cruelty. In one memorable scene he has a rival gangster – whom he suspects of involvement in his boss's disappearance – strung up with meat hooks, like a flying bat, and doused with boiling oil. Incredibly, the gangster survives, but Kakihara's real showdown is with Ichi.

Though utterly fantastic, and thus faithful to its manga source, *Koroshiya Ichi* is not dream-like. Instead its surrealism derives from the psychology of its characters, whose unspeakable acts point to their twisted inner selves. For all their violence, Kakihara is a frustrated masochist in search of the ultimate sadist, while Ichi is a lost child, wandering in a hell house of implanted memories.

In the work of Tsukamoto and Miike, as well as others of their generation, the surreal has few direct links with Europe modernism and traditional Japanese culture, both high and low. Instead, it derives energy and inspiration from not only postwar pop culture, but the psychodrama of adolescence, in which the boundaries between fantasy and reality, self and others are unstable and shifting, in which childish play alternates with existential terror.

Graeme Harper

EMOBILISM AND NEW 'FILM': SURREALISM IN THE POST-DIGITAL AGE

The Cinema of Complexity

It is now at least two decades since we entered the era of the Cinema of Complexity, yet few have concertedly considered its nature. The Cinema of Complexity, a term coined in 2004,[1] describes the condition of film in the late twentieth and early twenty-first centuries in which the form itself is no longer film, as it was once understood, but a complex interaction of no longer mechanical production techniques and their attendant human readings and responses. These were initiated by new technologies, but doubly supported by personal, cultural and societal shifts that contributed to the end of cinema as it was once understood and saw, in the period from the late 1970s to the present, the growth of a new form of 'film' (though, because of these shifts, this word itself now requires replacing).

As with Surrealism, the Cinema of Complexity is both a physical manifestation – not least an aesthetic one – and a reaction to societal change, acknowledging the role of the individual, and highlighting political, economic and social change essentially on the platform of changes in human understanding of our physical and psychic space. In essence, the Cinema of Complexity owes its foundation to a shift from mechanical to electronic media production and reproduction. However, it would not have developed had changes not occurred in both the receptive capabilities and the knowledgeability of individuals and social groups. The same is true of the tenets of Surrealism.

Changes in receptive capabilities and knowledgeability reflect changes in the material environment, changes in structures which act holistically, not least in economic and political terms, and yet these also impact on the makers and viewers of film in quite individual ways. For example, changes in copyright regulations in relation to technologies like DVD and internet music downloading have undoubtedly impacted on our daily lives, though not necessarily in one, holistic block. Changes in global attitudes to the outsourcing of the industrial needs of 'developed' countries' media industries to 'underdeveloped' countries have impacted likewise.

Empowered by the growth of a relatively media-literate audience (compared to early mass media audiences whose media knowledge-base was narrow) the Cinema of Complexity is a product of similar discourse of futurism that drove Surrealism's initial iteration, and contains within it similar pointers to the ways in which film text and film audience form a relationship, and both consciously and unconsciously build upon it.

The interpretative skills of today's film audiences are certainly not those that originally helped to determine the nature and style of film as it was understood before, and at, the birth of Surrealism. Distinctively, they find voice in a particular kind of non-linear dynamics. The arrival of the internet is often quoted as determining such forms of nodal thinking, thinking unbound by measured unitary movement. True indeed, the internet offers a 'webbed' sense of connectivity and interconnectivity (what is sometimes called, in computer programming, 'global optimisation'). However, the web is not the sole reason for the arrival of the Cinema of Complexity, much as machine culture of the First World War was not the sole reason for the birth of the Surrealist movement – though in both cases these things are related. Simply put, for more than two decades now we have been engaging in a change from analogism, through into a period of digitalism and now, most importantly here, to post-digitalism.

Post-digitalism, a condition in which *emobility* is at the fore, draws its discourse and its modes from a sense of space and time not connected with a location or with scientific time,[2] as it was once usefully called. Indeed, an analogous sense of such *emobilism* is the obvious one brought about by the use of mobile handset technology; if not, perhaps, by its national and regional service providers, certainly by its technical intentions.

The *emobile* is neither always static nor always moving, neither our inner nor our outer sense of place (that is, it is not based entirely on the physical and, as such, is detached from the solar or the sidereal, which require fixed points of reference), neither the real around us nor the virtual that is transmitted to us as simulated or simply transported reality. Our new post-digital sense of *emobility* – and it is no mistake that the word sounds like 'immobility' because one of the keys here is that even a thing that appears to be immobile is moving through time – is driven by progress toward the resolution of contradictions between scientific time and what Henri Bergson called 'pure time', lived time. In addition, it is driven by the ways in which our contemporary 'new media' technologies have utilised the moving visual and the enhanced aural to provide revolutionary challenges to our perceived sense of the world, both metonymically and metaphorically.

Here, thinking analogously, it is very easy to be reminded of the foundations of the Surrealist movement. As André Breton wrote in 1924, in the *Manifeste du surréalisme*:

> I believe in the future resolution of the these two states, in appearance so contradictory, which are dream and reality, in a kind of absolute reality, *surreality*, one might

call it ... pure psychic automatism, by which an attempt is made to express, either verbally, in writing or in any other manner, the true functioning of thought. The dictation of thought, in the absence of all control by reason, excluding any aesthetic or moral preoccupation. (In Nadeau 1968: 96)

And Breton, again, in the *Second Manifesto* (1930):

... mental vantage-point (*point de l'esprit*) from which life and death, the real and the imaginary, past and future, communicable and incommunicable, high and low, will no longer be perceived as contradictions. (In Nadeau 1968: 22)

The Cinema of Complexity, likewise, is not based simply on changing our points of reference within what might be called, paradoxically, a fixed sense of the movie (this being not unlike our fixed sense of time based on sidereal or solar calculations). Rather, the Cinema of Complexity is one element of the revolutionary change that is *emobilism*, begun in the late 1970s and linked indeed to an evolving new *esprit*.

The technologies that have driven post-digital *emobility* in our early twenty-first century, like the technologies that drove the foundational concepts of the early twentieth century (such as the X-ray machine, the telephone, the aeroplane, the motor vehicle) are highly pragmatic, functional and technically progressive. And yet, it has not widely been discussed that what they achieve in practical terms is matched, if not exceeded, by what they achieve in terms in altering our modes of consciousness.

So, for example, in 1895 the discovery of X-radiation by German physicist Wilhelm Conrad Roentgen formed the basis of a machine that would not only provide for breakthroughs in medical science but would change our perception of human shape, of the relationship between inner self and outer self, even of such psychology or religious notions as 'the mind' and 'the soul'. That is, if you could see inside the human being, where, in there, was the soul? X-ray, as novelists James Joyce and Thomas Mann quickly showed, in *Ulysses* (1922) and *The Magic Mountain* (1924) respectively, altered our perception of inner and outer, and began a process of dissolving previously held notions about the separation of the two. Similarly, the aeroplane, along with its conceptual stable-mate the rocket, not only changed the way we perceive distance but also changed our concept of size and, ultimately, impacted upon such long-held notions as those of 'place', 'home', 'nation' and even 'our world'. While the latter might seem a mighty claim, it only takes a brief comparison of the length of the journey from London to Sydney in the early twentieth century (around 45 days), by ship, with that from London to Sydney in the early twenty-first century (around 22 hours), by plane, to recognise that a sense of the world had to change in order to incorporate new ideas about travel, distance, time-taken, and even our psychological and physical states on arrival.

We can see the interaction between the psychological and the physical in the early twentieth century in relation to Surrealism itself. Emerging from Dada, Surrealism embraced the work of Freud, the psychoanalytical, not least in its general concern with the unconscious, and not inconsequentially through André Breton's specific personal interest in the severe mental breakdown seen in shellshocked patients in the First World War, and thus also in Freud's work on the machinations of the human mind. The interior vision, that sense of the self and of the world that seemed unreachable was now, through the technology of the X-ray and the techniques of psychoanalysis, approachable. All this became primary material for Breton's *First Manifesto of Surrealism*, for *Littérature* (1919–24) and for the journal that replaced it, *La Révolution Surréaliste* (*The Surrealist Revolution*), 1924–30.

And yet, such a focus on a central sense of Surrealism's *First Manifesto* and its early journals gives the impression that Surrealism was a united movement and, patently, this was not the case. It is true to say that most people associate it with the visual arts and here, between Ernst's mythical constructions and Dalí's hyper-realism, between Magritte's metaphors and Duchamp's irreverence, enough variation existed to confirm that an interest in Freud and a backdrop of the art of de Chirico did not unite all. Considering further that 'Surrealism began among poets' (Brandon 1999: 3), the term, first used by writer Guillaume Apollinaire in 1917 to describe a production of Jean Cocteau's ballet *Parade*, never did lend itself to being firm glue.

By the end of the 1920s, when the Georges Bataille-edited periodical *Documents* made more of the base instincts of human kind than of the magical aspects of dream, it was no surprise that Breton, attacking Bataille, produced the *Second Manifesto* and the journal *Le Surréalisme au Service de la Révolution* (*Surrealism at the Service of the Revolution*, 1930), which sought to readdress Bataille's variance from the official Surrealist line. Ultimately, however, even such an advocate as Breton was unable to accomplish the difficult trick of bringing together revolutionary arms, the tenets of Communism and the emotional and dispositional notions linked to psychoanalysis. Before the mid-1930s he and several other Surrealists had been expelled from the Communist Party.

What this relates is not merely a historic backdrop to the emergence of a new discussion on Surrealism here three-quarters of a century later, and the complex social, economic and political mix that surrounds a technological revolution that was digitalism. It also relates back to what Surrealism always considered it was attempting, and how the psychological and the agential interact with holistic changes in the physical world.

With the arrival of digital media technologies – many of them quickly found somewhere in the production and reception of film – it was inevitable that the cinema, as it had been from the last years of the twentieth century, would change, as would its reception. Could it be that, in terms of the intentions, feelings, meanings and, ultimately, expressions of this change, new Surrealist notions have emerged, notions perhaps closer to the original Surrealist worldview than even those attempted by the writers and artists of the early twentieth century?

Digital media technology has been the basis of a shift in individual and group attitudes to film and has, in a key sense, created the Cinema of Complexity. Beyond the

Internet, three digitally-based technologies might be taken as indicative of this shift and its ongoing results. These are: micro or 'home' computers, Compact Discs (CDs and CD-ROM), and Digital Versatile Discs (DVD and DVD-ROM).

Interlude: *échantillon surréaliste*

Before proceeding, a case must be made, firstly, for the approach taken to the addressing of digital surrealism, or *post*-digital surrealism as the case happens to be. This approach is synthetic, the result of a synthesis of analyses not founded solely in textual interpretation, or cultural analysis, or behavioural psychology; not solely in consideration of action, consciousness, or social structures, but in transcending the discursive boundaries of all these approaches in order to fill in the gaps in each approach.

A brief analytical interlude provides evidence of why this approach best avoids the fetishisation of appearance over our need to grasp the *real* relations that lie beneath appearance.

Though digitalism, much like analogism, has not alone provided change in filmic terms it has, as noted, required and informed changes in receptive capabilities and knowledgeability. The programme from the contemporary BBC website, *Film Network*, 'designed to showcase new British film talent by screening films and profiling the people who made them' provides ample evidence of what is meant here. The website www.bbc.co.uk/dna/filmnetwork currently includes the following digital films:

Sweet, by Alex Tanner:
> Two bored office workers have found a satisfying way to get themselves through the working day. However, their routine is disrupted with the arrival of a new employee and when these indulgences get out of hand their true feelings are finally revealed.

Baby Dogs, by Dave Anderson:
> A cut-out photo animation depicting what your dog would be talking about if he was down the local with his mates.

Brief Encounters, by Alison Edgar:
> A woman searches for her ideal partner in just fifteen seconds.

By the time reader logs onto this site these films will either no longer be posted there, or they will be archived in some other part of it. This, indeed, is the result of a certain method of delivery of these films to their audience and that delivery could indeed be called digital. So these are films made on digital technology and delivered on digital technology. However, they share a place on this website with films made not necessarily on digital technology, but delivered via digital means. This does not make them discernibly different; though as films made *in time*, they will be informed by differences brought about by today's digital technology. Similarly, were we to examine films made by analogue means or even, historically, before what we could identify as the impact of digital technologies their similarities to, and differences from, digitally produced films would not confirm or deny an analytical position in relation to them, though they would be informed by analogism.

Thus, to approach digitalism or post-digitalism as if it, *in itself*, produces a new mode of aesthetics, new forms of narrative, new themes and new filmic representations is naïve. What is needed is a synthetic analysis of the relationship between technological change, society as a whole and the individual. The film text, then, can be considered both a reflection of and a product of its environment.

Three digital technologies

Inaccessible names such as the Scelbi-8H Mini-Computer, the Altair 8800 and the IBM 5100; true domestic computing did not properly arrive until 1977 with the domestically named Apple Macintosh Apple II range of microcomputers. These had been preceded by quite a variety of mainly 'home-build' kit computers – with inaccessible names. While the names might seem insignificant the process of naming, and of adapting to new ways of describing what was to become a familiar home appliance, was part of our familiarisation with computer technology. In effect, these new media were connected not simply by their physical forms, nor merely by the act of using them, but by the often random thoughts of those first experiencing digital media's domestication. How like Breton's definition of Surrealism does this sound? Breton writes:

> Surrealism. *n.masc.* pure psychic automatism, by which an attempt is made to express, either verbally, in writing or in any other manner, the true functioning of thought. The dictation of thought, in the absence of all control by reason, excluding any aesthetic or moral preoccupation. (In Nadeau 1968: 97)

Not entirely incidentally, it was a 13-year-old girl who gave her father the name for the Altair 8800, finding it in an episode of the TV show *Star Trek* (1966–69). The story of the initial impact of digitalism is the story of exactly this kind of media convergence, the informing and interacting of one media form and another, and much of this being done at the point of individual human agency.

The Apple II brought computing fully to the layperson's personal space. It was the first domestic computer with colour graphics therefore referencing consumer sensory expectation born out of *colour* television, *colour* film, *colour* photography. It had expansion slots that made it appear as a hub of digitally-driven flexibility; the digital seemed open to your every-person needs. Its floppy disk and audio cassette systems allowed data retrieval and promoted tactility. This was not a hard-hearted mechanism, it wanted to assist you!

The Apple II was not only a technological innovation, it combined something that conceptually made of it a contradiction: it was both a potential work machine and an advanced device for play; neither a typewriter nor an arcade game but, in some way, both. It was not so¹ ly for the serious pragmatist or the jovial hedonist but, it made clear, it could be for both. Based in the domestic space it was, paradoxically, something that seemed to arrive from the science lab. Perhaps it is simplest to recall here Tristan Tzara writing in the *Dada Manifesto 1918*: 'I'm writing this manifesto to show that you can perform contrary actions at the same time, in one single fresh breath... (in Brandon 1999: 129). Tzara might well have been writing an advertisement for the Apple II. Or, perhaps alternatively, Tzara could have been describing one of Dalí's paintings: *The Burning Giraffe* (1936–37). Contrary actions, or what Surrealist Raymond Queneau recognised as a 'revolution that aims at the profound substance and order of thought' (in Nadeau 1968: 114) is at the heart of both of these, at the heart of digitalism and its successor *emobilism*.

Digitalism, from the start, was about reconciling needs, offering and providing alternatives, combining conscious and unconsciously induced functions, automatically. If there was anything that had the potential to do what Breton once described as the 'creation of a collective myth', digitalism in the form of the computer had that potential. And it did it, from the late 1970s, and largely because of the Apple II, in our personal domestic spaces.

The human being, however, is a creature that values tactility; thus the reason digitalism, in the form of the home computer, made much of its 'controllers', its 'keyboards', its 'mouse'. While based in numerical concepts, digitalism found its connection to humanity not in its *true* form, which was abstract, but in its *representation* of an interface based initially on touch. Disk technology was also that kind of tactile technology.

The Compact Disc, or CD, launched in 1982, contained within its digital audio data called 'sub-code', giving it a sense of being both what it appeared on the surface and what it was beneath. CD-ROM, launched three years later, provided access to data previously only able to be held on computer hard drives. Thus it made that digitalism founded in the domestic space by microcomputers, increasingly mobile. CD-ROM's one problem, as Brian Winston has pointed out, was that it had it 'limited capacity for full motion video' (1998: 238). This had still to be provided by videotape. Videotape itself had 'gone digital' in 1987. While home computers and CD/CD-ROM were promoting non-linear, trouble-free digitalism digital videotape seemed, at best, a compromise.

Launched in 1996 in Japan, though not arriving until 1997 in the USA and 1998 in Europe, DVD (Digital Versatile Disc or Digital Video Disc: tellingly, both terms were used) finally placed film on the same domesticated footing as music and computer data. That was, and is, its revolutionary contribution. Prior to DVD the possibility of a digital 'bridge' for film, from old to new technologies, had no platform on which to build. DVD, which could be played either on a freestanding player linked to a television, or on a computer, proved to be the key technology. As I have said elsewhere,³ what was at stake is so well summed up by Jim Taylor in his book *DVD Demystified* that it seems ponderous to try and paraphrase:

DVD is the ideal convergence medium for a converging world. We are witnessing watershed transitions from analogue TV to digital TV (DTV), from interlaced video to progressive video, from standard TV to widescreen TV and from entertainment to interactive entertainment. In every case DVD works on both sides, bridging from the 'old way' to the 'new way'. (2001: 2)

These three technologies, the home computer, the CD/CD-ROM and the DVD/DVD-ROM worked together to emphasise something significant about the digital world. That something was its willingness to be what Surrealist poet Pierre Reverdy called 'two sides of the same material' (in Nadeau 1968: 102). Alongside these three technologies, the Internet, the evolution from narrowband to broadband and mobile or cell phone, lead the way for *emobilism*.

Surrealism and digital technology

To reiterate the suggestion here: it is that the physical, in the form of new digital technologies, has united with the metaphysical and psychological, in the form of psychological, emotive, intentional and unintentional human acts, expressions and feeling, to produce new digital films, and to respond to film in new ways, because of *emobilism*. And that, in the development of digitalism and *emobilism* we have moved closer than ever to a Surrealist ideal. This can be seen not merely in the texts (digital films and films informed by digitalism) and in film production techniques (further, production-specific digital technologies) but also in methods of viewing (the emergence of new modes of individual and mass consumption of film).

In addition to the three technologies mentioned, the evolution of *emobilism* has been driven by use of the Internet and the prevalence and considerable expansion of mobile phone technology. This combination of disc technology, computer and mobility has brought to the fore many things that the original Surrealists found in cinema.

From Louis Aragon, for example:

We must open our eyes in front of the screen, we must analyse the feeling that transports us, reason it out to discover the cause of that sublimation of ourselves ... It isn't the sight of eternally similar passions, nor – as one would have liked to believe – the faithful reproduction of a nature that the Thomas Cook Agency puts within our reach, but the magnification of the kinds of objects that, without artifice, our feeble lives can raise up to the superior life of poetry. (In Hammond 1978: 51)

From Marcel Marién:

However one tries to resist them, the images of the cinema, studded with words and sounds, interlace themselves insidiously with the images that people our minds, that govern our lives, that *are* our lives. These images reveal themselves thus as the most efficacious of all the relays given to our senses and to our sentiments. (In Hammond 1978: 146)

From Ado Kyrou:

When watching a film I inevitably perform an act of will on it, hence I transform it, and from its given elements make it *my* thing, draw snippets of knowledge from it and see better into myself. (In Hammond 1978: 130)

And from Jean Goudal:

The cinema, then, constitutes a conscious hallucination, and utilises this fusion of dream and consciousness which Surrealism would like to see realised in the literary. These moving images delude us, by leaving us with a confused awareness of our own personality and allowing us to evoke, if necessary, the resources of our memory. (In Hammond 1978: 89)

Not to say, of course, that the original Surrealists were all in favour of the cinema or, if in favour, that they were in favour of *all* of it. In his *Selected Writings* Buñuel called it both a 'marvellous and dangerous weapon' (2000b: 136); while Man Ray talked of most films being too long and only containing ten or fifteen minutes of truly marvellous material. Dalí felt film was inferior to painting and sculpture, even to creative writing, and Breton himself maintained that cinema had not gone far enough, expressing a 'certain nostalgia for what cinema might have become' (in Hammond 1978: 76).

If Breton's nostalgia was driven (as it appeared to be) by a notion that the multi-dimensions of cinema could provide much more for an investigation of the relationship between the individual and the society, the public and private, the material and psychological; that it could in effect represent new insights into a world sub-divided by economic, political and even artistic discourse, then certainly the Cinema of Complexity emerging in this period of *emobilism* gives a good indication that these Surrealist ideals have more foundation here in the early twenty-first century than they did three-quarters of a century ago.

And yet, the word 'surreal' has been applied to a range of contemporary films that have relatively little to do with the ideas behind Surrealism. In this sense, its application is more a reflection of the prevalence of the idea that somehow, despite its origins with poets, it has always been the visual – somewhat playful and detached rather than politically committed – that has driven Surrealism. These assumptions that Surrealism was 'primarily concerned with the visual arts; that it was primarily about jokes; that it was designed with a beady eye to the market' could not be, as Ruth Brandon also notes, 'further from the truth' (1999: 3).

Such relatively mainstream Hollywood films as *The Big Lebowski* (1998), a post-hippie crime film about mistaken identity; *Fight Club* (1999), an adaptation from a novel by Chuck Palahnuik, and carrying an anti-materialist message; *A Beautiful Mind* (2001), a biopic about John Forbes Nash Jr., a mathematics prodigy with schizophrenia who won the Nobel Prize; and *Eternal Sunshine of the Spotless Mind* (2004), a drama/comedy about memory eradication, have all had the adjective 'surreal' applied to them. Similarly, *Tales from the Gimli Hospital* (1988) by Canadian filmmaker Guy Maddin, the work of American animators Stephen and Timothy Quay and of Lars von Trier in such films as *Zentropa* (1991), all have been subject to the label 'surrealist'. What seems to draw this definition is that these films appear to be non-linear, or meandering, or have elements in them that seem out of kilter with what might be called perceived reality. But that, despite any colloquial critical consideration, would not make them Surrealist.

From a different point of view, when Malcolm Le Grice talks about Surrealist Cinema in *Experimental Cinema in the Digital Age* he talks about the relationship between computers and early Surrealist cinema – but in reverse – noting that 'non-linear concepts which relate to the intrinsic feature of Random Access Memory in computers can be seen to have had their origins in many works' (2001: 318) and he lists *Un chien andalou* (*An Andalusian Dog*, 1929) and *L'Age d'or* (*The Golden Age*, 1930) as some of those origins. While in Shari Roman's *Digital Babylon: Hollywood, Indiewood and Dogme*, in an interview with American filmmaker John Bailey, Bailey notes in answer to the question 'If photography is freed-up art, is DV [digital video] freeing up film?'

> As far as I'm concerned, we're right at the infancy of whatever the interface is going to be, because digital technology is still so new, still so primitive in a way. From a point of view of students, it really empowers them. They can go off with no crew and virtually no equipment, even if they aren't producing anything of a very high quality. If they have something to say, if they have ideas and energies they want to get recorded, they can do it very easily. (In Roman 2001: 119)

This is not so far removed from the original Surrealist ideal: 'We have no talent', wrote Breton in the *Manifeste du surréalisme*, 'we who have made ourselves, in our works, the deaf receptacles of so many echoes, the modest *recording devices* that are not hypnotised by the designs they trace (in Nadeau 1968: 97).

And, finally, in *A History of Experimental Film and Video*, A. L. Rees suggests 'the same combination of art and technology which made up the activity of the first decades of artists' films are at work today – even down to the very images which are explored in digital forms as we have them now' (1999: 120).

Post-Digitalism and Surrealism

As digital technology, by definition, has been about storing and exchanging in a variety of electronic media, making it easily transferable, creating a system of production and consumption that is based on interconnectivity, empowerment of individuals to associate and intervene (through the web or the relative cheapness of recording or distribution devices), to cover and exchange knowledge, participate in entertainments, communicate without needing a fixed location or instrument, do several of these things at random or, indeed, at the same time, then post-digitalism is the result of the human reaction to this technology.

What are now seen as simple acts were, at the time of the birth of Surrealism, difficult, often impossible, notions. The Surrealists might indeed have sought out 'total liberation of the mind', the release of the imagination from 'slavery', the creation of 'a new kind of mysticism', 'memory and the pleasure of the eyes' (Nadeau 1968: 88, 114, 118) each of these drawing to a considerable extent on Freudian concepts, and each presented in different narratives as individual Surrealists considered the difficulty of working between concern with the aesthetics of dream and similarly with the brutality of revolutionary. They might have denounced a social order, and sought out Marxism as a political vehicle for ideas about the randomness and disorder creating opportunities for a new *ésprit*. They might have looked toward the overthrowing of intellectual values not in keeping with their desire to methodologically bridge from poet to scientist, without hierarchy. But, whether specifically relating to the cinema, or generally to the world around, they did not have the tools to accomplish what they sought to achieve. The collapse of the Surrealists' relationship with the Communists reflected the difficulty of the act that they were attempting. But, in the case of film, their relationship with cinema equally reflected the condition of the filmmaking and consumption at that time.

What then might Dalí, who openly favoured sculpture and painting and poetry over the cinema, make of today's digital media? How might Breton have reacted to the democratisation of film production brought about by the evolution of the digital video camera, computer-based film editing and digital sound recording? What might the Surrealists, in general, make of the interactive capabilities of DVD, in which the audience can pause and discuss the film, frozen there on the screen, or watch the filmmakers at work via the supplementary platform of the disc, before returning to the film? What might they have made of the act of streaming film on the web, downloading movies into the home, manipulating films in software packages, both your own and those of others?

Commercial and Humanist imperatives demanded that, rather than being seen as ontologically or epistemologically investigative, digitalism arrived as applied science. It was utilitarian. The initial differences between digital and analogue were linked with such things as convenience, speed, accessibility, multi-functionalism and quality. But the digital revolution – and it must be seen as a revolution, if not overtly political then certainly more than simply technological because such considerable change in the physical world could not help but produce substantial conceptual change – was followed by a human reaction.

Now, not quite thirty years since the arrival of the Apple II personal computer, not even twenty years since the arrival of the CD and then the DVD, and only just ten years since the effective opening of the Internet, to speak of film in the age of the Cinema of Complexity is to talk about concepts and ideas which bear a striking resemblance to those expressed by the Surrealists. Breton once wrote that 'almost all images, for instance, strike me as spontaneous' (1968: 280). If this kind of automatism is something we associate with the post-digital world, a world of *emobility*, as surely it is, then we are today closer to the Surrealist ideal than we were in any age previously.

Notes

1 See Graeme Harper (2005) 'DVD and the New Cinema of Complexity', in Nicholas Rombes (ed.) *New Punk Cinema*. Edinburgh: Edinburgh University Press, 89–101.
2 Using the term 'scientific time' in the manner adopted by Henri Bergson in such works as *Creative Evolution* (1911), New York: Holt.
3 Harper (2005) in Rombes (ed.), 89–101.

Bruce Jenkins

Postscript
THE IMPOSSIBLE CINEMA OF MARCEL BROODTHAERS[1]

> I don't know whether the result will be a work of art, but I am sure it will be cinema.
> Cinema in the sense that no other art, no science, can take its place ... If it doesn't
> involve an artist it involves at least a man.
> – Jean Vigo (1977/78: 23)

Seated before a small writing table located in a courtyard version of his *Musée d'Art Moderne* – instantiated here for the duration of a brief film as a sort of museum without walls – Marcel Broodthaers is writing with pen and ink. As his work proceeds, rain begins to pour down upon the author and his text. Broodthaers, stonefaced, continues his jottings despite the fact that the water has begun to transform his efforts into something approaching the work of a painter. The writing is completed with a signature that manages to survive the storm, the screen fades to black, and a title appears: 'Projet pour un texte.'

As with his debut artwork *Pense-Bête* (1964), a sculptural assemblage of bundled copies of his final volume of poetry inserted into plaster, *La Pluie* (*Projet pour un texte*) (1969) serves as a metaphor for Broodthaers' aesthetic-material transition from literary to visual artist. In *Pense-Bête* he obstructs the act of reading; in *La Pluie*, the act of writing. In each instance the denial of one work serves as the grounds for the creation of another: books stuck in plaster become a sculpture, a text drenched in rain becomes a movie.

No less allegory than biography, these transgressive acts situate Broodthaers within a history, both real and imagined, of radical artistic practice. The Dadaists exemplified this aspiration to sweep aside the discrete boundaries between artistic disciplines. Although engaged by their ideas, Broodthaers preferred the company of others. He acknowledged two such compatriots with a pair of prints produced in 1972 that celebrate the (apocryphal) careers of Charles Baudelaire, painter, and René Magritte, author. *La*

Pluie inscribes on film another seemingly counterfactual biography in its wry portrayal of 'Marcel Broodthaers, cinéaste'. One winces ('ceci n'est pas une pipe') and then, serenely, the logic of the associations overtakes their initial incongruity.

Marcel Broodthaers had initiated his work in film more than a decade before the production of *La Pluie* and a half-dozen years before *Pense-Bête* signalled his emergence as a visual artist. As a filmmaker, his career spanned nearly twenty years and involved some fifty projects. He worked in 16mm and 35mm (and occasionally in Super-8), produced documentaries, animation and short fiction pieces and screened his films in a variety of venues. A lifelong cinephile, Broodthaers invested even his most modest productions with citations drawn from classic narrative cinema; he made particular allusions to the films of Charlie Chaplin and Buster Keaton, Jean Vigo and Jean Renoir, as well as Orson Welles. This fascination with film is well evidenced in *La Pluie*, with its multiple references to Keystone sight gags, the 'Great Stoneface' Keaton, and the open-air primitiveness of the Lumières.

Broodthaers' sustained interest in the cinema, which underlay the use of film as a medium for his own art, remained steadfastly in the historical register throughout his career and thus decidedly out of sync with the prevailing critical norms of his times. Precisely, for instance, at that moment in the late 1950s and early 1960s when the leading young critics across Western Europe (at *Cahiers du cinéma* in Paris and *Movie* in London) were embracing the American cinema of Howard Hawks, Nicholas Ray and John Ford, the young Marcel Broodthaers was dressing up as 'Charlot' and introducing film programmes that mixed silent cinema (often appropriated from early newsreels and comedy shorts) with contemporary non-fiction films. In 1959, Jean-Luc Godard made his entry into feature filmmaking with the contemporary crime film *À bout de souffle* (*Breathless*) directed with Hawksian efficiency and an eye for the marketplace; it seemed distinctly modern in its audacious appropriation of popular culture. By contrast, Broodthaers' first film, produced around the same time, would have seemed quaintly anachronistic, reprising as it did the kinetic visual lexicon of the not-yet rediscovered 1920s avant-garde in a 'cinematic poem' dedicated to the work of Kurt Schwitters.

If Broodthaers rejected the concerns of the New Wave European cinéastes, he remained equally at odds with the aspirations of those avant-garde artists of the 1960s who were then beginning to realise works in film and video. Rejecting the label 'experimental' for his films, he withheld them from the alternative circuits of distribution and exhibition of the day and even went so far as to suggest that one of his works, *Un film de Charles Baudelaire* (1970), had been 'shot in the nineteenth century'.[2] Broodthaers' films share few affinities with the work of such roughly contemporaneous filmmakers as Stan Brakhage, Peter Kubelka or Michael Snow; nor do they echo the concerns of early video artists such as Bruce Nauman, Joan Jonas or Vito Acconci. Broodthaers demonstrated little interest in investigating either the materiality of the medium or its formal possibilities, on the one hand, or in utilising the more populist, visually degraded and dematerialised medium of video for artmaking, on the other. And while moving-image experimentation by artists would shift by the early 1970s almost exclusively to video, with its focus on the present tense of live recording, Broodthaers would continue mining connections to the past on celluloid.

The past that captivated Broodthaers was the cinema that had ended with the coming of sound in the late 1920s and the rapid consolidation of commercial filmmaking into corporate structures – a closure that was as chilling in the capitalist West as it was in the communist East. His entire output of more than forty films, made over a period of nearly two decades, remains faithful in its allusions to this earlier era. It is, nonetheless, not a body of work dedicated to mere cinephilic nostalgia. Broodthaers' systematic invocation of these early, pre-institutionalised film forms – by virtue of its art-world context and its overt allusion to those cinematic practices of the 1920s that had already marshalled these popular forms into the medium's first instance of a counter-practice – rather marked an attempt to reopen the problematics surrounding the possibilities for what the filmmaker Jean Vigo, in 1930, had called a 'social cinema' (1977/78: n. 1). Embracing a fairly broad range of alternative practices and social contexts – from such sporadic avant-garde endeavors as François Picabia and René Clair's Dadaist film interlude *Entr'acte* (1924), which aspired to further increase the outrage of the audience attending a performance of Les Ballets Suedois' 'Relâche', or Salvador Dalí and Luis Buñuel's Surrealist *Un chien andalou* (*An Andalusian Dog*, 1929), to the ideologically engaged historical films of Sergei Eisenstein (*Stachka/Strike*, 1925; *Bronenosets Potyomkin/Battleship Potemkin*, 1925; *Octyabr/October*, 1927) or the agitprop documentaries of Dziga Vertov – it was a cinema that, for all its overt heterogeneity, shared a common affinity: a singular fascination with the medium's earliest populist appeal (the joyous anarchy of slapstick and crude fantasy) and an epochal desire to channel this appeal into an instrument for social critique. It was a cinema, that is, which appropriated the medium's fledgling strategies of visual pleasure and refracted them through the prism of its various manifestos, creating in the process a practice that was both aesthetically advanced and socially corrosive, yet bearing the traces of cinema's own populist history.

Broodthaers launched his filmmaking career by attempting to create a sound-era practice capable of achieving the polyvalent forms of visual elaboration and social engagement imagined by these earlier filmmakers, revisiting both their own work and the pre-commercial, naïve cinema it appropriated. In his first film, *La Clef de l'horloge* (1957), for example, he explicitly revised one of the more celebrated avant-garde works of the silent era, Fernand Léger's non-narrative *Ballet mécanique* (1923–24), the painter's single work in the medium. Relying upon an arsenal of trick film techniques that would already have been viewed as antiquated by the early 1920s (and therefore available for artistic appropriation), Léger had created an improbable 'ballet' largely from inanimate objects – cooking utensils, dishes and glasses, pistons and flywheels – which he animated with the magical precision of a Georges Méliès or a Ferdinand Zecca. The few human subjects that appear in the film, by contrast, are relegated to mechanistic roles: the Parisian model Kiki is seen in close-up performing a limited repertoire of facial gestures (opening and closing her eyes, smiling and frowning), while the simple found performance of a washerwoman who climbs a set of stone steps is systematically repeated to mimic the movement and the functional output of a machine.

Broodthaers' film, subtitled '*Poème cinématographique en l'honneur de Kurt Schwitters*', was shot after-hours in the galleries of the Palais des Beaux-Arts in Brussels, which was hosting a major monographic exhibition of Schwitters at the time. The film's techniques – stark black-and-white cinematography, kinetic camerawork, montage of close-up details – hark back to the period of 'cinéma pur', to attempts at a Dadaist cinema and most directly to Léger's cubist film 'ballet', while making full use of what Walter Benjamin, writing from the perspective of the mid-1930s, had contended were cinema's distinctive visual techniques: 'Its lowerings and liftings, its interruptions and isolations, its extensions and accelerations, its enlargements and reductions' (1969: 237). Further suggesting the work's vintage origins is the opening credit sequence, where the artist's name, parsed and printed on two lines as 'Marcel Broo/dthaers', slyly invokes the figure of another Marcel (Duchamp) who, in his *Anémic cinéma* (1925), similarly experimented with primitive film techniques by setting a series of his roto-reliefs into motion.

The confluence of these filmic devices, over-determinedly derived from the 1920s avant-garde, with the works of Schwitters themselves (largely from the same period) endows *La Clef de l'horloge* with an oddly dual status. That is to say, it reads concurrently as a contemporary 'documentary' on Schwitters' art and as an imaginary film relic realised in the advanced forms of film practice of the period. In this way, the film neatly adumbrates Broodthaers' 'Museum Fictions' of the late 1960s and early 1970s. Engaging in a metahistorical form of aesthetic appropriation, it re-imagines a history (never realised) in which art and cinema pursue consonant courses of modernity. All of Broodthaers' subsequent filmmaking would employ similar time-shifting strategies – ones that could conjure up an array of impossible cinemas dating back, for example, to a nineteenth-century film by Charles Baudelaire or forward to a contemporary BBC-style filmed interview with the British philosopher Jeremy Bentham (1748–1832). In the late 1960s and early 1970s, he would even fashion a 1920s Surrealist cinema in a series of films that appropriately accommodated the work of his fellow Belgian artist René Magritte by reprising the figure of Magritte's celebrated pipe.

This latter body of work included no less than eight filmic variations on the theme of Magritte's *Ceci n'est pas une pipe*, a seminal work that Broodthaers credited as a personal influence:

> Magritte denies the aesthetic nature of painting (which does not prevent him, almost in spite of himself, from creating some beautiful paintings). *Ceci n'est pas une pipe* is the title of a painting as enigmatic as the smile of the Mona Lisa ... Still faithful to his initial purpose, he continues to elaborate a poetic language aimed at undermining that upon which we depend. (1987: 34)

As Broodthaers suggests in this brief homage, the enigma of the Magritte painting stems from the artist's resolute efforts to undermine 'that upon which we depend' – namely language and meaning. Broodthaers adapts Magritte's emblem of this loss – the contradictory image of the pipe and its self-negating caption – into a series of comic misadventures in the quest for meaning.

In the preliminary versions, *La Pipe (René Magritte)* (1968–70) and *Ceci ne serait pas une pipe* (1970), Broodthaers utilises animation techniques to suspend the pipe, placing it in mid-air before the garden wall of *La Pluie*. The pipe is levitated less for art-historical reasons (the Surrealism of the source) than for semantic ones. As Michel Foucault noted in his provocative analysis of the Magritte painting: 'The form reascends to its heaven from which the complicity of letters with space had momentarily brought it down: free from any discursive bond, it can go back to floating in its native silence' (1976: 10).[3] While replicating the shallow space of Magritte's illustration, Broodthaers jettisons the original transgressive inscription in favour of ones that recontextualise the image and begin to expose the cinema to the corrosive forces that Magritte had unleashed on painting. In *La Pipe (Figure noire)* (1968–70), for example, Broodthaers subtitles the entire sequence with the single word 'Figure', thereby reducing filmic representation to the level of illustration. In *Ceci ne serait pas une pipe*, he employs the transgressive device of marking objects with contradictory designations – the wall subtitled 'Figure I' and then 'Figure II', the smoking pipe labelled successively 'Figure III', 'Figure I' and 'Figure II', the final image of the extinguished pipe, subtitled 'Figure I et II'. Broodthaers interpenetrates word and image, denying meaning to both. The result is a rebus-like form emptied of reality and significance. Foucault best described it: 'Magritte allows the old space of representation to prevail, but only on the surface, for it is no more than a smooth stone, bearing figures and words: underneath, there is nothing' (1976: 16).

That which fills the void at the centre of representation forms the subject for Broodthaers' most elaborate appropriation of Magritte, in which he comically portrays attempts to find a source of meaning in the work of art either by recourse to the figure of the artist or, alternatively, to the processes of the unconscious. In *La Pipe satire* (1969), Broodthaers inserts himself into the work in the role of artist – masked, shirtless, wearing a sailor's cap, mysteriously exhaling smoke and eventually playing an accordion. The artist portrayed in *La Pipe satire* is neither Magritte nor Broodthaers but another fiction, a phantom, a citation: he is 'Père Jules', the old junk-collecting sailor of Jean Vigo's *L'Atalante* (1934), the maritime version of Baudelaire's ragpicker. In a like recourse to fiction, the meaning of the pipe is recuperated in the film, through the machinations of psychoanalysis, as a phallus, displayed by Broodthaers in close-up as a smoking briar pipe held between the thighs of a nude woman. By unfettering film from its referential bonds, Broodthaers allows cinema to float, like Magritte's pipe, in a sea of citation of other voices and other forms.

In considering these imaginary, anachronistic cinemas created by Broodthaers, one recalls the curious pronouncement of Abel Gance, the French filmmaker noted for his innovative adaptations of historical themes, that 'Shakespeare, Rembrandt [and] Beethoven will make films' (in Benjamin 1969: 221–2). Perhaps what Gance envisioned and Broodthaers attempted to achieve was a version of what Walter Benjamin, writing in 1920, had theorised – namely, that 'the medium through which works of art continue to influence later ages is always different from the one in which they affect their own age' (1996: 235). When Broodthaers dons the hat of a Charlot or Schwitters or Baudelaire, he is not merely dressing up; for beneath the garb and behind the camera, he is channelling their aesthetic discourse through his unique postwar sensibility. For Broodthaers, the cinema was a transformative medium, capable of preserving and recasting the art of the past (including that of his own making). But for all that, the film medium was not for him transparent; any form it assumes – even that 'zero degree' nearly achieved by the uninflected frontality of his own *mise-en-scène* – is marked by what we might label a 'photogenetic code', a metahistorical signature derived through conventional usage and ingrained in each generation of moviegoer. This aspect of the cinema was acknowledged in 1972 by the Cuban filmmaker Santiago Álvarez when he positioned his own non-fiction film practice 'as a challenge to the film genres instituted by capitalism, a challenge to the habits of watching films according to canons of commercial cinema, a challenge to the theories of intellectuals influenced by cinema's commercialism' (1980: 52).

Although less overtly political than Álvarez, Broodthaers, too, challenged the various cinemas championed by Álvarez's 'intellectuals'. His weapon, most often, was humour and in particular its lowest, most culturally denigrated form – slapstick. Broodthaers' cinema, in fact, consists in its entirety of comedy: parodies (as in the reportage of his 'Fiction Museum' openings, for example, replete with bus-tour footage and scenes chronicling the journey of empty art-shipping crates), primitive-style trick films (where objects, like Magritte's pipe, magically appear and vanish), or short slapstick narratives (almost all featuring the artist in Keatonesque scenarios). Such work, Broodthaers must have surmised, would be equally repellent to the bourgeois defenders of orthodox high culture and to the stylish partisans of the avant-garde. It is this latter challenge – which gives Broodthaers' films the status of *counter*-counter-cinema – that may seem most surprising. After all, the work of a contemporary artist during the period of late modernism would be expected to upset the cultural elite. But the concurrent dismissal of the counter-culture (an affront which Broodthaers claimed both on behalf of his films and the wider body of his art) positioned him uniquely apart from even the heterodox practice of the 1960s. Broodthaers' films emitted a multifaceted critique that included a suspicion of any canon (even those of the various anti-art-isms then forming) and a clear interest in avoiding absorption as 'experimental', 'avant-garde', or any other category of alternative practice. His model may well have been that of Buñuel, who in the 1920s had maintained a deep suspicion of and disdain for the various forms of 'avant-garde' filmmaking and who went so far as to refuse Jean Vigo's request to screen *Un chien andalou* in a ciné-club setting.[4]

Broodthaers' films resist categorisation within any of the rubrics of alternative cinematic practice (they are neither 'structural', 'concrete', 'direct', 'personal', 'mythopoetic', nor 'underground'). To corral them within such descriptions would be reductive. But to avoid categorisation would entail even more severe critical consequences: either to remain unknown (something in which they have demonstrated remarkable success) or, worse, to be comprehended as mere 'visual complements' to his other work. So let them be comedies, albeit comedies with a difference. These are all comedies out of time – often silent black-and-white shorts, made in the era of widescreen, Technicolor features, whose subjects are unlikely sources for humour: an amateur nautical painting shown in close-up details, an exhibition of lithographic prints of animals and insects in the gallery of the Palais des Beaux-Art, a man (Broodthaers) seated in front of the wax figure of Jeremy Bentham at University College, London. Broodthaers' invocation of silent comedy was never direct; rather it was always refracted through the lens of an earlier Dadaist appropriation of the incipient anti-social, anti-bourgeois elements that slapstick comedy had long ago provided its original audiences in the nickelodeons and vaudeville houses.

Thus Buster Keaton, born in the same year that the Lumières first publicly exhibited their cinématograph, becomes a recurrent presence in the films of Broodthaers. He makes his first appearance in *La Pluie* and reappears in *Eau de cologne* (1974), in which Broodthaers is seen seated outside the famous cathedral in Cologne clutching a potted palm tree. Here, wind rather than rain becomes his adversary. As in *La Pluie*, the artist impeccably maintains his composure and deadpan countenance against the elements; but now he adds a new component to the simple sight gag: a young woman appears and immediately bends over and exposes her bottom (some versions of the film have this scene repeated). While certainly not a reference to the films of Keaton, this enduring gesture of dismissal does have a precedent in 1920s cinema, in which vulgarity was often used for social ends – as, for example, when bared bottoms and exposed undergarments are deployed in the Dadaist comedy *Entr'acte* to satirise the aesthetic experience of ballet and undermine the solemnity of a funeral procession; or when, in the ironic city symphony *A propos de Nice* (1930), Jean Vigo pricks the vanity of the leisure class by stripping bare one of its young sunbathing minions.[5] Such intertextuality would become a leitmotif of Broodthaers' narratives and a means to provide works that seem so determinedly out of time and category with a discontinuous affiliation in his imaginary aesthetic discourse. They are, in effect, the 'key to the clock' that unites these moments of radical practice in time.

One of the most elaborate instances of the complex intertextual invocation of classic cinema in Broodthaers' films and one of his most surreal comes in *Berlin oder ein Traum mit Sahne* (*Berlin or Dream with Cream*, 1974), a work that again invokes the Keaton figure in the guise of the artist. Here Broodthaers is cast as 'Ein Künstler' (an artist) who enjoys a teatime repast served by his real-life daughter, Marie-Puck ('Das Mädchen'). As the film opens, Marie-Puck stands by a window in the apartment next to a potted palm, a recurring element of Broodthaers' installations and films. She carries the palm across the room to another window and pauses to watch as a barge in the river below passes under a bridge. Meanwhile, the artist, seated at the table, smokes his pipe and looks in the direction of a toy parrot perched under a hanging light fixture. In the first sight gag, Broodthaers lowers his pipe and stares intently at the parrot, now gently swaying on its perch. An egg lies beneath it on the table. The artist briefly picks it up, shoots an inquisitive look to the bird, and puts it back. As he resumes his pipe smoking and nods off, Marie-Puck waters the palm and prepares a plate of pastries. Accordion music is heard on the soundtrack. Broodthaers awakens, dons his reading glasses to scan the newspaper, and in a classic gesture from the slapstick era, lays them down into a dish of cream. In true Keatonesque fashion, Broodthaers replaces the glasses on his face, oblivious to the cream-opaqued lenses, and proceeds to read his newspaper. Another barge is seen in a long take passing under a bridge, and the film ends with a shot of people passing an outdoor café decorated with potted palms.

While the comic dénouement of *Berlin...* locates the work squarely within the canon of classic silent comedy (the titled cream serving as a metonymic signifier of the ubiquitous cream pies of slapstick), its German locale and the interpolation of the barge imagery suggest another intertextual reading, again to Vigo. References to the French filmmaker had occurred earlier in Broodthaers' films – obliquely in the Baudelaire film (a map image of a Pacific island shown twice in the film bears a name nearly identical to that of Vigo's biographer, Salles Gomes) and more visibly in *La Pipe satire*, with its invocation of le père Jules from Vigo's *L'Atalante*. While the presence of such allusions imbues these earlier films with the sort of triangulated histories Broodthaers so favoured (the invocation of le père Jules, for example, provides Magritte's pipe with an ethnographic past as part of the sailor's eccentric booty), in *Berlin...* the citation opens onto more complex issues of aesthetics and politics.

Broodthaers' representation in *Berlin...* of the barge traffic on the river is an undeniable reference to *L'Atalante*, a romance set on the canals of France in which the German actress Dita Parlo portrays a young bride married to a French bargeman.[6] Mapping this rather arcane and romantic cinematic citation onto what is otherwise a simple farce would be both curious and idle if the motivation for doing so were a matter of simple homage. What, then, accounts for the way in which the two allusions (Vigo and Keaton) meet and cohabit in *Berlin...*? In *L'Atalante*, Vigo's bargeman is constrained by the rigors of working-class life until, abandoned by his new bride, he discovers the true meaning of love. Diving into the murky canal water, her image appears to him in an epiphanic, dreamlike vision, and he realises the imaginative leap of faith that is necessary to sustain both his marriage and his life. In *Berlin...* Broodthaers reprises the themes at the heart of the Vigo film – the links between imagination, faith and freedom – and condenses them onto the Keatonesque figure of the dreaming artist. The central visual gag (Broodthaers reading through the cream-covered glasses) recalls the blurry vision through which Vigo's bargeman had discovered his emotional truth. Here, Vigo and Keaton join forces to describe the central challenge of the artist: to discover the essential emotional truth that underlies the everyday world.

While Broodthaers focuses on cinema's past in order to assemble his poignant, comic allegories of the artist's circumstance, he nonetheless never fails to address the social and political moments in which his films are made. According to its voice-over narration, for example, *Figures of Wax* (1974) was 'made between the two elections', while *Un voyage à Waterloo* (1969) was produced to document 'the itinerary of a voyage to Waterloo in the golden frame of the Bicentennial of the birth of Napoleon'.[7] Broodthaers described the anthology of nine short films he organised under the title *Rendez-vous mit Jacques Offenbach* (1972) by referencing a 1971 speech by US President Richard Nixon: 'This programme covers the period which has seen the birth and developement [sic] of inflation and its consequences'.[8] The brief portrait film *Monsieur Teste* (1974) revealed Broodthaers' comic automaton (a cartoonish and smiling rosy-cheeked, balding middle-aged figure) perusing the pages of the international edition of the August 1975 issue of *L'Express* magazine, its cover a mixture of current affairs ('Giscard Au Zaire') and human interest ('L'Amour Après 60 Ans').

The Battle of Waterloo (1975), Broodthaers' final and most ambitious film, begins with a clear acknowledgment of the context of its production: 'This film was made on the occasion of an exhibition at the I.C.A. New Gallery, London, 14th June 1975 (on the day of The Trooping of the Colour)'. Like *Un jardin d'hiver* (1974), shot eighteen months earlier to document his installation of the same name at the Palais des Beaux-Arts in Brussels, the film provides a detailed inventory of the elements of the gallery installation it accompanies. But despite the ostensible documentary nature of the project, the film operates equally in the mode of *Berlin...*, with the filmmaker weaving an intertextual narrative out of cinematic citations as he draws upon both the actions set within the interior space and the actuality of the streets below.

The film's title begins to suggest the nature of Broodthaers' intertextual construction. Unlike *Un jardin d'hiver* or his earlier *Musée d'Art Moderne, Département des Aigles, Section du XIXième Siècle* (1968), it does not name the exhibition it purports to document. Rather, the exhibition we are shown in *The Battle of Waterloo* is the artist's *Décor* show at the Institute of Contemporary Arts (ICA) in 1975, in which he had assembled an array of mostly rented objects in two galleries: a nineteenth-century room and a contemporary one. The former (filmed here by Broodthaers with such nineteenth-century techniques as the static tableau and proto-trickfilm ruses) contained a mixture of military artifacts (two cannons, a revolver, barrels of rum and gin), Louis XIV furnishings (silver candelabras, upholstered chairs) and a grouping of Broodthaersesque potted palms. The second gallery (filmed in a more contemporary mode using continuity editing, close-ups and point-of-view shots) similarly juxtaposed the martial and the domestic in an arrangement of white patio furnishings (table, umbrella and chairs) flanked by shelves displaying automatic rifles. In the filmed version we also see, outside on the street below, the British Trooping of the Colours parade (this filmed directly in the style of the Lumière brothers' turn-of-the-century actualities), with rows of red-coated beefeaters marching past a crowd of spectators.

Into the documentation of this exhibition and celebration, Broodthaers introduces a character (the 'Actress'), who is seen seated at the table of the contemporary room picking apart a jigsaw puzzle that depicts the Battle of Waterloo. Cinematic references immediately begin to accrue around two film classics: Abel Gance's *Napoléon* (1927) and Orson Welles' *Citizen Kane* (1941). The Gance film, an acknowledged masterpiece of silent cinema, was an epic biographical study of its titled character. No less epic nor less acclaimed, Welles' fictional biography focused on the life of another powerful figure, a newspaperman who manipulates world affairs but bungles his own private ones. Broodthaers' jigsaw-puzzle scene condenses citations to both films by directly referencing the climactic moment of the Gance work (here displaced as the subject of the puzzle) while simultaneously invoking a highly symbolic moment in the Welles film, in which the protagonist's wife is seen in the baroque interior of their private estate obsessively playing with such puzzles. With cinematic citations that recall themes of imperialism and power, the film proposes several sets of parallel tales: of two imperialist nations (France and the US), of two film auteurs and of two tragic, overreaching protagonists. It is these miniature narratives that provide the key to the spatial duality that had characterised the *Décor* installation itself and that help to clarify the complex ideological and metahistorical discourse operative in that show.

If Napoleon had *fought* his way to the throne of imperialist power in the nineteenth century, Kane *bought* his way to a similar kind of power in the twentieth. Kane, it must be remembered, not only ruled a politically powerful publishing empire but was a cultural imperialist as well, an obsessive acquirer of increasingly grotesque art and artifacts. The two figures, Napoleon the imperialist and Kane the capitalist, meet up in the final image of *The Battle of Waterloo*, in which the image of Napoleon is displaced from battle and from history onto the label of a cognac bottle, a potent signifier of late twentieth-century consumption. The new imperialism is advertising, and the Trooping of the Colours outside reminds us that pageantry is no less a potent form of political advertising. Using these themes from the film as a guide, we can now read the deployment of artifacts within the two galleries of the *Décor* installation as specific object lessons on the relationship between power and culture.

Broodthaers ends his film career in *The Battle of Waterloo* with a persuasive demonstration of the cultural force that cinema has wielded across this century in both the social and aesthetic realms. Populist in its appeal and ubiquitous in its societal presence, the cinema became an ideal tool for Broodthaers to deploy in his artmaking. He used it both as a medium and as a point of reference, creating filmed works rich in their allusions to popular forms that could speak in a language unavailable to the 'higher' arts. Broodthaers' cinematic allusions serve as a kind of *lingua franca* that is capable of mediating the worlds of art and activism, and as a kind of shorthand for the broader concerns of his art. So, for example, when he speaks the language of Vigo in *Berlin oder ein Traum mit Sahne*, he communicates in marvelously distilled form both his solidarity with the worker and a programme for artistic practice. When he speaks the language of Welles in *The Battle of Waterloo*, he provides the key to the interpretation of his own eclectic oeuvre as a comment on the commodification of culture.

Broodthaers emerges as something of a missing link, mediating between the end of a lost modernist cinema and the beginning of postmodern visual culture. He was the last artist to ply the craft of Léger and Vigo, of Keaton and Welles, a filmmaker who knew that while there was no future to the medium, its past could be the site for a lifetime of complex aesthetic intervention. For Broodthaers, filmmaking represented less an opportunity to indulge his cinephilia through homage (though it was that too) than an attempt to deploy an archaic form of popular culture in the service of a larger aesthetic enterprise. His films are the work of the amateur – the lover – who seeks in the cinema not only a refuge from the gallery's demand for the object (a concern he shared with many in his own generation of artists) but a rich lode of iconography to appropriate for his own art.

No artist and certainly no filmmaker of the postwar era has borne such clear witness to the originating potential of film, a medium that intrigued from the start of this past century onward intellectuals and immigrants, magicians and merchants, artists and entrepreneurs, revolutionaries and reactionaries. Decidedly out of step with his own generation in cleaving to the quaint cinema of the past – its slight comedies, its obscure experiments, its grandiose epics – in reclaiming a cultural space for it, and in weaving it into his own artistic programme, Broodthaers placed his films at risk of being misunderstood, dismissed, or even forgotten. It was a risk he probably felt was worth taking. Reanimating these seemingly insignificant bits of cinematic detritus was a sustaining mission for him – for, as Chaplin claimed of the humble humour in his own work, 'it heightens our sense of survival' (1966: 226). When Broodthaers created his first artwork, he claimed to have succumbed to the idea of 'inventing something insincere';[9] these little films, by contrast, are deeply sincere and serve as his testament to the power of a medium that has managed for more than a century to endure.

Notes

1 This essay derives from writings originally published in *Marcel Broodthaers*, exhibition catalogue (Minneapolis and New York: Walker Art Center and Rizzoli, 1989) and *Marcel Broodthaers Cinéma*, exhibition catalogue (Barcelona: Fundació Antoni Tàpies, 1997).

2 Marcel Broodthaers, unpublished notes on *Un Film de Charles Baudelaire*, in the Broodthaers archive, Brussels.

3 Broodthaers was apparently well acquainted with the Foucault essay and, according to a postscript to the publication circular for *A Voyage on the North Sea*, planned to publish his own edition of Foucault's text.

4 Buñuel's disdain for the avant-garde is described in Phillip Drummond's 'Textual Space in *Un chien andalou*', *Screen*, 18, 3, 62; Vigo recounts the story of Buñuel's refusal in 'Toward a Social Cinema' (1977–78: n. 1).

5 For a broader discussion of the political implications of comedy in *Entr'acte*, see Nöel Carroll's 'Entr'acte, Paris and Dada', *Millennium Film Journal*, 1, 5–11.

6 See Marina Warner's excellent analysis of the film in her *L'Atalante* (London: British Film Institute, 1993), to which my discussion here is indebted.

7 Marcel Broodthaers, unpublished note in the Broodthaers archive, Brussels.

8 Ibid.

9 Marcel Broodthaers, cited in Michael Compton, 'In Praise of the Subject', *Marcel Broodthaers*, exhibition catalogue (Minneapolis and New York: Walker Art Center and Rizzoli, 1989, 25). Broodthaers made the statement in an introduction he wrote for an exhibition announcement for his first monographic show, at the Galarie Saint-Laurent, Brussels, 10–25 April 1964.

BIBLIOGRAPHY

Aitken, Ian (1992) *Film and Reform: John Grierson and the Documentary Film Movement.* London: Routledge.

___ (2000) *Alberto Cavalcanti: Realism, Surrealism and National Cinemas.* Trowbridge: Flicks Books.

Álvarez, Santiago (1980 [1968]) in Michael Chanan (ed.) *Santiago Álvarez.* London: British Film Institute, 27–30.

Anderson, Lindsay (1954) 'Only Connect: Some aspects of the Work of Humphrey Jennings', *Sight and Sound*, April–June, 181–6.

Anon. (2004) 'Chaotic Cinema'; http://www.wayney.pwp.blueyonder.co.uk (accessed 16 February 2007).

Aragon, Louis (1926) *Le Paysan de Paris.* Paris: Gallimard.

___ (1978 [1918]) 'On Décor', in Paul Hammond (ed.) *The Shadow and Its Shadow: Surrealist Writings on Cinema.* London: British Film Institute, 28–31.

Aranda, Francisco (1985) *Luis Buñuel.* New York: De Capo Press.

Artaud, Antonin (1976 [1927]) 'Cinema and Reality', trans. Helen Weaver, in Susan Sontag (ed.) *Antonin Artaud: Selected Writings.* Berkeley: University of California Press, 150–4.

Balakian, Anna (1971) *André Breton: The Magus of Surrealism.* New York: Oxford University Press.

Ballard, Phil (2003) 'Magic Against Materialism: Czech Animator Jiří Barta interviewed'; http://www.kinoeye.org/03/09/ballard09.php (accessed 31 October 2004).

Barker, Martin, Jane Arthurs and Ramaswami Harindranath (2001) *The Crash Controversy: Censorship Campaigns and Film Reception.* London: Wallflower Press.

Barr, Charles (ed.) (1986) *All Our Yesterdays: 90 Years of British Cinema.* London: British Film Institute.

Barrier, Michael (1999) *Hollywood Cartoons: American Animation in its Golden Age.* New York: Oxford University Press.

BBC http://www.bbc.co.uk/dna/filmnetwork.

Bell, Michael S. (2004) www.bway.net/~monique/history.htm.

Belz, Carl (1972) 'The Terror of the Surreal', in Roy Huss and Theodore J. Ross (eds) *Focus on the Horror Film*. New Jersey: Prentice-Hall, 144–8.

Benjamin, Walter (1969 [1936]) 'The Work of Art in the Age of Mechanical Reproduction', trans. Harry Zohn, in *Illuminations*. New York: Schocken Books, 217–52.

___(1996 [1920]) 'The Medium Through Which Works of Art Continue to Influence Later Ages', (ed. Marcus Bullock and Michael W. Jennings) in *Walter Benjamin Selected Writings Volume I: 1913-1926*. Cambridge, MA and London: The Belknap Press of Harvard University Press, 235.

___ (1999 [1927]) *The Arcades Project*, trans. Howard Elland and Kevin McLaughlin. Cambridge, MA and London: Harvard University Press.

Bergmark, Johannes 'Butoh: Revolt of the Flesh in Japan and a Surrealist Way to Move', in *Mannen På Gatan*; http://www.bergmark.org/butoh.html. (accessed 2 December 2004).

Bigsby, C. W. E. (1972) *Dada and Surrealism*. London: Methuen.

Bondil-Poupard, Nathalie (2001) 'Such Stuff as Dreams are Made On: Hitchcock and Dalí, Surrealism and Oneiricism', in Dominique Païni and Guy Cogeval (eds) *Hitchcock and Art: Fatal Coincidences*. Montreal: Montreal Museum of Fine Arts, 155–71.

Brandon, Ruth (1999) *Surreal Lives: The Surrealists 1917-1945*. New York: Grove Press.

Brassaï, Gyula Halasz (1997) *Marcel Proust sous l'emprise de la photographie*. Paris: Gallimard.

Breton, André (1949) *Entretiens: 1913-1952*. Paris: Gallimard.

___ (1962 [1924, 1930, 1934]) *Manifestes du Surréalisme*. Paris: Jean-Jacques Pauvert.

___ (1965 [1936]) 'Crise de l'objet', in *Le Surréalisme et la peinture*. Paris: Gallimard, 275–81.

___ (1966 [1924]) 'The First Surrealist Manifesto', in Patrick Waldberg, *Surrealism*. New York: McGraw-Hill, 66–75.

___ (1969 [1924, 1930, 1934]) *Manifestos of Surrealism*, trans. Richard Seaver and Helen R. Lane. Ann Arbor: University of Michigan Press.

___ (1972a [1936]) 'Crisis of the Object', in *Surrealism and Painting*, trans. Simon Watson Taylor. London: MacDonald, 275–280.

___ (1972b [1940] *Anthologie de l'humour noir*. Paris: Jean-Jacques Pauvert.

___ (1978a [1921]) 'Max Ernst', trans. Ralph Manheim, in *What is Surrealism? Selected Writings*, edited and introduced by Franklin Rosemont. London: Pluto Press, 7–8.

___ (1978b [1933]) 'The Automatic Message', trans. Guy Ducornet, in *What is Surrealism? Selected Writings*, edited and introduced by Franklin Rosemont. London: Pluto Press, 97–109.

___ (1978c [1951]) 'As in a Wood', in Paul Hammond (ed.) *The Shadow and Its Shadow: Surrealist Writings on Cinema*. London: British Film Institute, 42–5.

___ (1988a [1921]) 'Max Ernst', *Oeuvres Complètes* I. Paris: Gallimard, 309–46.

___ (1988b [1924]'Les pas perdus' in *Oeuvres Complètes I*. Paris: Gallimard, 193–308.

___ (1992a [1933]) 'Le Message automatique', *Oeuvres complètes* II. Paris: Gallimard, 375–

92.

___ (1992b [1937]) 'L'Amour fou', *Oeuvres complètes* II. Paris: Gallimard, 673–785.

___ (1999 [1951]) 'Comme dans un bois' in *Oeuvres Complètes III*. Paris: Gallimard, 902–7.

___ (2002 [1928]) 'Surrealism and Painting', in *Surrealism and Painting*, trans. Simon Watson Taylor. Boston: MFA Publications, 1–48.

Bronfen, Elisabeth (1992) *Over Her Dead Body: Death, Femininity and the Aesthetic*. Manchester: Manchester University Press.

Broodthaers, Marcel (1987) 'Gare au défi! Pop Art, Jim Dine, and the Influence of René Magritte', trans. Paul Schmidt. *October*, 42 (Fall), 34.

Buñuel, Luis (1982) *Mon dernier soupir*. Paris: Robert Laffont.

___ (1985) *My Last Breath*. Glasgow: Flamingo.

___ (2000a [1958]) 'The Cinema, Instrument of Poetry', in Paul Hammond (ed.) *The Shadow and Its Shadow*, third edition. San Francisco: City Lights Books, 112–16.

___ (2000b) *An Unspeakable Betrayal: Selected Writings of Luis Buñuel*, trans. Garrett White. Berkeley: University of California Press.

Cabarga, Leslie (1976) *The Fleischer Story*. New York: Nostalgia Press.

Carroll, Noel (1977–78) 'Entr'acte, Paris and Dada', *Millennium Film Journal*, 1 (Winter), 5–11.

Carroll, Lewis (1993 [1887]) *Alice's Adventures in Wonderland and Through the Looking-Glass*. London: Dent.

Chaplin, Charles (1966) *My Autobiography*. New York: Pocket Books.

Charney, Leo and Vanessa R. Schwartz (1998) *Cinema and the Invention of Modern Life*. Berkeley: University of California Press.

Chessick, Richard D. (1987) 'The Search for the Authentic Self in Bergson and Proust', in Maurice Charney and Joseph Reppen (eds) *Psychoanalytic Approaches to Literature and Film*. London and Toronto: Associated University Press, 19–36.

Christie, Ian (2000) *A Matter of Life and Death*. London: British Film Institute.

Christley, Jaime (2004) 'Chris Marker/senses of cinema'; http://www.sensesofcinema.com/contents/directors/02/marker (accessed 16 February 2007).

Ciment, Michel and Lorenzo Codelli (1989) 'Entretien avec Jan Švankmajer', *Positif*, 345, 45–7.

Clifford, James (1986) *Writing Culture: The Poetics and Politics of Ethnography*. Berkeley: University of California Press.

Cocteau, Jean (1992 [1988]) *The Art of the Cinema*. London: Marion Boyars.

Cohen, Mitchell S. (1975) 'Looney Tunes and Merrie Melodies', *The Velvet Light Trap*, 5, (Fall), 33–7.

Corliss, Richard (1975) 'Warnervana', *Film Comment*, 21, November/December, 11–19.

___ (1989) 'Fourteen Carat Oomph', *Film Comment*, 25, July/August, 40–6.

Critchley, Simon (2002) *On Humour*. London and New York: Routledge.

Culhane, John (1987) *Walt Disney's Fantasia*. New York: Abradale Press and H.N. Abrams.

Culhane, Shamus (1986) *Talking Animals and Other People*. New York: De Capo Press.

Dalí, Salvador (2000 [1932]) 'Abstract of a Critical History of the Cinema', in Paul Hammond (ed.) *The Shadow and Its Shadow: Surrealist Writings on Cinema*. San Francisco: City Lights, 63–7.

Deneroff, Harvey (1999) 'The Innovators 1930–1940: The Thin Black Line', *Sight and Sound*, 9, 6, 22–4.

Downing, Lisa (2003) *Desiring the Dead: Necrophilia and Nineteenth-Century French Literature*. Oxford: Legenda.

Drummond, Phillip (1977) 'Textual Space in *Un chien andalou*', *Screen*, 18, 3 (Autumn), 55–119.

Duchamp, Marcel (1975) *Duchamp du signe. Ecrits*. Paris: Flammarion.

Eiren (Motion Picture Producers of Japan); http://www.eiren.org/toueki/kakodata.htm.

Eisenstein, Sergei M. (1997), *Memuary*, 2 vols. Moscow: Muzei kino.

Ellis, Jack (2000) *John Grierson*. Illinois: Southern Illinois University Press.

Elsaesser, Thomas (1987) 'Dada/Cinema?', in Rudolf Kuenzli (ed.) *Dada and Surrealist Film*. New York: Willis Locker and Owens, 13–27.

Foster, Andy and Steve Furst (1996) *Radio Comedy 1938–1968*. London: Virgin.

Foster, Hal (1993) *Compulsive Beauty*. London: MIT Press.

Foucault, Michel (1976) 'Ceci n'est pas une pipe', trans. Richard Howard, *October*, 1, 10, 6–21.

Freud, Sigmund (1963 [1905]) *Jokes and their Relation to the Unconscious*, trans. James Strachey. New York: W. W. Norton.

___ (1977 [1905]) *Sigmund Freud on Sexuality*. Harmondsworth: Penguin.

___ (1981 [1905]) *On Sexuality: Three Essays on Sexuality*. Harmondsworth: Penguin.

___ (1982 [1900]) *The Interpretation of Dreams*. Harmondsworth: Penguin.

Fuentes, Víctor (2000) *Los mundos de Buñuel*. Madrid: Ediciones Akal.

Fukuma, Kenji (1992) *Ishii Teruo*. Eigakon: Wise Shuppan.

Furniss, Maureen (1998) *Art in Motion: Animation Aesthetics*. New York: Libbey.

García Lorca, Federico (1994) *Obras completas*. Madrid: Akal Bolsillo.

Gómez, Joseph (1976) *Ken Russell: The Adaptor as Creator*. London: Frederick Muller.

Goudal, Jean (2000 [1925]) 'Surrealism and Cinema', in Paul Hammond (ed.) *The Shadow and Its Shadow: Surrealist Writings on Cinema*. San Francisco: City Lights, 84–94.

Gould, Michael (1976) *Surrealism and the Cinema*. London: Tantivy Press.

Grant, John (2001) *Masters of Animation*. London: Batsford.

Grierson, John (1933) 'The Documentary Producer', *Cinema Quarterly*, Autumn.

___ (1939) 'The Documentary', *Fortnightly Review*, 8.

Hacker, Jonathan and David Price (1991) *Take 10: Contemporary British Film Directors*. Oxford: Oxford University Press.

Hames, Peter (ed.) (2007) *The Cinema of Jan Švankmajer: Dark Alchemy* (second edition). London: Wallflower Press.

Hammond, Paul (ed.) (1978) *The Shadow and Its Shadow: Surrealist Writings on Cinema*. London: Britsh Film Institute.

___ (ed.) (2000) *The Shadow and Its Shadow: Surrealist Writings on Cinema*. Francisco:

City Lights.

Hardy, Forsyth (ed.) (1966) *John Grierson on Documentary*. London: Faber.

Harper, Sue (1997) "'Nothing to Beat the Hay Diet'': Comedy at Gaumont and Gainsborough', in Pam Cook (ed.) *Gainsborough Pictures*. London: Cassell, 80–98.

Hawkes, John (1972) 'A Conversation on *The Blood Oranges* between John Hawkes and Robert Scholes'; http://www.brown.edu/Departments/Literary_Arts/projects/hawkes/scholes.htm (accessed 13 February 2007).

Higson, Andrew (1986) 'Britain's Outstanding Contribution to the Film: The Documentary Realist Tradition', in Charles Barr (ed.) *All Our Yesterdays*. London: British Film Institute, 72–97.

Hitchcock, Alfred (1997a [1936]) 'Why "Thrillers" Thrive', in Sidney Gottlieb (ed.) *Hitchcock on Hitchcock*. London: Faber & Faber, 109–12.

___ (1997b [1960]) 'Why I Am Afraid of The Dark', in Sidney Gottlieb (ed.) *Hitchcock on Hitchcock*. London: Faber & Faber, 142–5.

Hopewell, John (1986) *Out of the Past: Spanish Cinema After Franco*. London: British Film Institute.

Ilie, Paul (1968) *The Surrealist Mode in Spanish Literature: An Interpretation of Basic Trends From Post-Romanticism to the Spanish Vanguard*. Ann Arbor: University of Michigan Press.

Imber, David G. (1999) 'David Lynch: Mainstream Subterranean', in Takimoto Makoto (ed.) *The Kinema Junpo Filmmakers Series: David Lynch*; http://www.maniform.com/prolix/lynch/htm (accessed 21 February 2007).

Infante, Cabrera (1991) *A Twentieth Century Job: Cabrera Infante's Film Criticism, 1954–1960*. London: Faber & Faber.

Ingdahl, Kazimiera (1994) *A Graveyard of Themes: The Genesis of Three Key Works by Iurii Olesha*. Stockholm: Almqvist and Wiksell International.

Jackson, Kevin (ed.) (1993) *The Humphrey Jennings Film Reader*. New York: Carcanet Press.

Jennings, Humphrey (1995 [1985]) *Pandaemonium: the Coming of the Machine*. London: Picador Papermac.

Johnson Sweeney, James (1946) Interview with Marcel Duchamp in 'Eleven Europeans in America', *The Museum of Modern Art Bulletin* (New York), XIII, 4–5.

Johnson, Vida T. and Graham Petrie (1994) *The Films of Andrei Tarkovsky: A Visual Fugue*. Bloomington: Indiana University Press.

Jones, Chuck (1989) *Chuck Amuck: The Life and Times of an Animated Cartoonist*. New York: Farrar, Strauss and Giroux.

Kanfer, Stefan (2000) *Serious Business: The Art and Commerce of Animation in America from Betty Boop to Toy Story*. New York: De Capo Press.

Kenez, Peter (1992) *Cinema and Soviet Society, 1917–1953*. Cambridge: Cambridge University Press.

Kleinberg, S. J. (1999) *Women in the United States*. London: Macmillan.

Kovács, Steven (1980) *From Enchantment to Rage: The Story of Surrealist Cinema*. London and Toronto: Fairleigh Dickinson University Press.

Kuenzli, Rudolf (1986) 'Surrealism and Misogyny', in Rudolf Kuenzli (ed.) *Dada and Surrealist Film*. New York: Willis, Locker and Owens, 1–12.

___ (ed.) (1990) 'Surrealism and Misogyny', *Dada/Surrealism*, 18, 17–26.

Kyrou, Ado (1978 [1967]) 'Eroticism=Love', in Paul Hammond (ed.) *The Shadow and Its Shadow: Surrealist Writings on Cinema*. London: British Film Institute, 124–6.

Langer, Mark (1975) 'Max and Dave Fleischer', *Film Comment*, 11, 1, 48–56.

___ (1992) 'The Disney-Fleischer Dilemma: Product Differentiation and Technological Innovation', *Screen*, 33, 4, 343–60.

Le Grice, Malcolm (2001) *Experimental Cinema in the Digital Age*. London: British Film Institute.

Leach, Tomas (2004) 'Introduction to Jennings'; http://www.zenbullets.com/britfilm.

Leslie, Esther (2002) *Hollywood Flatlands: Animation, Critical Theory and the Avant-garde*. London: Verso.

Levy, Julian (1995 [1936]) *Surrealism*. New York: Da Capo.

Lovell, Alan and Jim Hillier (1972) *Studies in Documentary*. London: Secker and Warburg.

Mabire, Jean-Marie (1965) 'Entretien avec Philippe Soupault', *Etudes cinématographiques*, 38–9, special issue 'Surréalisme et cinéma', 29.

Macdonald, Kevin and Mark Cousins (1998) *Imagining Reality: The Faber Book of Documentary*. London: Faber.

Maltin, Leonard (1975) 'TV Animation: The Decline and Pratfall of a Popular Art', *Film Comment*, 11, 1, 76–81.

___ (1987) *Of Mice and Magic*. London: Plume.

Matthews, J. H. (1971) *Surrealism and Film*. Ann Arbor: University of Michigan Press.

___ (1976) *Towards the Poetics of Surrealism*. New York: Syracuse University Press.

McCabe, Bob (1999) *Dark Knights and Holy Fools: The Art and Films of Terry Gilliam*. London: Orion.

Medem, Julio (2001) *Lucía y el sexo*. Madrid: Ocho y Medio.

Mellor, David (ed.) (1987) *A Paradise Lost*. London: Lund Humphries.

Mes, Tom (2003) *Agitator: The Cinema of Takashi Miike*. Godalming: Fab Press.

___ (2005) *Iron Man: The Cinema of Shinya Tsukamot*. Godalming: Fab Press.

Miles, Adrian (1995) Chris Marker website: http://cs.art.rmit.edu.au/projects/media/marker (accessed 17 February 2007).

Mogg, Ken (1999) *The Alfred Hitchcock Story*. London: Titan Books.

___ (2006) *New Publications*; http://www.labyrinth.net.au/muffin/publications.c.html

Moix, Terence (1983) 'Con Buñuel en su casa mexicana', *Fotogramas*, September, 14–15.

Morris, C. B. (1972) *Surrealism and Spain*. Cambridge: Cambridge University Press.

Muybridge, Eadward (1955 [1890]) The Human Figure in Motion. New York: Dover Publications Inc.

Nadeau, Maurice (1968) *The History of Surrealism*. London: Cape.

Nesbet, Anne (2003) *Savage Junctures: Sergei Eisenstein and the Shape of Thinking*. London: I. B. Tauris.

Nowell-Smith, Geoffrey (1986) 'Humphrey Jennings, Surrealist Observer', in Charles Barr (ed.) *All Our Yesterdays: 90 Years of British Cinema*. London: British Film Institute.

Olesha, IuMan Ray (1934) 'Stogii iunosha', in *Novyi mir*, 8, 66–89 .

O'Pray, Michael (1984) *Primitive Phantasy in Cronenberg's Films*. London: British Film Institute.

___ (1996) *Derek Jarman: Dreams of England*. London: British Film Institute.

___ (2007) 'Jan Švankmajer, a Mannerist Surrealist', in Peter Hames (ed.) *The Cinema of Jan Švankmajer: Dark Alchemy* (second edition). London: Wallflower Press.

Paglia, Camille (1998) *The Birds*. London: British Film Institute.

Parfenov, L. A. (1999) *Zhivye golosa kino: Govoriat vydaiushchiesia mastera otechestven-nogo kinoiskusstva (30-e–40-e gody). Iz neopublikovannogo*. Moscow: Belyi bereg.

Park, James (1984) *Learning to Dream: The New British Cinema*. London: Faber & Faber.

Persson, Per (1998) 'Towards a Psychological Theory of Close-ups', *Kinema*, 9, (Spring) 1998, 24–42.

Peterson, James (1989) 'A War of Utter Rebellion: Kinugasa's Page of Madness and the Japanese Avant-garde of the 1920s', in *Cinema Journal*, 29, 1, 36–53.

Petley, Julian (1986) 'The Cabinet of Jan Švankmajer: Prague's Alchemist of Film', *Monthly Film Bulletin*, 53, 629, 188.

Petric, Vlada (1987) *Constructivism in Film: The Man with the Movie Camera – A Cinematic Analysis*. Cambridge: Cambridge University Press.

Pirie, David (1973) *A Heritage of Horror: The English Gothic Cinema 1946–1972*. London: Gordon Fraser.

Poloka, Gennadii (1996) 'Uvazhenie k sobstvennym traditsiiam', in Vitalii Troianovskii (ed.), *Kinomatograf ottepeli. Kniga pervaia*. Moscow: Materik, 204–15.

Poš, Jan (1990) *Výtvarníci animovaného filmu*. Prague: Odeon.

Powell, Michael (1992 [1986]) *A Life in Movies: An Autobiography* (second edition). London: Mandarin.

Prickett, Stephen (1979) *Victorian Fantasy*. Brighton: Harvester Press.

Proust, Marcel (1957 [1913]) *Swann's Way*. New York: Penguin.

Putterman, Barry (1998) 'A Short Critical History of Warner Bros. Cartoons', in Kevin S. Sandler (ed.) *Reading The Rabbit: Explorations in Warner Bros. Animation*. New Jersey and London: Rutgers University Press, 29–31.

Ray, Man (1933) 'L'Age de la lumière', *Minotaure*, 3–4.

___ (1963) *Self-Portrait*. Boston: Little, Brown.

___ (1965) 'Temoignages', *Etudes cinematographiques*, 38/39, 43–6.

Ray, Paul (1971) *The Surrealist Movement in England*. Ithaca: Cornell University Press.

Rees, A. L. (1999) *A History of Experimental Film and Video: From Canonical Avant-Garde to Contemporary British Practice*. London: British Film Institute.

Remy, Michel (1999) *Surrealism in Britain*. Aldershot: Ashgate.

Richie, Donald (2001) *A Hundred Years of Japanese Film*. Tokyo: Kodansha International.

Roberts, Graham (1999) *Stride Soviet*. London: I. B. Tauris.

___ (2001) *Man with the Movie Camera*. London: I. B. Tauris.

Rodley, Chris (1997) *Lynch on Lynch*. London: Faber & Faber.

Roman, Shari (2001) *Digital Babylon: Hollywood, Indiewood and Dogme*. Los Angeles: Lone Eagle.

Rombes, Nicholas (2005) 'DVD and the New Cinema of Complexity', in Nicholas Rombes (ed.) *New Punk Cinema*. Edinburgh: Edinburgh University Press, 89–101.

Rosemont, Franklin (ed.) (1978) *What is Surrealism?: Selected Writings*. New York: Pathfinder.

Roth, Laurent and Raymond Bellour (1997) *Qu'est-ce qu'une Madeleine?* Paris: CGP.

Rouff, Jeffrey (1998) 'An Ethnographic Surrealist Film: Luis Buñuel's *Land Without Bread*', *Visual Anthropology Review*, 14, 1, 45–57.

Rucar de Buñuel, Jeanne (1991) *Memorias de una mujer sin piano, escritas por Marisol Martín del Campo*. Madrid: Alianza.

Salfellner, Harold (1988) *Franz Kafka and Prague*. Prague: Vitalis.

Sánchez Vidal, Agustín (1984) *Luis Buñuel; obra cinematográfica*. Madrid: Ediciones JC.

___ (1993) *El mundo de Buñuel*. Zaragoza: Caja de Ahorros de la Inmaculada.

Sandro, Paul (1987) *Diversions of Pleasure; Luis Buñuel and the Crises of Desire*. Columbus: Ohio State University Press.

Sárközi, Radek (2004) *Czech Surrealism after World War Two*; http://www.ceskaliteratura. cz/studie/sur.htm (accessed 2 November 2004).

Sas, Miryam (2001) *Fault Lines: Cultural Memory and Japanese Surrealism*. Palo Alto: Stanford University Press.

Schilling, Mark (2001) 'Donald Richie: Being Inside and Outside Japanese Cinema', *The Japan Times*, 18 March; http://www.japantimes.co.jp/cgi-bin/getarticle.pl5?ff20010318a1. htm.

___ (2003a) *The Yakuza Movie Book: A Guide to Japanese Gangster Films*. Berkeley: Stone Bridge.

___ (2003b) *Nickelodeon: Far East Film*. Udine: Centro Espressioni Cinematografiche.

Schwarz, Arturo (1969) *The Complete Works of Marcel Duchamp*. London: Thames and Hudson.

Short, Robert (2003) *The Age of Gold: Surrealist Cinema, Persistence of Vision, Volume 3*. New York: Creation Books.

Shvarts, Evgenii (1999) *Drakon. Klad. Ten. Dva klena. Obyknovennoe chudo i drugie proizvedniia*. Moscow: Gud'ial Press, 269–339.

Sinyard, Neil (1985) *The Films of Richard Lester*. London: Croom Helm.

Smoodin, Eric (1993) *Animating Culture: Hollywood Cartoons from the Sound Era*. New York: Rutgers University Press.

Solzhenitsyn, Alexander (1978) *Cancer Ward*, trans. Nicholas Bethell and David Burg. Harmondsworth: Penguin.

Stern, Emil (2000) 'Hitchcock's *Marnie*: Dreams, Surrealism, and the Sublime', in *The Hitchcock Annual 1999–2000*. Detroit: Wayne State University Press, 30–50.

Stone, Rob (2001) *Spanish Cinema*. Harlow: Longman.

Storey, John (ed) (1994) 'Postmodernisms', in *Cultural Theory and The Study of Popular*

Culture: An Introduction. New York: Harvester Wheatsheaf, 146–70.

Sulieman, Susan Rubin (2003) *Surrealist Black Humour: Masculine/Feminine.* http://72.14.207.104/search?q=cache:70BNChExTsJ:www.surrealismcentre.ac.uk/publications/papers/journal1/acrobat_iles/ (accessed 22 May 2005).

Sussex, Elizabeth (1975) *The Rise and Fall of British Documentary.* London: University of California Press.

Synessios, Natasha (2001) *Mirror: The Film Companion.* London: I. B. Tauris.

Taylor, Jim (2001) *DVD Demystified,* second edition. New York: McGraw-Hill.

Taylor, Paul (2005) 'The Pornographic Barbarism of the Self-Reflecting Sign', in Hillel Nossek, Annabelle Sreberny and Prasun Sonwalkar (eds) *Media and Political Violence.* New York: Hampton Press, 349–66.

Thompson, Ben (2004) *Sunshine on Putty: The Golden Age of British Comedy.* London: Fourth Estate.

Thomson, David (2003) *The New Biographical Dictionary of Film.* London: Secker and Warburg.

Truffaut, François (1984) *Hitchcock by Truffaut.* London: Paladin.

Tsukamoto, Shinya (2003) *Tsukamoto Shinya Dokuhon Yomihon: Futsu Size no Kyojin.* Tokyo: Kinema Junposha.

Vigo, Jean (1977/78 [1930]) 'Toward a Social Cinema', trans. Stuart Liebman, *Millenium Film Journal,* 1, 23.

Waldberg, Patrick (1966) *Surrealism.* New York: McGraw-Hill.

Warner, Marina (1977) 'Voodoo Road', *Sight and Sound,* August, 8–10.

___ (1993) *L'Atlante.* London: British Film Institute.

Wells, Paul (1998) *Understanding Animation.* London: Routledge.

___ (2000) *The Horror Genre: From Beelzebub to Blair Witch.* London: Wallflower Press.

___ (2002a) *Animation and America.* Edinburgh: Edinburgh University Press.

___ (2002b) *Animation: Genre and Authorship.* London: Wallflower Press.

White, Mimi (1984) 'Two French Dada Films: *Entr'acte* and *Emak-Bakia*', *Dada/Surrealism,* 13, 37–47.

Williams, Linda (1981) *Figures of Desire: A Theory and Analysis of Surrealist Film.* Berkeley: University of California Press.

Winston, Brian (1995) *Claiming the Real.* London: British Film Institute.

___ (1998) *Media Technology and Society, A History: From The Telegraph to the Internet.* London: Routledge.

___ (1999) *Fires Were Started.* London: British Film Institute.

Wollen, Peter (1977) 'Compulsion', *Sight and Sound,* April, 14–18.

Wood, Guy (2005) 'El festival de Cannes: Elemento facilitador de la presencia e influencia de Luis Buñuel en *La caza* de Carlos Saura', paper given at Second International Conference on Latin(o) American and Iberian Cinema, University of Hawaii at Manoa, 4 November 2005.

Wood, Michael (1981) 'The Corruption of Accidents', in Andrew Horton and Joan Magretta (eds) *Modern European Filmmakers and the Art of Adaptation.* New York: Frederick

Ungar, 329–43.

___ (1992) 'Double Lives', *Sight and Sound*, 1, 9, 20–3.

Wright, Basil (1971) *The Long View*. London: Secker and Warburg.

Zhdanov, Andrei (1977) 'Soviet Literature: The Richest in Ideas, the Most Advanced Literature', in Maxim Gorky and H. G. Scott (eds) *Soviet Writers' Congress 1934: The Debate on Socialist Realism and Modernism in the Soviet Union*. London: Lawrence and Wishart, 15–24.

INDEX